Deconstruction, Femin...

Deconstruction, Feminism, Film

Sarah Dillon

EDINBURGH
University Press

For Gav

Edinburgh University Press is one of the leading university presses in the UK. We publish academic books and journals in our selected subject areas across the humanities and social sciences, combining cutting-edge scholarship with high editorial and production values to produce academic works of lasting importance. For more information visit our website: edinburghuniversitypress.com

© Sarah Dillon, 2018, 2019

Edinburgh University Press Ltd
The Tun – Holyrood Road
12 (2f) Jackson's Entry
Edinburgh EH8 8PJ

First published in hardback by Edinburgh University Press 2018

Typeset in Adobe Garamond Pro by
Manila Typesetting Company, and
printed and bound in Great Britain
by CPI Group (UK) Ltd, Croydon,
CR0 4YY

A CIP record for this book is available from the British Library

ISBN 978 1 4744 3419 5 (hardback)
ISBN 978 1 4744 3422 5 (paperback)
ISBN 978 1 4744 3420 1 (webready PDF)
ISBN 978 1 4744 3421 8 (epub)

The right of Sarah Dillon to be identified as author of this work has been asserted in accordance with the Copyright, Designs and Patents Act 1988 and the Copyright and Related Rights Regulations 2003 (SI No. 2498).

Contents

List of Figures	vi
Acknowledgements	vii
Abbreviations of Works Cited by Jacques Derrida	ix
Introduction: Departing from Proust	1
1 Deconstruction, Feminism, Film	14
I It-Woman vs We-Women	17
II Singular Spectatorship	24
2 Supplanting Spectrality	40
I The Incidental Philosopher	41
II Feminist *Trompe L'Oeil*	47
III Feminist Camp Artifice	53
3 Feminist Countersignature	66
I Female Infidelity	69
II Adaptation as Reproduction	78
III Phenomenal Film	82
IV Dorsal Philosophy	88
4 Auto/biography	97
I Biography, or, the Realist Paradox	98
II *Quer* Autobiography (directed sideways)	109
5 How Do I Look?	129
I He Can't See Queerly	130
II Metonymic Reading	139
III Veering from Borges	144
Bibliography	151
Filmography	162
Index	163

Figures

2.1	The ungrammatical knife	43
2.2	Pascale and the knife	44
2.3	Marianne on Marx's tomb	49
2.4	Exposure of the *trompe l'oeil*	49
2.5	Rape scene	53
2.6	Performance artist Stuart Brisley	54
2.7	Performance artist Stuart Brisley	54
2.8	Pascale and Marianne keeping it real	58
2.9	Pascale and Marianne camping it up	58
3.1	Filmmaker Joanna released	76
3.2	Sophie and Theo reunited	76
3.3	Martin McQuillan and playground	80
3.4	Joanna reproducing portrait	80
3.5	Lucy reproducing poster	81
3.6	Lucy reproducing portrait	81
3.7	Sophie, wide shot without audience	87
3.8	Sophie, medium shot	87
3.9	Sophie, wide shot with audience	87
3.10	Marian Hobson reading from Derrida's 'Envois'	92
4.1	Derrida's wife Marguerite leaving their home in Paris	104
4.2	Split screen: Derrida and Geoffrey Bennington above; Derrida's apartment below	106
4.3	Derrida's sideways glances (1)	113
4.4	Derrida's sideways glances (2)	113
4.5	Derrida's sideways glances (3)	113
4.6	Sarah Polley at the mixing console	118
4.7	Six-second pause on Sarah Polley	119
5.1	Denaturalising heterosexuality	136
5.2	Entering the world of the two young girls	138
5.3	The Director transcribes Borges' 'Covered Mirrors'	146
5.4	The Director transcribes more of Borges' 'Covered Mirrors'	146

Acknowledgements

I have carried this book for sixteen years. As I explain in the Introduction, it was conceived in 2001 in Loughborough when, as a PhD student, I listened to Derrida talk at John Schad's 'Life After Theory' conference. The ideas fertilised that day have divided and multiplied over the years. I've produced essays that tackled some but not all of them. I've taught classes which helped my thinking develop, as encounters with the best students do. I've had two job moves and two children along the way: inevitably, this slowed things down, a phenomenon both frustrating but also productive, since it meant the book had time for its own unhurried gestation. It is certainly a different book to the one I would have produced without the interruptions of starting a family; I am equally sure that it is a better one. In fact, I do not think it could have been written until now.

Many people have touched my life and thought over those fifteen years, contributing in their individual ways to the book's development, leaving traces of their intellectual DNA. In particular I would like to thank Mark Breeze, Angus Brown, Joanna Callaghan, James Clackson, Tom Conley, David Cunningham, Jennifer Cooke, Michael Dillon, Zara Dinnen, Lucy Fife Donaldson, Bob Eaglestone, Elspeth Gillespie, Xiaolu Guo, Sarah Jackson, Dragan Kujundžić, Laura MacMahon, Laura Marcus, Leonie Mellinger, Cillian Ó Fathaigh, Joanna Page, J. D. Rhodes, Nicholas Royle, Richard Rushton, John Schad, Murray Smith, Alice Thorpe, David Trotter, Kate Wilkinson and Emma Wilson. A special word goes to my friend Nora Bartlett whose love of life was unsurpassed. She died too soon, as this book was being finished. She adored film and I wish she had been able to read this book – I think she would have delighted in it.

I would like to thank the anonymous readers for Edinburgh University Press, who provided detailed and helpful feedback on the draft manuscript, and my editor Gillian Leslie for her faith in this project and her enthusiasm and support, just when it was needed most.

Punctum Books have given kind permission to reproduce in revised form in Chapter 1 some material from my essay 'Derrida and the Question of "Woman"', in Christian Hite (ed.), *Derrida and Queer Theory* (Brooklyn:

Punctum Books, 2017), pp. 108–30. Opening material in the Introduction has been extracted and adapted from my journal article 'Life After Derrida: Anacoluthia and the Agrammaticality of Following', *Research in Phenomenology* 36 (2006): 97–114, with a licence to reproduce obtained from Brill. High-quality original files for stills in Chapter 3 from *Love in the Post* were kindly provided by Joanna Callaghan. My thanks to Benoît Peeters and Marie-Françoise Plissart for giving me permission to reproduce photographs from *Right of Inspection* in Chapter 5, and for providing high-quality copies of the images © Les Impressions Nouvelles/Marie-Françoise Plissart, 2017. Details of the most recent French edition of *Droit de Regards* are available at https://lesimpressionsnouvelles.com/catalogue/droit-de-regards/ (last accessed 18 September 2017).

Finally, there have been a special few people whose company – intellectual and otherwise – has been constant over the past decade and a half. To them in particular I give my thanks, for supporting me when I was in danger of collapsing, and for keeping my feet on the ground when I was in danger of taking off: my parents, Mick and Jeannette Dillon; my sister, Jayne Dillon; my children, Isaac and Charlotte. Above all, I acknowledge my husband, fellow feminist and cinephile, Gavin McHugh. He turned me on to film in the first place and for that, for his unfailing support of my career, and for everything else, I dedicate this book to him.

Abbreviations of Works Cited by Jacques Derrida

A	'Aletheia', trans. Pleshette DeArmitt and Kas Saghafi, *The Oxford Literary Review* 32.2 (2010): 169–88.
ACM	'A Certain "Madness": Must Watch Over Thinking', with François Ewald, *Educational Theory* 45.3 (September 1995): 273–91.
AF	*Archive Fever: A Freudian Impression*, trans. Eric Prenowitz (Chicago and London: University of Chicago Press, 1996).
AI	'"*As if* I were Dead": An Interview with Jacques Derrida', in John Brannigan, Ruth Robbins and Julian Wolfreys (eds), *Applying: To Derrida* (London: Macmillan, 1996), pp. 212–26.
ASR	*Athens, Still Remains: The Photographs of Jean François Bonhomme*, trans. Pascale-Anne Brault and Michael Naas (New York: Fordham University Press, 2010).
C	'Choreographies', with Christie V. McDonald, *Diacritics* 12.2 (Summer 1982): 66–76.
CAS	*Copy, Archive, Signature: A Conversation on Photography*, trans. Jeff Fort (Stanford: Stanford University Press, 2010).
CG	'Cinema and Its Ghosts: An Interview with Jacques Derrida', with Antoine de Baecque and Thierry Jousse, trans. Peggy Kamuf, *Discourse* 37.1–2 (Winter/Spring 2015): 22–39.
CM	'Circumfession', in Geoffrey Bennington and Jacques Derrida, *Jacques Derrida* (Chicago: University of Chicago Press, 1993).
CS	'Countersignature', trans. Mairéad Hanrahan, *Paragraph* 27.2 (2004): 7–42.
D	In Frédéric Brenner, *Diaspora: Homelands in Exile voices* (London: Bloomsbury, 2004).
DIS	*Dissemination* (London: Athlone Press, 1981).
DOD	'Derrida on *Derrida* – Q and A with Jacques Derrida', in Kirby Dick and Amy Ziering Kofman, *Screenplay and Essays on the Film* Derrida (Manchester: Manchester University Press, 2005), pp. 110–17.
DRB	'The Deaths of Roland Barthes', trans. Pascale-Anne Brault and Michael Naas, in Peggy Kamuf and Elizabeth Rottenberg (eds),

	Psyche: Inventions of the Other, Volume 1 (Stanford: Stanford University Press, 2007), pp. 264–98.
E	'Envois', in *The Post Card: From Socrates to Freud and Beyond*, trans. Alan Bass (Chicago: University of Chicago Press, 1987).
EC	*Echographies of Television: Filmed Interviews*, with Bernard Stiegler, trans. Jennifer Bajorek (Cambridge: Polity Press, 2002).
FT	'following theory: Jacques Derrida', in Michael Payne and John Schad (eds), *life.after.theory* (New York: Continuum, 2003), pp. 1–51.
GD	'The Ghost Dance: An Interview with Jacques Derrida', with Mark Lewis and Andrew Payne, trans. Jean-Luc Svoboda, *Public* 2 (1989): 60–74.
GOD	*The Gift of Death*, trans. David Wills (Chicago and London: The University of Chicago Press, 1995).
JD	*Jacques Derrida*, with Geoffrey Bennington (Chicago: University of Chicago Press, 1993).
MB	*Memoirs of the Blind: The self-portrait and other ruins*, trans. Pascale-Anne Brault and Michael Naas (Chicago: University of Chicago Press, 1993).
NW	'The Night Watch (over "the book of himself")', trans. Pascale-Anne Brault and Michael Naas, in Andrew J. Mitchell and Sam Slote (eds), *Derrida and Joyce: Texts and Contexts* (Albany: State University of New York Press, 2013), pp. 87–108.
OF	*Of Hospitality*, with Anne Dufourmantelle, trans. Rachel Bowlby (Stanford: Stanford University Press, 2000).
P	*Positions*, trans. Alan Bass (London: The Athlone Press, 1981).
PF	*The Politics of Friendship*, trans. George Collins (London: Verso, 2005).
RI	'Right of Inspection', trans. David Wills, in Marie-Françoise Plissart, *Right of Inspection* (New York: The Monacelli Press, 1998).
SP	*Speech and Phenomena*, trans. David B. Allison (Evanston, IL: Northwestern University Press, 1973).
TLM	*Tourner le mots: Au bord d'un film*, with Safaa Fathy (Paris: Galilée, 2000).
TP	*The Truth in Painting*, trans. Geoff Bennington and Ian McLeod (Chicago: University of Chicago Press, 1987).
TW	'Two Words for Joyce', trans. Geoffrey Bennington, in Derek Attridge and Daniel Ferrer (eds), *Post-structuralist Joyce: Essays from the French* (Cambridge: Cambridge University Press, 1994), pp. 145–59.
V	'Videor', trans. Peggy Kamuf, in Michael Renov and Erika Suderburg (eds), *Resolutions: Contemporary Video Practices* (Minneapolis: University of Minnesota Press, 1996), pp. 73–7.

WA	'"Le Parjure," *Perhaps*: Storytelling and Lying', trans. Peggy Kamuf, in *Without Alibi* (Stanford: Stanford University Press, 2002), pp. 161–201.
WB	'Women in the Beehive: A Seminar with Jacques Derrida', in Alice Jardine and Paul Smith (eds), *Men in Feminism* (New York and London: Routledge, 1987), pp. 189–203.

There now exists, in a certain way, an unequaled offer or demand for deconstruction, in writing as well as in film. The thing is to know what to do with it.
>	Jacques Derrida, 'Cinema and Its Ghosts' (2015)

Really close up is the thing.
>	Lisa Cholodenko, 'Talking About Women' (2004)

Introduction: Departing from Proust

The thinking for this book began on a very specific date: Saturday 10 November 2001. On that day I listened to Jacques Derrida deliver a lecture at John Schad's 'Life After Theory' conference, published the following year in *Without Alibi* under the title '"Le Parjure," *Perhaps*: Storytelling and Lying'. That day my desire to probe the feminist fault lines in Derrida's work was conceived; this book is the product of that desire. In '"Le Parjure," *Perhaps*', Derrida develops the idea of *the anacoluthon*, a substantivised figure derived from the grammatical term *anacoluthia*: literally, a want of grammatical sequence; the passing from one construction to another before the former is completed. Derrida is drawn to this figure by its significance in his friend J. Hillis Miller's work on the relationship between narrative and perjury, and he is concerned to investigate further the 'indissolubly ethico-literary question of testimonial narration and of fiction' (*WA* 170). He does so through a reading – informed by the connotations of the anacoluthon – of Henri Thomas' novel *Le Parjure* (1964). So Derrida finds the figure of the anacoluthon in Hillis Miller's work, but Hillis Miller found it in Proust, and his attention was drawn to the passage in Proust by a footnote on the anacoluthon in Paul De Man's *Allegories of Reading* (1979), and – adding a further link to these chains of texts and men – Paul De Man, perhaps, provided the real-life model for the character of Stéphane in *Le Parjure*. In defiance of the exclusion of women from this lineage, in the essay I wrote in the wake of Derrida's death – 'Life After Derrida: Anacoluthia and the Agrammaticality of Following' (2006) – I sought to add my female voice to this masculine transmission of thought, developing yet again the concept of the anacoluthon. But I did not do so from a feminist perspective, and I was plagued by a regret that in entering into the male lineage I was relinquishing the power of alternative female spaces of thought and relationality. In this book, finally, I embrace those spaces and brandish their power. I do so as part of the dual feminist *modus operandi* of critique and generation which I will elaborate in this Introduction. This methodology enables *both* the critique of the masculine tradition of thought *and* the feminist generation of new thought and ideas through recentred attention to that which has been excluded from that tradition – as I will explain in Chapter 1, a position occupied by women and film.

In their discussions of the anacoluthon, both Hillis Miller and Derrida quote a passage from Proust's *The Captive* or, as it is sometimes translated, *The Prisoner*, a volume of *In Search of Lost Time* in which the narrator describes his lover Albertine's use of anacolutha, and the effect they have:

> To tell the truth, I knew nothing that Albertine had done since I had come to know her, or even before. But in her conversation (she might, had I mentioned it to her, have replied that I had misunderstood her) there were certain contradictions, certain embellishments which seemed to me as decisive as catching her red-handed [*qui me semblaient aussi décisives qu'un flagrant délit*], but less usable against Albertine who, often caught out like a child, had invariably, by dint of sudden, strategic changes of front, stultified my cruel attacks and retrieved the situation. Cruel, most of all, to myself. She employed, not by way of stylistic refinement, but in order to correct her imprudences, abrupt breaches of syntax not unlike the figure which the grammarians call anacoluthon or some such names [*de ces brusques sautes de syntaxe resemblant un peu à ce que les grammairiens appellant anacoluthe ou je ne sais comment*]. Having allowed herself, while discussing women, to say: 'I remember, the other day, I . . . ,' she would suddenly, after a semi-quaver rest, change the 'I' to 'she': it was something that she had witnessed as an innocent spectator, not a thing that she herself had done. It was not she who was the subject of the action [*Ce n'était pas elle qui était le sujet de l'action*]. (Proust cited in *WA* 168)

Albertine's 'abrupt breaches of syntax' consist in anacoluthic moments of hesitation, and subsequent pronominal shifts from 'I' to 'she'. Since they are used in order to avoid the disclosure of her infidelity to Marcel, Derrida reads Albertine's anacolutha as revelatory of an intimacy between the anacoluthon and the way in which the very idea of fidelity is dependent upon a denial of – and, at the same time, is always potentially compromised by – the discontinuity of the self that Albertine's pronominal shifts exploit. More than this, the anacoluthon offers itself as a figure for Derrida's idea of (in)fidelity, a following that is also a not following, which is key to his concept of inheritance and defines his deconstructive relationship to the texts he reads and writes on (Dillon 2006).

However, while Albertine provides the anacoluthic model for the relationship that binds these men, she remains definitively external to it – as Hillis Miller notes, 'the example of the eternal feminine, evasive and unpossessable' (cited in *WA* 169). Whereas Albertine originates textual and verbal relationality, in Thomas' novel *Le Parjure*, Stéphane's wife Judith has the power to end it, to abort the word, to 'keep' this last word. This seems both a relief – she is the word's 'guardian' – but also a dangerous termination. The transmission of the word falters and, indeed, ends in the possession of 'an impassive and at bottom inaccessible woman' (*WA* 198) who is wholly external to the male line that has up until now secured its transmission. For Derrida, Judith stands in opposition to 'all these acolytes who do not accompany . . . Paul de Man, Henri Thomas, Stéphane Chalier, Father Chalier, the narrator Hillis Miller,' and Derrida himself (*WA* 199). Her presence exposes 'a kind of *idiocy* of man, of the two men who have understood nothing, the two acolytes, the perjurer and his witness' (*WA* 198). While they are 'sleeping in the same body in some way', she 'keeps watch, is stirring about, making decisions, and so on' (*WA* 198). It is only she who has the power to arrest the endless narrative chains of storytelling and lying, to perform the decisive action that terminates those chains and ends not just the novel but also Derrida's discussion of it – the figure of the Woman ends '"Le Parjure," *Perhaps*' just as she ends other texts by Derrida, including *Otobiographies* and *Pas d'hospitalité*. In her decisiveness and her ability to act, Judith exposes the idiocy of these speaking and writing men. But, at the same time, Derrida says, 'one feels an accusation on the horizon: a couple of men united as one, "a single idiot," brothers, in sum, seems to denounce the woman' (*WA* 198). Both Albertine and Judith therefore occupy ambivalent positions in these male narrative chains. They are figures of power – of dissimulation and of action respectively – and yet they are also powerless, excluded from the brotherhood of the male by which they are represented.

Rather than thinking philosophically about Albertine's anacolutha, after all these men, including the narrator himself, I want to pay attention instead to the literary context in which they occur. *The Prisoner* is a deeply disturbing novel, a case study of the narrator's paranoiac jealousy and obsessive control. Unsure whether he loves Albertine or not, nevertheless the narrator wishes to keep her to himself and carries an absolute 'horror' (Proust 2002: 21) of her 'taste for women' (Proust 2002: 22) and the sexual relationships he believes she engages in with them. The narrator therefore takes Albertine from Balbec, where they meet, and secludes her in his house in Paris, keeping track of her movements and analysing every word and action for evidence of her sapphic infidelities. The novel is told in the first person, exclusively from the male narrator's perspective. Not only is he paranoid, he is also unrelentingly sexist, treating Albertine as little more than a pet to be summoned at will, casually disregardful of women in general. Consider, for example, his observation that 'superior intelligence in a woman always having interested me so little that if I remarked on it to one or other of them, it has always been from mere politeness' (Proust 2002: 11), or his unwavering belief in 'the stupid banality of women's humour' (Proust 2002: 14). Albertine has no presence in this novel other than that mediated through the narrator: there is never a shift in narrative perspective that would allow the reader access to her thoughts and feelings; her direct speech, what little there is of it, is only ever reported by the narrator.

It is in this context that the passage cited by Hillis Miller and Derrida occurs, and taking into account this context provokes an alternative feminist line of thought and enquiry. For Albertine's anacoluthic pronominal shifts from 'I' to 'she' erase her lived experiences, partaking of the narrator's persistent othering of women. In doing so, Albertine relinquishes her agency and identity for the narrator in words, as he wishes her to do so in reality. At the same time, however, the anacolutha only function in this way because there *is* something to conceal, because Albertine *does* have agency, because she *does* exist as an 'I' who desires, acts and speaks independently of oppressive male control. But this independence is never visible in the novel. As Eve Kosofsky Sedgwick notes in her discussion of Albertine in *Epistemology of the Closet*, Albertine resides in an 'inchoate space' (1991: 231), exempt from sight. Her female homosexuality, in contradistinction to the male homosexuality embodied in M. de Charlus, is, if not quite invisible, more precisely what Terry Castle determines 'apparitional', that paradox of a visible absence:[1]

> With all their plurality of interpretive paths, there is no way to read the Albertine volumes without finding same-sex desire *somewhere*; at the same time, that specificity of desire, in the Albertine plot, notoriously refuses to remain fixed to a single character type, to a single character, or even to a single ontological level of the text. (Sedgwick 1991: 231).

Sedgwick rightly notes that, in Albertine, the figure of the lesbian becomes definitional of the figure of the woman, that absolutely unknowable, unpresentable Other for both the male narrator and male author: 'Albertine's female connections with women [are] in their very lesbianism, of the essence of the female – centrally and definingly located within femininity' (Sedgwick 1991: 234). The idea and threat of the free independent woman is represented most powerfully in the figure of the lesbian – whether indeed that lesbianism is actual or imagined – since, as Castle notes, 'lesbianism poses an ineluctable challenge to the political, economic, and sexual authority of men over women. It implies a whole new social order, characterized – at the very least – by a profound feminine indifference to masculine charisma' (Castle 1993: 62).

There are two feminist responses possible to the othering and silencing of Albertine as lesbian and woman in Proust. One is critique – to expose precisely those operations of othering and silencing in order to subject them to feminist analysis, both within the body of Proust's work in particular and in

Western literature more generally. In this mode, Albertine's anacolutha might be read as grammatical versions of the blocking gestures Castle identifies in literature about lesbians which serve to derealise lesbianism, manifesting it only as apparitional (1993: 33–4). It is important to note, as Castle does in relation to Diderot, that these gestures are authorial, perhaps even more so in the case of Proust since Albertine's anacolutha are mediated through two male authors – the narrator and Proust himself. In this reading, the anacolutha function as authorial gestures that displace and avoid the representation of lesbianism, even as it haunts the text and its male authors who are consumed by the panic Castle identifies as underwriting these blocking gestures: 'a panic over love, female pleasure, and the possibility of women breaking free – together – from their male sexual overseers' (Castle 1993: 34).[2] The other possible feminist response is to step away from the masculine chains of signification – even if we have inserted ourselves into them as radical critics – in order to place women centre stage and enable us to speak for ourselves. Jacqueline Rose's novel *Albertine* (2001), in which she attempts to give Albertine the voice and inner life she lacks in Proust's work, would be a good example of this second mode of generative response.

This duality of feminist thought and action – the combined force of critique and generation – is exactly what Teresa de Lauretis believes constitutes the double-action of feminism:

> the critique of all discourses concerning gender, including those produced or promoted as feminist, continues to be as vital a part of feminism as is the ongoing effort to create new spaces of discourse, to rewrite cultural narratives, and to define the terms of another perspective – a view from 'elsewhere'. (de Lauretis 1987: 25)[3]

However, that 'elsewhere' is of course 'here', in the everyday lived realities of women as opposed to the masculine imagined 'otherness' of the figure of Woman. As de Lauretis says, 'that "elsewhere" is not some mythic distant past or some utopian future history: it is the elsewhere of discourse here and now, the blind spots, or the space-off, of its representations' (de Lauretis 1987: 25). As noted above, the dual-action of feminism – critique and generation – constitutes this book's *modus operandi* in relation to Derrida's work. At the same time, it bears similarities to the method of deconstruction itself which necessarily involves two phases: a reversal of the system in order to intervene in it, for to 'take an attitude of neutralizing indifference with respect to classical oppositions would be to give free rein to the existing forces that effectively and historically dominate the field' (*DIS* 6); *and* a step away from, outside of, that very system, in order to go further, to generate thought that is 'more radical or more daring' (*DIS* 6). 'These two operations', Derrida says, 'must be conducted in a kind of disconcerting *simul*, in a movement of the entire field that must be coherent, of course, but at the same time divided, differentiated, and stratified' (*DIS* 6). In each chapter of this book, then, Derrida's thought is subject to critique which exposes what it offers feminism and film, and where its limitations or problems lie; at the same time, each chapter explores cinematic (and, in Chapter 5, photographic) sites of female–female intimacy in order to generate new thought and insight from those 'elsewheres' of masculine discourse which the book places centre stage.

Chapter 1, 'Deconstruction, Feminism, Film', opens with an engagement with Plato's *Phaedo*, and Derrida's readings of it, in order to establish the structural exclusion of women and popular art at the origins of the Western metaphysical tradition, and highlight the suspension of an interrogation of this exclusion in Derrida's work. The first section proceeds to address the relationship between deconstruction and feminism, teasing out Derrida's deconstruction of the figure of Woman, exploring where he repeats, and is complicit in, Western metaphysics' othering of Woman, as well as what possibilities deconstruction offers for thinking beyond this. The work of key female commentators on Derrida, including Elizabeth Grosz and Gayatri Chakravorty Spivak, is foregrounded here to facilitate the phase of critique. This is followed by a justification of my turn to film to pursue these questions further, and generate new thought, because of film's status as a privileged site for the feminist negotiation of the relationship between Woman and women. The book's close analyses of films therefore function as a form of generative feminist philosophy that produce new knowledge. In the second half of the chapter, I shift focus to an assessment of the relationship between deconstruction and film, arguing that Derrida's treatment of film is structurally comparable to his treatment of the question of Woman. Against the backdrop of an overview of existing work on deconstruction and film, I propose that a new approach to Derrida's work developed out of feminist film theory reveals Derrida's contribution to film theory to lie in his ideas about film as a singular experience and the empowerment this affords the postcinematic feminist spectator. Remaining with the idea of the singular, the chapter closes by introducing the book's other key feminist methodology – close reading – which I perform throughout the book and elaborate further theoretically in the final chapter.

In Chapter 2, 'Supplanting Spectrality', I begin the book's cinematic engagements with the film perhaps most often discussed in relation to deconstruction and film, since within it Derrida reflects on cinema – Ken McMullen's *Ghost Dance* (1983). Previous scholarship unquestioningly prioritises the interview with Pascale Ogier in which Derrida makes these comments on film, focusing thematically on technology and spectrality.

In contrast, informed by Michael Riffaterre's theory of reading, I pay close attention to ungrammatical elements of the film's mise-en-scène in order to expose how spectrality is in fact linked critically in the film with Derrida, the academy and the masculine narcissism of mainstream cinema. In contrast, a feminist reading of the film, including attention to the leading couple – Marianne and Pascale – reveals that *Ghost Dance* opens up the possibilities of female agency free from male control. I conclude that while these feminist possibilities remain potential rather than actual, fantastical rather than realistic, in *Ghost Dance* and its key filmic influence, Jacques Rivette's *Céline et Julie vont en bateau: Phantom Ladies Over Paris* (1974), they are more fully realised in the female-directed films which are the subjects of the following two chapters.

Chapter 3, 'Feminist Countersignature', moves from a film in which Derrida appears to one which responds to his work. Joanna Callaghan's *Love in the Post: From Plato to Derrida* (2014) is a film rich to the point of mise-en-abyme in women engaging in critical and creative responses to Derrida's thought, as well as generating new thought and insight out of spaces of female–female intimacy. In *Love in the Post*, Callaghan engages in a creative response to, and feminist critique of, the epistolary 'Envois' section of Derrida's *The Post Card* (1987) by making a film about a filmmaker called Joanna making a film in response to 'Envois'. With a female–female extra-marital affair at its core, *Love in the Post* performs a specifically *feminist* countersignature of 'Envois', inserting women into structures of philosophic and other forms of inheritance-as-(in)fidelity, and exploring in practice the possibilities of a feminist film-philosophy. The central two sections of the chapter explore two aspects of the film's feminist philosophical work: in the first, I argue that the film generates an alternative concept of relationality and inheritance based not in an idea of (in)fidelity but in the idea of reproduction – both aesthetic and sexual – and the centrality of women to it; in the second, I explore how *Love in the Post* is able to materialise women in their embodied reality *and* perform the possibility of gender and sexual indeterminacy, of multiple possible signatories and addressees, a feat to which Derrida's 'Envois' only aspires. The chapter concludes that *Love in the Post* avoids an excess of fidelity to Derrida by this feminist countersignature, and by cinematically countersigning the idea of countersignature itself – a textual metaphor – by presenting an alternative cinematic way of figuring the relationship between film and philosophy.

Whereas Chapter 3 considers a film that responds to just one of Derrida's works, Chapter 4 considers a film which responds to Derrida's life and work more broadly, Kirby Dick and Amy Ziering Kofman's *Derrida* (2002). *Derrida* has been heralded from within Derridean circles as a path-breaking experimental film, Derridean in form in its foregrounding of the delusions and dangers of biography and in its pronounced self-reflexivity. However, placing the film in the context of the history of feminist experimental documentary filmmaking, and in the context of Dick and Kofman's wider feminist film oeuvre, this chapter reveals that the film is neither original in its experimentation nor in fact experimental enough, and that Derrida's arguments about biography – foregrounded in the film – are only saying what feminist filmmakers have always already known. The second part of this chapter moves from a concern with biography to a concern with autobiography, reading *Derrida* as Ziering Kofman's autobiographical expression of her relationship with him. As such, Ziering Kofman takes her place as yet another of the women within this book – myself, Pascale, Joanna (real and fictional), Sophie (another character in *Love in the Post*) – who are responding to and departing from Derrida and his work. Moving on from Derrida, in the generative part of this chapter I seek to develop an alternative theory of autobiography out of the feminist autobiographical cinematic tradition, focusing on Michelle Citron's *Daughter Rite* (1978) and its contemporary heir, Sarah Polley's *Stories We Tell* (2012). This move enables me to close the chapter by returning to Derrida's work from the recentred feminist 'elsewhere', in order to provide a new interpretation of Derrida's deconstructive autobiographical practice in 'Circumfession'.

While the first four chapters of the book address feminist responses to Derrida's work, and explore female–female sites of generation of new ideas in relation to deconstruction and film, the final chapter turns the tables. In Chapter 5 it is Derrida, not us, who is the respondent, in a text he was solicited to write in response to Marie Françoise Plissart's photonovel *Right of Inspection* (1985). Here, the lesbian feminist work comes first, front and centre; it is the provocation for Derrida's thought, rather than vice versa. Derrida never wrote on a feminist or lesbian film, so the inclusion of a photonovel rather than a film in the final chapter of the book is not merely justified, it is essential: to rule out an engagement with *Right of Inspection* here simply because it is not a film would have been to miss the only opportunity available to examine what happens when Derrida attempts to 'read' a lesbian feminist visual work. This chapter begins by offering a detailed close reading of *Right of Inspection*, contending that while Derrida's accompanying polylogue does attempt to address the questions the photonovel raises about looking – how one does so and who has the right to do so – his reading is limited by a failure on his part to recognise and take up the embodied lesbian subject position I show is created by the work. In the second section I argue that what Derrida's essay does offer the feminist film critic, however, is a theoretical account of *metonymic reading* which delineates and justifies the close-reading methodology employed throughout this book. While the book begins by departing from Proust, it ends by veering from Borges: at the heart of *Right of Inspection* lies an extract from one of Borges' short stories which offers a surprising metonymic clue to the power of feminist critical and creative practice.

The texts under primary analysis in the chapters of this book have been chosen since together they constitute a body of visual works closely associated with Derrida and deconstruction: this is the first time they have been considered together as such, and the first time many of them have been read in their cinematic, or photographic, contexts, rather than merely their philosophic one. At the same time they all, interestingly, feature female–female intimacy. In Chapters 2 and 3, the relationships between Pascale and Marianne, between Céline and Julie, and between Joanna and Sophie are apparitionally lesbian, rather than explicitly so. In Chapter 4, the female–female intimacy explored is not lesbian at all, but rather that between a woman and herself, as well as between a woman and her mother. In contrast, the very focus of Chapter 5 is the visibility and representation of the lesbian. In all these variant cases, however, whether the lesbian is apparitional, absent or powerfully visible, these female–female intimacies provide productive sites of knowledge and representation, generative 'elsewheres' to male-dominated technologies of thought and institutional discourses. In cinematic terms, these visual works remain, as de Lauretis notes sites of feminist generation so often do, 'in the margins of hegemonic discourses' (de Lauretis 1987: 18) – they are all, to more and lesser extents, experimental and avant-garde. One of the intentions of this book is to put them in the limelight. It is in these spaces made visible that not just, as de Lauretis proposes, 'the terms of a different construction of gender can be posed' (1987: 25), but the terms of a different construction of key concerns also of film studies: realism, artifice, narrative, adaptation, autobiography, the still, and how we look at and read the visual. In my experience, in fact, such feminist spaces offer the possibility of a different construction of almost everything of importance, with the power, as de Lauretis says, to 'have effect and take hold at the level of subjectivity and self-representation: in the micropolitical practices of daily life and daily resistances that afford both agency and sources of power or empowering investments' (de Lauretis 1987: 25). It is therefore more important than ever that spaces of feminist thought and practice become mainstream. And in relation to film this is indeed beginning to happen. This book is a scholarly contribution to the wider cultural attention to feminism and film which began in the 1970s but which has gained renewed momentum and prominence in the UK and the US in the past few years. A new generation of feminist filmmakers, critics and scholars is now taking on the challenges, and moving forward the debates, begun by the first wave of feminist filmmakers, critics and scholars in the 1970s. In *Political Animals: New Feminist Cinema* (2015), Sophie Mayer argues that 'what's "new" about the twenty-first century "new feminist cinema" […] is its negotiation of a transgenerational feminist film history of four decades within a reflexive awareness of the interruption and re-vision of feminisms, and interconnectedly of film cultures, in the new millennium' (6).

Renewed attention to, engagement with and interrogation of feminism and film is today to be found everywhere, from production through distribution to popular and scholarly reception. To give just a few examples, founded in 2013 in New York City but now encompassing local chapters across the world, the feminist film collective *Films Fatales* has created a grassroots community of collaboration and support for female film directors.[4] The 2015 Woodstock Film Festival had a Spotlight on Women in Film & Media, featuring more films by female directors than ever before in its sixteen-year history, as well as hosting a panel discussion on women in film and media.[5] In the UK, the queer feminist film-curating collective *Club des Femmes* has been active since 2007, the London Feminist Film Festival launched in 2012, and the Director of the London Film Festival 2015 declared 2015 'the year of the strong woman' (Fordy 2015). There are now also a host of online organisations dedicated to feminist coverage of media and popular culture, including film.[6] More mainstream, at the 2015 Oscars, Patricia Arquette used her acceptance speech to call for equal pay in the film industry, prompting many other female actresses also to raise the issue. In October 2015, in response to repeated reports regarding inequality and sexism in the film industry, the US federal Equal Employment Opportunity Commission began interviewing female directors to determine if formal action ought to be taken to combat discrimination against female film and TV directors (Robb 2015; Child and Smith 2015). Seven months later, in May 2016, the EEOC widened 'its circle of interview subjects to include studio executives, producers, agents, actors and male directors' (Keegan 2016). In February 2017, *Deadline* reported that 'the EEOC is in settlement talks with the major studios to resolve charges that they systemically discriminated against female directors' (Robb 2017). No report from the EEOC has yet been published as this book goes to press, however, and the new US Administration's ongoing reshuffle of the EEOC poses potential threats to the continuation and effectiveness of the investigation. Alicia Malone's new book, *Backwards and in Heels: The Past, Present and Future of Women Working in Film* (2017), is the most recent work to highlight the contribution women have made to film, the discrimination that persists, and the work still to be done.

Academic scholarship, as I understand it, is not divorced from this world of attention and activity but part of it, making its own contribution in its own singular ways. In 2015, issues of feminism and film rose to heightened academic visibility. It was the year which saw: the publication of *Feminisms: Diversity, Difference and Multiplicity in Contemporary Film Cultures*, an editorial collaboration between an established and an emerging feminist scholar – Laura Mulvey and Anna Backman Rogers respectively – which assesses new developments in feminist film theory and culture against the backdrop of their histories; an international symposium on 'Independent Film (and) Women' at the University of Liverpool;[7] and the launch of a new book series, *Visionaries*, edited by Lucy Bolton and Richard Rushton, the first ever to be devoted exclusively to female filmmakers, their work, influence and status.[8] In 2017, the new intersectional feminist and LGBTQIA+ journal *MAI: Journal of Feminism and Visual Culture* was founded by Anna Backman Rogers, with the aim of becoming the basis for an intersectional feminist and queer collective of scholars, writers, artists and activists; and a four-year research project funded by the Arts and Humanities Research Council, 'Calling the Shots: Women and Contemporary Film Culture in the UK', is now underway at the University of Southampton, UK, to investigate the role and place of women in the UK film industry.[9] The importance of this academic work is emphasised by the British Film Institute's Filmography of British Film, launched as this book went to press, which shows that there is still enormous work to be done to achieve gender equality in front of and behind the camera in UK film.[10] As *The Guardian* reports, 'the filmography, which analyses more than 10,000 films and 250,000 cast and crew members, reveals that less than 1% of films made between 1913 and 2017 had a majority female crew and only 7% since 2000; only 4.5% of all films have been directed by a woman' (Brown 2017).

This book takes its place, then, within this context of renewed attention to issues of feminism and film in the industry, in wider culture and in academia. In turn, this renewed attention to feminism and film is itself part of a wider resurgence of feminism and its political importance in response to renewed threats to women's rights in the UK and US, and the increasing visibility of violations of those rights across the world. This book's contribution to feminism and film, and to feminism more widely, is unashamedly scholarly not in order to close down dialogue but to open it up. In that sense, the theories developed here, the scholarly readings produced, are not independent of filmmaking and reception nor, in fact, of the lived experiences of real people; rather, they are driven by art and by life, and, it is hoped, can feed back into both of those realms. There are parts of this work that do not intersect with other circles of experience, activity or ideas: this book does not, for instance, address important intersectional feminist issues such as race, class and transgender concerns; the female characters in the films under discussion are white and cis-gendered. But there is no intention to imply by this that such women encompass all women; no intention to commit the 'deadly metonymy', as Hortense J. Spillers has it, of universalising from the singular experience of white women (1984: 78). Rather, I hope that the work performed here will be of use and inform debate and scholarship in those intersecting fields of enquiry, and that while not encompassing the whole of what it means to be, for example, a woman of colour, or a woman not cis-gendered, or a woman with disabilities, that the 'we' in this work might at least provide some common ground where the experiences of being different kinds of women do intersect. For united in our differences we must stand.

Notes

1. See Castle (1993), especially 'The Apparitional Lesbian' (pp. 28–65), for her foundational arguments regarding lesbianism and apparitionality: 'It is perhaps not surprising that at least until around 1900 lesbianism manifests itself in the Western literary imagination primarily as an absence, as chimera or *amor impossibilia* – a kind of love that, by definition, cannot exist. Even when "there" (like Stein's Oakland) it is "not there": inhabiting only a recessive, indeterminate, misted-over space in the collective literary psyche. [. . .] it is reduced to a ghost effect: to ambiguity and taboo. It cannot be perceived, except apparitionally' (30–1).
2. Other feminist critiques of Proust, in particular in relation to his representation of lesbianism, can be found in Ladenson (2000) and Chapter 6 of Huffer (2013).
3. De Lauretis considers the feminist requirement to inhabit both of these modes of response to be a contradiction, that the condition of possibility of feminism (both theoretical and actual) is one of tension between 'the critical negativity of its theory, and the affirmative positivity of its politics' (1987: 26). I do not see these two modes of response as in tension, as pulling in opposite directions, but as part of a combined dual action.
4. Full details regarding *Films Fatales* are available at http://www.filmfatalesnyc.com/ (last accessed 18 September 2017).
5. The Woodstock 2015 Press Release can be found at http://wffpress.squarespace.com/women-in-film-2015/ (last accessed 18 September 2017).
6. See, for example, bitchmedia in the US at https://bitchmedia.org/about-us and the F-Word in the UK at http://www.thefword.org.uk/about/ (both last accessed 18 September 2017).
7. Unfortunately, the proceedings of the symposium were not recorded and there are no plans to publish the proceedings. The event was held on Thursday 21 May 2015 at the University of Liverpool, organised by Yannis Tzioumakis.
8. Details of the series and the call for submissions can be found at https://edinburghuniversitypress.com/series-visionaries.html (last accessed 18 September 2017).

9. More information can be found on the 'Calling the Shots' website available at https://www.southampton.ac.uk/cswf/project/index.page? (last accessed 21 September 2017).
10. The Filmography is available at https://filmography.bfi.org.uk/ (last accessed 21 September 2017).

CHAPTER ONE

Deconstruction, Feminism, Film

In *The Gift of Death* (1995) Derrida enters into dialogue with Plato's *Phaedo*, Western metaphysics' founding meditation on death. He explains how, in this text, Socrates defines philosophy as 'the attentive anticipation of death, the care brought to bear upon dying, the meditation on the best way to receive, give, or give oneself to death, the experience of a *vigil* over the possibility of death, and over the possibility of death as impossibility' (*GOD* 12–13). The *Phaedo* thus establishes a necessary and irreducible intimacy between philosophy and death such that, as Socrates puts it, 'all who actually engage in philosophy aright are practising nothing other than dying and being dead' (Plato 2009: 64a4–6). This assertion has haunted the Western philosophical tradition all the way down to Kierkegaard, Heidegger and Jan Patočka, all of whom are Derrida's interlocutors, in addition to Plato, in *The Gift of Death*. What Derrida fails to address, however, is who and what are excluded – at the very beginning – from this philosophical tradition: women; popular art; and the body. At the start of his detailed account of Socrates' death, Phaedo explains how, on the day decreed for Socrates' death, he and Socrates' other companions visited him in prison as usual, only to find him already with company:

> On entering we found Socrates, just released, and Xanthippe – you know her – holding his little boy and sitting beside him. When she saw us, Xanthippe broke out and said just the kinds of things that women are given to saying: 'So this is the very last time, Socrates that your good friends will speak to you and you to them.' At which Socrates looked at Crito and said: 'Crito, someone had better take her home.'
> So she was taken away by some of Crito's people, calling out and lamenting . . . (Plato 2009: 60a1–9)

With his wife Xanthippe removed, Socrates does not immediately embark on his philosophical dialogue, however, but reflects on the curious interdependence of pleasure and pain, and, importantly, on art, not philosophy's, potential to evoke it. Socrates' reflection here prompts Cebes to quiz him about his recent creative activities. Since coming to prison Socrates has indulged, for the first time, in the writing of poetry: he has made up poems 'putting the tales of Aesop into verse' and has written a 'hymn to Apollo' (Plato 2009: 60d1–2). Cebes reports that people, especially Evenus, have been asking what Socrates has had in mind, 'in making them up after you'd come here, when you'd never made up anything before?' (Plato 2009: 60d2–4). In reply, Socrates explains that he has produced art, rather than philosophy, for the first time, in response to a recurring dream he has had 'often in my past life' (Plato 2009: 60e5–6). Until now, he has interpreted the dream's imperative to '"make art and practise it"' (Plato 2009: 60e8) as an instruction 'to do the very thing that I was doing, to make art, since philosophy is a very high art form, and that was what I was making' (Plato 2009: 61a1).[1] Now that his trial is over but the festival of Apollo (during which no death sentences may be carried out) has delayed his execution, however, Socrates is led to question his previous interpretation of the dream. In the face of death he has decided to, as it were, hedge his bets: 'I thought that in case it was art in the popular sense that the dream was commanding me to make, I ought not to disobey it, but should make it; as it was safer not to go off before I'd fulfilled a sacred duty, by making verses [ποιήματα] and thus obeying the dream' (Plato 2009: 61a6–61b2).

At the opening of the *Phaedo* we thus discover that, in the interim between sentence and execution, on the verge or cusp of death, Socrates is led to question the form of art he should have been making *throughout his entire life*. Facing death, Socrates does not just produce popular art for the first time, but wonders if this is in fact *always what he should have been producing*. The enormity of this admission should not be ignored. But it is. Socrates' companions do not respond in any way to this explanation of his activities, but rather take up his closing suggestion that Cebes should say goodbye to Evenus from him and tell him 'if he's sensible, to come after me as quickly as he can' (Plato 2009: 61c–61c1). It is this provocative advice that leads into the rest of the dialogue's arguments for the proposition that to philosophise is to learn how to die, which can be summarised as follows: since the body is a hindrance to thought and the soul alone can gain access to truth, the philosopher must aim to take leave of the body in order to access truth through the mind alone; but the soul is only parted from the body in death, therefore 'those who practise philosophy aright are cultivating dying' (Plato 2009: 67e4–5). In Socrates' arguments in the *Phaedo*, the rejection of the body is structurally necessary for philosophical access to truth. In order to make those arguments, the body (with all its inconvenient fleshy needs and desires), the woman (with all her inconvenient emotions and interruptive speech) and popular art have been exorcised in both senses of this term – that is, they have been called forth in order to be expelled.

Derrida returns to this moment in the *Phaedo* in his reflections on the photographs of Jean-François Bonhomme, published posthumously in *Athens, Still Remains* (2010), but he makes no comment on the banishment of Woman. Initially, he makes little too of Socrates' creative writing. Derrida does not indicate which translation (if indeed it is a translation) of the *Phaedo* he is working from here, but it seems to be one that renders μουσική as 'music' (*la musique*, in Derrida's original French), not 'art'. Derrida therefore reduces Socrates' experiments in art forms other than philosophy to merely paying 'a debt by composing music to offer to the god whose votive festival was responsible for deferring his death' (*ASR* 51). But a few pages later he returns again to Socrates' dream only to present a surprising misreading of this moment in the *Phaedo*. Derrida cites the key passage in which Socrates says, quite clearly, that he has turned to art ('music', as Derrida has it) in case he has been misinterpreting his dream throughout his life and this is what he always should have been making, rather than philosophy. But Derrida elides the two, equating music with philosophy, in order to argue that in philosophising Socrates has always already met the demands of the dream: 'Socrates is certain that that's what he has always done' (*ASR* 55), says Derrida, whereas this in fact could not be further from the truth. In order to shore up this misreading, it is necessary for Derrida to omit from his citation the crucial lines 'as it was safer not to go off before I'd fulfilled a sacred duty, by making verses and thus obeying the dream' (61a6–61b2), which clearly indicate that his creative activities are *different to* the philosophical activities on which he has focused until now.

Through selective citation and misreading, Derrida fails to engage with the import of Socrates' artistic activities prior to his death. Equally, he fails to address the use and abuse of Woman and women in this dialogue, and elsewhere. For instance, Derrida yokes to his discussion of the *Phaedo* the moment in the *Crito* when 'tall and beautiful, clothed in white, a woman calls him by name in order to give him this rendez-vous, the moment of death' (*ASR* 51). Here the figure of Woman becomes synonymous with death, but Derrida does not pause to reflect on the use of Woman again just as a figure, an empty disembodied signifier, within the masculine philosophical discourse. Returning to *The Gift of Death*, after exploring the aporia of (ir)responsibility in the biblical story of Abraham and Isaac, and in Melville's 'Bartleby the Scrivener', Derrida does finally reflect on the absence of Woman. He observes that

> It is difficult not to be struck by the absence of woman in these two monstrous yet banal stories. It is a story of father and son, of masculine figures, of hierarchies among men (God the father, Abraham, Isaac; the woman, Sarah,

is she to whom nothing is said; and Bartleby the Scrivener doesn't make a single allusion to anything feminine whatsoever, even less to anything that could be construed as a figure of woman). (*GOD* 75–6)

This observation leads Derrida to pose a series of questions regarding the Woman, sacrifice and death which, in a characteristic gesture, he leaves unanswered: 'Let us leave the question in suspense' (*GOD* 76).[2] A feminist response to Derrida's work must not leave the question of Woman in suspense. Rather, it must ask, and answer, the question of Woman in Derrida. Such a process reveals the feminist fault lines in Derrida's work: there is no excess of fidelity here; but it also reveals the contribution that Derrida's work can and does make to feminist thought. In the first section of this chapter I concentrate on the relationship between deconstruction and feminism, arguing that film offers a privileged site for a feminist philosophy able to negotiate the relationship between philosophy and social reality, and conceptualise we-women rather than It-Woman – a conceptualisation Derrida does not manage to achieve in his work. In the second half of the chapter I turn to the relationship between deconstruction and film in order to argue that Derrida's attention to the singular – in his work on film, and as essential to deconstruction as a mode of reading – enables a theorisation of a new agential postcinematic female spectator.

Women, popular art and the body, exorcised at the origins of philosophy, return as key modes of thought in this book, insisting on their presence and the access to truth they provide. This book is concerned precisely with the importance of 'just the kinds of things that women are given to saying' (Plato 2009: 60a4–5) for I, this embodied woman, Sarah, refuse a philosophical tradition in which I, along with any other woman, is only she to whom nothing is said. Let us instead be both seen and heard on our own terms. To make a start, then, at speaking . . .

I It-Woman vs We-Women

The question of Woman in deconstruction consists of two interrelated parts: the first is the question of the relation between Woman and women, that is, between a philosophical or ontological concept of Woman and the political and everyday realities of embodied female subjects; the second is the question of the relation between women and men, the question of sexual difference. As Gayatri Chakravorty Spivak elaborates in her review essay of Derrida's *La carte postale* (1981) – 'Love Me, Love my Ombre, Elle' (1984) – Derrida uses Woman as *the* figure of deconstructive undecidability, part of a process of resexualising phallogocentric discourse that is integral to his deconstruction of Western metaphysics. Spivak focuses upon the place of '"woman" in the development of Derrida's own vocabulary' (1984: 21), arguing that '"woman" on the scene of Derrida's writing, from being a figure of "special interest," occupies the place of a general critique of the history of Western thought' (1984: 22). She substantiates this claim with reference to a range of Derrida's texts in which Woman represents the possibility of critique of the history of Western phallogocentrism, in which She enables, in fact, the possibility of deconstruction. In *Spurs*, for instance, Spivak explains that 'woman is taken, via Nietzsche, as a name for citationality' (1984: 22) and becomes, as she also does in 'The Double Session', the figure via which Derrida performs a critique of the proper; in 'To Speculate: On Freud', when 'Derrida uses the concept of semi-mourning (*demi-deuil*) to describe the conduct of the text, once again the abyss-structure that can be named "woman" is invoked' (1984: 23). Woman takes its place in Derrida's work alongside other terms such as '*différance*', 'parergon', 'writing', 'the supplement', but Spivak goes further than this, arguing that 'it is by no means one among many Derridean themes' (1984: 23). Rather, for Spivak, 'it is perhaps the most tenacious name for the limit that situates and undermines the vanguard of every theory seeking to be adequate to its theme' (1984: 23).

This raises the question, however, of the relation between Woman and women, and how, if at all, Derrida's philosophical use of Woman is any different to the use of Woman in Western metaphysics. The answer to these questions lies in what Derrida repeatedly talks of as the two phases of deconstruction.[3] The first phase of deconstruction reverses the oppositional hierarchies of metaphysics so, here, Derrida's use of Woman repeats, by merely reversing, the philosophical gesture of phallogocentrism: where previously the masculine has been privileged philosophically, Derrida philosophically privileges the feminine. Derrida uses Woman at this stage precisely because of, and for, its oppositional power. Such a move does not, however, address the question of the relationship between Woman and women – there is in fact no apparent connection between it-Woman and we-women. Nor, in fact, is this relationship addressed in the second phase of deconstruction which focuses not on Woman and women, but on gender, understood as a question of sexual difference. In this phase, not just women, but even the empty signifier supposedly attached to her, Woman, are in fact elided. In the two interviews in which he is asked to directly address the question of Woman – 'Choreographies' (1982) and 'Women in the Beehive' (1984) – Derrida introduces the thought of the gift and the time and movement of dance in order to refigure (sexual) relationality in a way intended to deconstruct the oppositional relationship between man and woman but also the oppositional relationship between philosophy and politics, the abstract and the concrete, which have been the grounds for many challenges to his use of the figure Woman.

Derrida does *not* use Woman in this second phase of the deconstruction of sexual difference in order to rethink (sexual) relationality otherwise than as opposition, for if that relation is no longer one of opposition, Woman no longer retains any oppositional power. The ideas of the gift and of the dance offer productive new modes for thinking (sexual) relationality other than through the lens of oppositional sexual difference, but this move leaves suspended the question of the relationship between Woman and women.[4]

In 'Ontology and Equivocation: Derrida's Politics of Sexual Difference' (1997), Elizabeth Grosz defends Derrida from critique on these grounds, articulated for instance in Rosi Braidotti's argument that Derrida's work is 'part of a tendency within contemporary theory to use the metaphor of Woman to question the status of truth, knowledge, and subjectivity at the expense of women's concrete social struggles' (1997: 78).[5] In Derrida's defence, Grosz draws attention to the way in which representation determines the real: 'I am not, of course, claiming that there are no real women, but that real women are the consequences or effects of systems of representation and inscription' (1997: 79). Revisiting the question of the relationship between deconstruction and feminism after Derrida's death, Grosz highlights Derrida's importance for feminist thought. In particular, in a long footnote she schematises 'how Derrida shares many common political and conceptual concerns with feminist theory' (1997: 92). These include: his critique of phallogocentrism; his deconstructive reading practice, which focuses on the excluded and its constitutive role; his commitment to reading as a political act, that is, his emphasis on the necessary relationship between the theoretical and the practical; the confronting way in which his work forces feminism to recognise its position as potentially constricted by its relativity to the power structure it challenges; and, his replacement of the traditional philosophical and psychoanalytic representation of Woman as lack with Woman as excess and undecidability, as that which challenges metaphysical logic of self-identity and presence.[6]

Alongside Grosz, Spivak takes her place as another key feminist open to the possibilities of deconstruction, while at the same time recognising the feminist limitations of Derrida's thought. As elaborated above, in 'Love Me, Love my Ombre, Elle', she identifies Woman as a 'privileged figure' (1984: 24) in Derrida's writing, a consequence of his critique of Western thought as phallogocentrism. But Spivak's essay is also characterised by a revealing ambivalence in relation to this movement in Derrida's writing, in particular in relation to the question of the relation between Woman and women, between this persistent question of the relationship between philosophy and social reality. Spivak first opens up this question in her discussion of *La carte postale* when she asks 'why should we read an elaboration of such a problematics given the urgency of "the rest of the world"?' (1984: 20), a question to which, as she indicates, she returns in her conclusion. She acknowledges, as Grosz does, that feminist rejection of deconstructive thought has primarily been driven by a perception of the divorce within it between theory and practice, between philosophy and reality. But Spivak understands Derrida's project 'as an undoing of such oppositions' (1984: 21). What Derrida's work reveals is the extent to which 'even the most abstract-seeming judgements are arrived at by way of, even constituted by, unwittingly value-laden story lines' (Spivak 1984: 21). Derrida's writing exposes the habitual and thus unquestioned narratives – 'so practised that they seem self-evident logical propositions' (Spivak 1984: 21) – that determine the structures that create social reality and that determine the actions of subjects functioning in that reality. Accordingly, by drawing attention to the values of such narratives, and by creating counter-narratives, such as the resexualisation of philosophical discourse under the name of Woman, Derrida's writing performs a twofold function: it undoes the division between the philosophical and the social, between, as Spivak calls them, the concrete and the abstract; and, it provides alternative grounds for judgements and decisions, alternate philosophical narratives that can determine social structures and actions otherwise.

This, at least, is Spivak's explanation of the relation between the thought of Woman and the concrete reality of women in Derrida's writing. But the scene of writing of Spivak's own text betrays an uncertainty on this point. Following her summary of Derrida's treatment of Woman and the hymen in 'The Double Session', there occurs a passage in which the grammar is revealing:

> Of course these deductions are based on a curious view of woman and an implicit identification of (male) pleasure ('sem(e)-ination') as the signified, however besieged. To see indeterminacy in the figure of women might be the effect of an ethicolegal narrative whose oppressive hegemony still remains largely unquestioned. Yet it must be recognized that the deduction allows Derrida's reading of Nietzsche and Mallarmé to make woman the mark of the critique of the proper. (Spivak 1984: 22)

The power and import of the opening 'of course' is unclear: why should this so evidently be the case? In the second sentence, the use of the infinitive form of the verb 'to see' removes the necessity for a grammatical subject; it thus remains undecidable *who* is performing this act of seeing, which leaves unquestioned, which indeed perpetuates, the oppressive hegemony of a 'certain' – speaking more plainly, patriarchal – ethicolegal narrative. The careful grammatical undecidability of Spivak's own text alleviates the necessity for her to formulate a direct criticism of Derrida – since the subject here could equally be Mallarmé – and his figuration of Woman as 'indeterminacy'; a criticism which might raise the question of how, if at all, this movement in Derrida's texts is really any different to the elision of women by the abstraction of Woman in Western metaphysics. That this question might indeed be troubling Spivak's text is revealed in the anomalous use of the plural 'women' in the second sentence of this passage, rather than the singular 'woman' which is used consistently throughout the rest of the text. 'The word "woman"' (Spivak 1984: 23) may well take its place in Derrida's writing in the chain of terms such as *différance* and writing, but the relation between 'the word "woman"' and women remains unthought. Even as Spivak recognises the feminine operation of undecidability in Derrida's text, she cannot but ask, if only in a footnote, 'does such a "generalization" of woman negate "woman in the narrow sense"?' (1984: 24, n. 9).[7]

At the beginning of 'Love Me', Spivak promises that she will 'offer some criticism of such a use of the figure of woman' (1984: 25) in the final section of the essay. It is to this section that the reader might expect to turn, then, in order to discover what conclusions, if any, Spivak comes to in answer to this question:

> What we have in *La carte postale*, then, is a spectacle of how a male philosopher trained in the School of Plato and Hegel and Nietzsche and Heidegger acknowledges the importance of sexual difference and tries to articulate the name of woman. He does not deny that he is tied to the tradition. He cannot show his readers womankind made heterogeneous by many worlds and many classes. Although such a philosopher can wish to deconstruct the methodological opposition between empiricism and structuralism [*Grammatology* 162], in fact it is a binary opposition he often seems to honor, with the privilege going to structure . . . Thus it would be unwise to look in Derrida for a deconstitution of the history of the concept 'it-woman' – as opposed to 'we-men' – where the line between empiricism and structuralism would shift and waver. Yet we might want to attend to him because the tradition that he is thus 'feminizing' or opening up has been the most prestigious articulation of the privileging of man. He thus shows us the dangers of borrowing the methodological imperatives of that tradition uncritically. (Spivak 1984: 35)

For Spivak, Derrida's position in relation to the question of Woman is delimited by his gender, his training and the location of his thought firmly within the Western philosophical tradition he deconstructs. Accordingly, given such disabling limitations, Derrida should be valued for what he does manage to achieve – a feminising of phallogocentric discourse – and acquitted for what he cannot: 'he cannot show his readers womankind made heterogeneous by many worlds and many classes'. Despite Derrida's wish to deconstruct the opposition between empiricism and structuralism, he is still (poor helpless male philosopher) bound by it, as a result of which it would be unwise (unkind, unfair) of us, his readers, to expect from Derrida any sustained deconstruction of the philosophical reduction of women to Woman in which his refigurations partake. In attempting to excuse Derrida here Spivak in fact leaves him vulnerable and exposed, dependent upon the wise generosity of his readers to absolve him of his philosophical and political shortcomings. Spivak summarises her attitude towards deconstruction in 'Displacement and the Discourse of Woman' (1997): 'first, deconstruction is illuminating as a critique of phallocentrism; second, it is convincing as an argument against the founding of a hysterocentric to counter a phallocentric discourse; third, as a "feminist" practice itself, it is caught on the other side of sexual difference' (1997: 60). 'I learn from Derrida's critique of phallocentrism,' Spivak writes, 'but I must then go somewhere else with it' (1997: 48). In '"Woman's Place" in Derrida and Irigaray' (1997), Ellen T. Artmour echoes Spivak's rhetoric of forgiveness and the need to move on from Derrida's thought:

> Certainly we (women) need something more. But do we really want (or can we expect) the 'something more' from a 'man'? (I would argue, furthermore, that Derrida will always be marked as such, no matter how he disguises himself – and I suspect he is aware of that.) Can a 'man' give 'it' to us? (68)

Artmour insists, like Spivak, that 'the site from which Derrida begins (the man-who-desires-woman and/or truth) limits what he can see and do' (1997: 74).

Like Grosz, Spivak and Artmour, I recognise what Derrida's work has to offer feminist thought, but I also recognise its limitations. I am interested in both a feminist philosophical development and critique of Derrida's thought, as well as in stepping away from Derrida, and from the metaphysical tradition of which he remains a part, in order to generate new thought. If not in Derrida's work, then, where might we turn for a deconstruction of the history of it-Woman? Where does the line between empiricism and structuralism, between philosophy and reality, shift and waver? What mode of thought enables us, as Ellen K. Feder and Emily Zankin note Derrida's work does not, 'to conceptualise women among ourselves' (1997: 28)? Where can we see an exploration of we-women who represent, as Geoffrey Bennington regrets Woman cannot, 'a plural difference which would affect the whole of metaphysical thought' (Bennington 1993: 225)? The answer is in film. As a technology of gender, film is able to address what Karen Barad calls 'the entanglement of matter and meaning' (2007) without disregarding or privileging one over the other. As such, film represents a privileged site for exploring 'the inter-implication of the discursive and the material in which no priority is given to either side' (Gonzalez-Arnal et al. 2012: 3). In other words, as a *visual* medium, film foregrounds the empirical world of matter and embodied lived realities, while as a visual *medium*, it foregrounds that matter and bodies are always mediated semiotically. The line between empiricism and structuralism, philosophy and reality, shifts and wavers. In films made by women, foregrounding women, we-women deconstruct it-Woman, exploiting and interrogating 'the discrepancy, the tension, and the constant slippage between Woman as representation, as the object and very condition of representation, and, on the other hand, women as historical beings, subjects of "real relations"' (de Lauretis 1987: 10). As Laura Mulvey noted recently, given film's 'exemplary place in "the society of the spectacle"', film practice and film theory have 'enabled feminists to grasp the gap between "women" in their social content and [. . .] "women" as a signifier that referred to the male psyche and the patriarchal unconscious' (Mulvey in Rogers and Mulvey 2015: 21).

It is for these reasons that I turn to film as the most productive site both to explore and challenge the question of Woman in Derrida's work, and as a site 'elsewhere' to philosophy from which to generate new thought. There are also two further reasons for turning to film. The first is that Derrida's work is often defended from feminist criticism of his abstraction of Woman and elision of women – by himself and others – with the argument that he incorporates feminine or female voices into his dialogic and polylogic texts. Under the heading 'Sexual Difference' in 'Derridabase' (1993), Geoffrey Bennington mounts precisely this defence, pointing to the intervention of a 'female' voice 'in dialogues or polylogues such as "Restitutions" . . . , "Pas" . . . , the "reading" of *Droits de regards*, or *Feu la cendre*' (1993: 204). He also notes that in *Glas* 'the "déjà" (but also the signature and the countersignature) is associated with the mother' and that in 'At This Very Moment in This Work Here I Am' it is in 'a dialogue also involving a female voice' (Bennington 1993: 204) that Levinas is suspected of the phallogocentric consequences of neutralisation. There are three major issues with such a defence.[8] One is ethical, that is, the problematic ethics of a man speaking as or for a woman, especially given, as Elizabeth Harvey notes, 'the cultural silence of women that subtends and enables male ventriloquization of their voices' (1992: 13). The other is literary, that is, the limitations of Derrida's stylistic ability – he is simply not a skilled enough creative writer to convincingly portray an alternative subject position to his own. The third is the problem of (dis)embodiment, a further iteration of the Woman–women issue. As de Lauretis notes, 'the question of woman for the male philosopher is a question of style (of discourse, language, writing – of philosophy)' (de Lauretis 1987: 32). For feminist thinking, however, the question of women is both a question of the social and semiotic production of gendered subjects, and a question of the adequate representation of women and the diverse realities of our embodied lived experiences. We need media that enable us to speak for, and appear as, ourselves. Film offers the potential to do just that, disrupting Derrida's security in the voice with the need also to negotiate the mediation of bodies.

The final reason for turning to film is because thinking with and through the works of visual art under analysis in this book enables the type of feminist philosophy of which Clare Colebrook is in pursuit when she observes:

> Philosophy may not just be a question of ideality, pure truth, universalizable ethics, and transcendental conditions. There have been other ways of thinking about truth – aesthetic, ethical, and pragmatic ways of establishing truth. And these ideas of truth do not rely on a negation or exclusion of particularity or contingency. (1997: 95)

I have argued elsewhere, in my literary scholarship, that the complexities and uneven textures of singular literary texts rupture the seductively smooth perfection of theoretical polemic, that literary equivocation deranges theoretical surety (Dillon 2015c). In the second half of this chapter I want to examine the power and importance of the singular – my preferred term to Colebrook's 'particularity' or 'contingency' – in Derrida's thinking about film in order to offer a new perspective on how Derrida's thought might be read in relation to feminist film theory and criticism. As paradoxical as this assertion might at first appear, thinking through the singular provides the opportunity for a more complex consideration of we-women – of the diverse pressures on us, as well as of our powers and possibilities – than the reductive it-Woman ever could.

II Singular Spectatorship

David Wills observes that 'Derrida has never been unaware of reactions to his writing by feminists, or reticent about addressing those reactions, although one could argue that he waits until he is solicited' (1988: 23); the same might be said of Derrida's writing on film. In fact, women and film seem to have occupied a similar position in Derrida's life and work – loved but mysterious; sources of pleasure but held at a distance from the serious business of philosophy; essential, but excluded. In *Derrida: A Biography*, Camilla Adami remembers, 'I often used to provoke him [. . .] which disconcerted him a little, since he was more used to talking to men. In spite of his love of women and his closeness to feminism, he still had a bit of a misogynistic side, like many men of his generation' (Adami cited in Peeters 2012: 266). Regarding film, Benoît Peeters observes that, 'unlike Deleuze, who wrote two major works on the subject, there was nothing of the "cinephile" about Derrida. What he sought from cinema first and foremost was a way of freeing himself from taboos and forgetting his work' (2012: 434). While in his later work Derrida produced, independently, a number of texts on the visual arts, his direct reflections on film were always solicited. In his interview for *Cahier du cinéma* conducted on 10 July 1998 and on 6 November 2000, Derrida is absolutely frank that his relationship to cinema is one of pleasure and escape, not one of thought. Cinema is, for him, 'a way of forgetting work' (*CG* 24); when he was a student, 'it often acted on me like a drug, entertainment par excellence, uneducated escape, the right to wildness' (*CG* 24). Cinema is of value for Derrida precisely because it is pure entertainment: 'as for me, as quite an avid spectator, I remain, I even plant myself on the side of the popular: cinema is a major art of entertainment. One really must let it have that distinction' (*CG* 25). He repeats the point again – 'it plays the role of pure feeling of escape' (*CG* 25), and again – 'for me, the movies are a hidden, secret, avid, gluttonous joy – in other words, an infantile pleasure. This is what they must remain [. . .]' (*CG* 25), and again – he surrenders to films out of 'childish enjoyment' (*CG* 25). With this repeated disavowal, Derrida is making his position in relation to cinema quite clear; it is the interviewers who solicit him to treat it seriously, against his natural inclination. And Derrida is troubled by this solicitation: his relationship to film as pure entertainment puts him in a difficult position – 'no doubt it is what bothers me a bit in talking to you because the space of *Cahiers* signifies a cultivated, theoretical relation to cinema' (*CG* 25), a cultivated, theoretical relation that Derrida does not share. As a result, Derrida's reflections on film, his theories of film, are best understood as presented here and elsewhere in the subjunctive mood: 'if I were to write about film,' he says, 'what would interest me above all is its mode and system of belief' (*CG* 27).[9] 'If I were to write about film': the subjunctive mood expresses a state of unreality – here, the *possibility* that Derrida might write about film – but one that *has not yet occurred*.

Derrida's writing about cinema is only ever subjunctive; it indicates the possibility, not the reality, of what he might say if he were to write about film. And it is the subjunctive nature of his reflections on film, here and elsewhere, that often render them, in a similar way to his comments on sexual difference, facile.[10] He is proposing only the possibility of what he might write or think; he never develops a sustained or complex theory of film, nor is his thought ever complicated or enriched by the close reading of a filmic text. This does not mean, of course, again similarly to his thoughts about women, that he has nothing to say when his thoughts are solicited. Just as his work has significantly influenced feminist thought – whether in modes of adoption, rejection or negotiation – the subjunctive possibilities of Derridean film thought have prompted what is now a significant body of theoretical and critical work at the intersection of deconstruction and film. This work can be divided into four categories:

1. work, dating primarily from the 1980s and early 1990s, that attempts to develop a Derridean theory of film as *écriture*.[11] Such work has failed to take hold because in its concentration on film as writing, as a differential system of traces, it does not address the phenomenality of film and its medium specificity. For film critics and theorists driven to investigate how films work and what cinema is, this body of writing simply does not provide compelling or convincing answers to such questions.[12]
2. work, dating primarily post-2000, that explores a theme in a film or films via Derrida's thinking on that topic, for example violence, the supplement, the signature, the postal, the animal, hauntology, forgiveness, autoimmunity, the political or friendship.[13] This work is being produced by a generation of film critics for whom Derrida is not a new thinker but an established and key philosophical interlocutor. Such work disproves Brunette's assertion in 1998 that 'if the mission and focus of film studies is seen as the formal and thematic interpretation of individual films, deconstruction has little to offer' (1998: 91).
3. work that returns to classical film theory in a deconstructive mode, and/or in the light of Derrida's thought, for instance recent re-examinations of such figures as Jean-Louis Baudry, André Bazin, Sergei Eisenstein, Jean Epstein and Siegfried Kracauer. In their introduction to a recent special issue of *Discourse* on Derrida and film, James Leo Cahill and Timothy Holland identify this kind of historiographic work as 'most exciting and surprising', arguing that recent returns to classical film theory 'have certainly benefited from a style of deconstructive engagement that, even when not invoking Derrida's name in direct citation, has come to carefully rethink and reengage with texts, phenomena, and lines of thought once considered fully accounted for and exhaustively read' (2015b: 16).[14]
4. recent work that changes the pre-existing directionality of enquiry; that is, whereas 1–3 take Derrida's thought into film studies (albeit in different modes), work in this category looks to manifest a theory of film latent within Derrida's oeuvre. This is film scholarship, as Timothy Holland puts it, 'that is more or less concretely "about" Derrida's work' (2015: 44). Holland's own work belongs here, in its attempt to prove that 'cinema inhabits a more privileged place within deconstructive thought than may be assumed' (2015: 49), as does Akira Mizuta Lippit's *Cinema Without Reflection* (2016), which begins with the assertion that 'Derrida gestures toward cinema, speaking of and to it in passing, provoking a series of spectralities that allow him to appear and disappear in the passage. His is a

theory of cinema *en passant*' (1). Such work primarily focuses on Derrida's contribution to a long-standing concern with the relationship between cinema and spectrality (on which more below and in Chapter 2), although Lippit extends this into further reflections on autobiography and narcissism. Work in this category is new and impressively inventive, in the double sense of that word. For instance, in his search for 'a secret thesis on film' (Lippit 2016: 2) within Derrida's work, Lippit is engaged in a process of discovery (the first meaning of invention: 'to come upon', 'discover', 'find out'), the success of which is predicated more on the inventiveness of Lippit's own intellectual abilities (inventive in the second sense of the word, that is, 'to devise', 'contrive', 'feign' or 'make up') than on the actual presence of such a thesis within Derrida's work.[15]

Existing accounts of the relationship between deconstruction and film are characterised by a shared move: they argue for the importance of Derrida's work to film while, at the same time, they insist on the still hidden or unacknowledged place of Derrida's work in film theory and criticism. Despite providing a prolific overview of scholarly literature engaged with Derrida, deconstruction, film and media theory, Cahill and Holland still conclude that 'the impact of deconstruction on the field remains largely implicit, tactical, and rarely called by name' (2015b: 15).[16] This account echoes the assessment of other commentators: in *Film Theory: An Introduction* (in both the 1988 first edition and the 2006 second edition), Robert Lapsley and Michael Westlake argue that 'within film theory Derrida is perhaps best conceived of as a structuring absence' (65); echoing their terminology directly, but without acknowledgement, in 1996 Anthony Easthope asserts that 'the writing of Derrida performs as a structuring absence in the work of *Screen*' (189), also adding his own metaphorical twist: 'in *Screen* the influence of Derrida's writing appears like a fish in water, never openly breaking the surface' (Easthope 1996: 187); in 1998, Brunette asserts that 'the application of Derridean thought to film has been important but largely indirect' (91); in 2009, Louise Burchill suggests that the presence of Derrida's work in film theory is 'of the order of a "palimpsestic" infiltration' (165); in 2012, Laura McMahon observes that 'specific frameworks for theorizing film in relation to Derrida's writing remain relatively underdeveloped' (511 n. 4). I do not intend to repeat this move. From the weight of evidence above it is no longer necessary to see Derrida as a hidden figure in film theory and criticism – his subjunctive reflections might hint only at the *possibility* of what he would say if he were to write about film, but those possibilities have been made realities by other thinkers and writers who have actualised in myriad ways what can be said and thought at the intersection of deconstruction and film.

This book's thinking about deconstruction and film, then, is not an isolated Derridean intervention into a field that has previously suppressed, repressed or ignored Derrida's influence; rather, it is a feminist intervention into what is now an established field of thought and practice with many important thinkers working on that terrain. My starting point, then, is not that of previous commentators – namely, to investigate what, if anything, there is to be said about Derrida and film. Rather, I want to explore what is interesting from a feminist perspective in what Derrida said about film, and to examine how his thoughts about film might connect with or contribute to feminist film theory and criticism. As a result, I am not interested in Derrida's reflections on spectrality in his solicited ideas about film, although, given the prominence attributed to them, the move away from this focus forms part of the work of the next chapter. It is now well-established that Derrida's reflections on film repeatedly identify the shared embeddedness of deconstruction and film in the logic of spectrality. The most explicit statement of this takes place, appropriately, on film, during Derrida's cameo appearance in Ken McMullen's *Ghost Dance* (1983), in which Derrida plays himself playing himself. In an improvised response to the actress Pascale Ogier's question, 'Do you believe in ghosts?', Derrida observes that 'the cinema is the art of ghosts, a battle of phantoms . . . It's the art of allowing ghosts to come back.' He gives voice to his belief that

> ghosts are part of the future and that the modern technology of images, like cinematography and telecommunication, enhances the power of ghosts and their ability to haunt us. In fact, it's because I wished to tempt the ghosts out, that I agreed to appear in a film.[17]

We find similar observations throughout Derrida's solicited work on technology, for example in 'The Ghost Dance', an interview in *Public* in 1989, where Derrida reiterates that 'the experience of ghosts . . . is accentuated, accelerated by modern technologies like film, television, the telephone. These technologies inhabit, as it were, a phantom structure. Cinema is the art of phantoms' (*TGD* 61).[18] For deconstruction, the logic of spectrality – both the non-contemporaneity of the present with itself and the open possibility of the phantasmatic return of the past and arrival of the future – is an absolute necessity. As Derrida says in the transcription of filmed interviews collected in *Echographies of Television*, 'without this possible coming-back, and if we refuse to acknowledge its irreducible originality, we are deprived of memory, heritage, justice, of everything that has value beyond life and by which the dignity of life is measured' (*EC* 23). As the art of ghosts, as the medium of that spectral return, it is clear that Derrida considers film to bear an essential affinity with deconstruction.

Derrida returns to this topic in the *Cahiers du cinéma* interview, which is entitled (by the interviewers rather than Derrida himself) in order to highlight the spectral theme: 'Cinema and Its Ghosts'. Previous commentary on the interview also focuses on Derrida's ideas about film and spectrality, but it does so at the expense of observing and interrogating the novel element of Derrida's reflections in this interview – his introduction of the idea of singularity as a key part of his experience and understanding of cinema.[19] In a crucial section of the interview, Derrida analyses the relationship between the collective and the individual, the general and the singular, in cinema. He warns against too easy assumptions about the collective experience of cinema-going. In fact, for him what marks cinema as different from, for instance, theatre is 'the solitude of the spectator' (*CG* 2). In opposition to theatre, a form of spectacle which creates the audience as a collective presence, what makes Derrida happy at the movies is 'the power of being alone in the face of the spectacle, the disconnection that cinematic representation supposes' (*CG* 29). Derrida values cinema-going as a singular experience of the spectacle:

> I don't like to know that there is a viewer next to me, and I dream, at least, of finding myself alone, or almost, in a movie theater. So I wouldn't use the word 'community' for the movie theater. I wouldn't use either the word 'individuality,' too solitary. The suitable expression is that of 'singularity,' which displaces, undoes the social bond, and replays it otherwise. (*CG* 29)

What is of feminist value in Derrida's theory of cinema – were he to have one – lies not in the oft-repeated idea of spectrality, but here, in this idea of cinema as a general experience of the singular. What defines cinema, its mode and system of belief, is its interplay between the general and the singular: 'There exists, at the root of the belief in cinema, an extraordinary conjunction between the masses – it's an art of the masses, which addresses the collectivity and receives collective representations – and the singular. The mass is dissociated, disconnected, neutralized. At the movies, I react "collectively," but I also learn to be alone' (*CG* 29). Derrida's interviewers do not solicit more thought on this point but move on to the question of testimony; the potential, feminist and otherwise, of his subjunctive theory of cinema as a general experience of the singular remains only a possibility yet to be developed, one which I wish to pursue here.

Samuel Weber is one of the few commentators to note the importance of Derrida's reflections on the singular experience of film. In interview with Peggy Kamuf, Weber identifies Derrida's focus 'on the spectrality of the medium and on the *solitude* of the film spectator' (2015: 159) as two elements of his ideas about cinema that have rendered his thought less influential in film than, for instance, Deleuze's.[20] While Weber uses the word '*solitude*', it is important to note that Derrida does not – he dismisses describing cinema-going as an 'individual' experience because that word is 'too solitary'. As Weber notes elsewhere, 'singularity for Derrida was always an aporetic concept that involved communication with others, and never just a self-identity. It is not the same, therefore, as the individual' (2014: 190). For Derrida, the singular does not dispense with the general but introduces and plays out new forms of relationality between the singular and the general, the individual and the communal. Derrida was, Weber says, 'trying to rethink the relation of the singular, of a singular experience, to commonality' (2014: 190). While Derrida does not pinpoint which individual and which community, which singularity and which generality, his subjunctive reflections can be understood in the context of the history of feminist film theory regarding the agency – or lack thereof – of the individual female spectator.

In the now canonical essay, 'Visual Pleasure and Narrative Cinema' (1975), Laura Mulvey argues that classical Hollywood cinema determines the position that the female spectator can adopt – since film objectifies the woman, female spectators must either enter into a masochistic identification with the women-object on screen, or they must engage in spectatorial transvestism by adopting the male gaze, the only spectatorial position offered by Hollywood film. The *agential* female spectator is in fact an impossibility according to Mulvey's theory, for it is only through the self-consciousness of avant-garde film – in which the foregrounding of the material existence of the filmic process punctures the illusion of the narrative – that film can escape the ideological constraints that bind Hollywood cinema. The female spectator herself does not have the agency to effect that resistance, although she may take up a different subject position to that of the male gaze, such as that of 'passionate detachment' (1975: 18), if it is created for her by avant-garde film. In this respect, Mulvey's essay remains embedded in the apparatus theory of the 1970s in which cinema is believed to constitute its subject, interpellating him according to the dominant ideology, with only certain films able to rupture this effect through exposing the mechanisms of the film-work.[21] Much feminist theory since Mulvey's essay has taken issue with this aspect of Mulvey's theory, but perhaps the strongest challenge to this lack of an agential female spectator has come out of Black feminist film theory, in particular bell hooks' essay 'The Oppositional Gaze: Black Female Spectators' (1993).[22] There, hooks confronts theory with practice, philosophy with reality, examining Black female spectatorship and its social reality.

According to hooks, in Black American history the politics of the gaze means something totally other to the way in which it has been construed by Mulvey and White feminism film theory; it is the politics of the gaze inherited from the racialised power structure of the right to look during slavery:

'The politics of slavery, of racialized power relations, were such that the slaves were denied their right to gaze' (hooks 1993: 288). Whereas for Mulvey the withdrawal of the right to look for women results in a cinematically enforced passivity, with no option but transvestism and the inhabitation of the masculine viewing position, in stark contrast, hooks makes a powerful political argument that the withdrawal of the right to look creates an oppositional gaze full of agency:

> all attempts to repress our/Black people's right to gaze had produced in us an overwhelming longing to look, a rebellious desire, an oppositional gaze. By courageously looking, we defiantly declared: 'Not only will I stare. I want my look to change reality.' Even in the worse circumstances of domination, the ability to manipulate one's gaze in the face of structures of domination that would contain it, opens up the possibility of agency. (hooks 1993: 289)

For Mulvey, the sexual politics of the gaze is imbricated in a sexually differentiated structure of domination which offers those dominated no site for active resistance. For hooks, the racial politics of the gaze is imbricated in a racially differentiated structure of relations of power – understood in a Foucauldian sense – which thereby affords those dominated the possibility for active resistance through the power of the oppositional gaze. In Black feminist film theory, cinema does not determine the viewer's subject position. Rather, as Manthia Diawara puts it, 'every narration places the spectator in a position of agency; and race, class and sexual relations influence the way in which this subjecthood is filled by the spectator' (Diawara 1990: 33 cited in hooks 1993: 290). For Mulvey in 'Visual Pleasure', the critical self-consciousness that would expose and disrupt the structures of domination inherent in the gaze is only possible in self-referential avant-garde film. For hooks, the power of that critical self-consciousness resides in the spectator herself:

> Black female spectators who refused to identify with White womanhood, who would not take on the phallocentric gaze of desire and possession, created a critical space where the binary opposition Mulvey posits of 'woman as image, man as bearer of the look' was continually deconstructed. (hooks 1993: 295)

Placing Derrida's observations on the singularity of the film spectator in the context of this feminist film theory about the spectator actualises the subjunctive potential of his reflections. That is, understanding the film spectator as singular delivers agency back to that spectator who is not constrained in her response by the film itself, or its apparatus, but rather exercises agency in negotiating her relationship as spectator to the generality that is both other viewers and the film itself. hooks' choice of verb, then, to describe the action of the agential female spectator is appropriate; in her activity, in her negotiation of the relationship between her singular experience and the generality of film and spectatorship, she does indeed continually *deconstruct* Mulvey's opposition between woman as exclusively object and the gaze as exclusively male.[23]

Mulvey's thoughts on cinema have of course evolved since her 1975 essay. Introducing her more recent work in *Death 24x a Second* (2006), Mulvey observes that 'then, I was absorbed in Hollywood cinema, turning to the avant-garde as its binary opposite. Now, I think that the aesthetics of cinema have a greater coherence across its historic body in the face of new media technologies and the new ways of watching films that they have generated' (Mulvey 2006: 7). The rise of digital has foregrounded the agency of the spectator, causing Mulvey to reformulate her theories of spectatorship and rendering Derrida's thoughts about singular spectatorship immediately relevant. For in the twenty-first century, watching film is no longer only, or even primarily, a cinema-going experience; developments in digital cinema and viewing platforms mean that Derrida's dream of there being no viewer next to him, of being alone in front of the screen, is now a common element of the viewing experience for the many people who watch films alone on computer, tablet or smartphone screens. Moreover, such devices change the way we view film; we can pause, move backwards, move forwards, watch deleted scenes, Director's cuts, 'making-of' interviews and more. My relationship with the film I am watching is now malleable, singular. And the way I engage with a film, the experience I have of it, may be radically different to that of someone else. Film viewing is now, then, in a way never so before, a singular experience; and reconceiving film viewing as a singular not a collective experience offers a new feminist politics of film spectatorship.[24] As a result of the singular, malleable ways in which we now interact with films, spectatorial agency is now a product of our apparatus of film consumption, not just gifted to us by avant-garde film or seized by us in an act of defiant opposition. We are no longer, or very rarely, under a cinematic illusion; we now have an unprecedented power to constitute ourselves as subjects and spectators.

There is a final way in which I develop Derrida's focus on the singular as a contribution to feminist film criticism in this book. This pertains not to his specific attention to the singularity of the film viewer, but the general attention across his work to the singularity of the text: 'a consistent deconstruction', he says in *Echographies of Television*, 'is a thinking of singularity, and therefore of the event, of what it ultimately preserves of the irreducible' (*EC* 6). Deconstruction is a general theory of the singular. I owe this formulation to Barnaby Norman who, in 'Time of Death: Herzog/Derrida' (2013), proposes that if we are to retain Barthes' ideas of the *punctum* and the *studium* then we have to 'reckon with the theory of photography as a general theory of the singular' (208).²⁵ Norman and I are opposed, however, in our understanding of the meaning of a general theory of the singular in relation to Derrida's work: for Norman, it denotes Derrida's problem, inherited from Blanchot and others, of 'how to say the unique in the language of the universal' (2013: 208). In his representation of the problem, 'language [. . .] can only *mean* as a power of generalisation, the singular cannot have a voice, and, ultimately, we have to say that the singular is in principle excluded from presenting itself *as such*' (Norman 2013: 208). I understand the problem to be the inverse; language and other systems of signification can only *mean* in the singular event, the general cannot have a voice and is excluded from presenting itself as such. Hence the importance of spectrality for Derrida in that the general is evoked, conjured, by the singular – the singular exorcises (that is, brings forth) the general but only ever as spectre.

If you want to 'do deconstruction', Derrida says in '"*As if* I were Dead"', 'then you have to perform something new, in your own language, in your singular situation, with your own signature, to invent the impossible and to break with the application, in the technical, neutral sense of the word' (*AI* 217–18). In this book, I 'do deconstruction' in relation to film in a singular way, in a way that incorporates and moves on from the existing categories of work on Derrida and film outlined above. I 'do deconstruction' of film by paying attention to the singular text and focusing on singularities in or of that text.²⁶ By focusing on singular filmic details I develop a deconstructive film critical practice that elucidates a film in its singularity and in doing so also contributes towards an ongoing analysis of the intersection of those discursive contexts within which I situate it. My readings are 'singular events, singular gestures, singular performatives' (Derrida, '"*As if* I were Dead"' 218) but, as Derrida notes, the singular replays the general, otherwise. More precisely, throughout this book, the singular functions metonymically: my singular readings invoke general theories. (I will return to the idea of metonymic reading at more length in the final chapter.)

Close reading is not a new methodology in film criticism. As Stephen Croft notes, it characterised much work in film criticism prior to the theoretical turn of the 1970s, when theoretically driven approaches challenged, and to some extent displaced, empirical criticism (Croft 1998: 311).²⁷ But close reading occupies a particularly problematic place in feminist theory. On the one hand, it is suspect, since paying attention to the detail is contaminated with ideas around the masculine fetishisation of the female image. For instance, in 1975 Mulvey identified in classical Hollywood film a structurally defining dualism of arresting spectacle – feminine, and kinetic narrative – masculine. The idea of 'pausing' the film voluntarily in criticism seems to participate in the fetishisation of the woman who 'bursts through the world of illusion as an intrusive, static, one-dimensional fetish' (Mulvey 1975: 18). At the same time, however, Mulvey recognises the disruptive potential of this irruption, the threat that the female image poses to the inexorable movement of masculine narrative. This potential is actualised in particular in lesbian and queer film criticism in which attention to the detail enables the subversion of the heteronormative narrative. Feminist film theory is divided between these two poles, as Judith Mayne outlines them: 'depending on your point of view, lesbian readings of isolated scenes are successful appropriations and subversions of Hollywood plots, or naïve fetishizations of the image' (Mayne 1991: 103); the same might also be said for feminist close reading more generally. In this book, I want to reclaim the deconstructive feminist power and potential of close reading. Rather than being trapped in a masculine problematic of fetishisation, I demonstrate that attention to detail can and is a feminist critical act. My readings of singular elements of specific films are thus agential acts of film criticism that challenge the ideological closure of narrative.[28]

In 'On Screen, In Frame' (1976), Stephen Heath defines film as 'a perpetual metonymy over which narrative lays as a model of closure' (261). While the perpetual metonymy of film's images leaves open the space for the interpretative desires of the spectator, narrative directs and positions the subject. Engaging with film in a deconstructive feminist mode means eschewing an analysis of narrative in favour of attention to the metonymic potential of specific elements of a film's signifying practices; doing so opens up the signifying possibilities of film beyond those imposed by the closure of narrative and demands and develops the interpretative power of the feminist spectator. In film, narrative prescribes a reading and inscribes a subject; reading non-narratively, reading metonymically, paying attention to the non-narrative detail, in essence, 'doing deconstruction', opens up a reading and empowers the interpreting subject. 'Frame, narrative placing, subject inscription cut short the interminable movement of the signifier' (Heath 1976: 261); deconstructive film criticism preserves it. Heath says that 'the problem, the political problem, for film in its intervention can be given as the transformation of the relations of subjectivity and ideology' (1976: 264). What this chapter has argued, and what the subsequent chapters of this book demonstrate, is that feminist deconstructive film criticism addresses and redresses that political problem by transforming the relations of subjectivity and ideology, positioning the singular subject as an empowered spectator paying attention to the metonymic potential of singular filmic details. As such, feminist deconstructive film criticism constitutes a political intervention in the field.

Notes

1. The original Greek word being translated into the English as 'art' here is 'μουσική', which Henry George Liddell and Robert Scott's *A Greek Lexicon* defines as 'any art over which the Muses presided, esp. Poetry sung to music'.
2. In 'The Sacrifice of Sarah' (2005), Peggy Kamuf notes that 'the "question of woman" has been posed (and suspended) repeatedly in Derrida's writings and at many different points of articulation with a larger cultural text' (105), but, in an excess of fidelity to Derrida, she also leaves the question suspended.
3. See, for example, *DIS* 4–6, discussed in the Introduction in relation to my own feminist *modus operandi* in this book. See also *P* 41–2, and *C* 71–2, in which Derrida and Christie McDonald discuss these phases in relation to questions of gender and feminism.
4. See Dillon (2011) and Dillon and Schad (2017) for a fuller exploration of what Derrida's theories of the gift and of dance offer to a rethinking of sexual relationality beyond sexual difference, the necessity of which is one of de Lauretis' key concerns in *Technologies of Gender* (1987).
5. See the rest of Grosz's essay for a useful engagement with feminist thinkers critical of Derrida's work, including Rosi Braidotti, Somer Brodrib, Nancy Fraser, Alice Jardine, Margaret Whitford and Michael Ryan. Another key feminist critic of Derrida's work is Joan Copjec: see Ewa Plonowska Ziarek (1997) for a useful presentation of, and engagement with, her position. Penelope Deutscher's work offers a sustained feminist philosophical engagement with Derrida's thought (1997, 2005, 2007, 2013), and Judith Newton and Nancy Hoffman (1988), in a special issue of *Feminist Studies* on deconstruction and feminism, critically interrogate what the former offers the latter.
6. The two key collections of essays that engage positively with the relationship between deconstruction and feminism remain Feder and Zankin (1997) and Holland (1997). See also Rey Chow (2006), in which attention is drawn to the work of key feminists for whom poststructuralist thought, including deconstruction, has been crucial; these include Nancy Armstrong, Judith Butler, Luce Irigaray, Teresa de Lauretis, Peggy Kamuf, Naomi Schor, Jenny Sharpe, Kaja Silverman, Gayatri Chakravorty Spivak, Robyn Wiegman and Linda Williams. See also Diane Elam (1994), who provides an introduction to deconstruction and feminism by considering them alongside each other, rather than, as this book does, by exploring their intersections.
7. There are a number of further moments at which Spivak's ambivalence regarding her own account of Derrida and the question of Woman betrays itself in the text. In her discussion of 'Plato's Pharmacy', for instance, she comments that 'the mother's son is directly related to another name for undecidability: writing . . . the phallocentric philosopher systematically resists the possibility that all discourse is dependent upon the producer's absence, and thus irreducibly illegitimate – a mother's son' (1984: 25) – she adds, but only as an undeveloped parenthetical aside: '(The daughter is not in sight.)' (1984: 25). In a more explicit

moment of criticism she refuses Derrida the benefit of the doubt in relation to his masculinist treatment of orgasm: 'although I know that Derrida *might* be *parodying* that Platonism which, identifying orgasm with semination – as in the male – declares in the *Laws* that the law of nature is coupling destined for reproduction [*Dissemination* 152–3]; I cannot not think that, like Normal Mailer and his thousand ancestors, he might also be *repeating* it; and repeating his own critique of Freud, I would withhold the benefit of the doubt: "description takes sides when it induces a practice, an ethics, and an institution, therefore a politics assuring the tradition of its truth"' (1984: 27). Spivak draws attention to a lack of 'a deconstitution of the sedimentation' (1984: 28) of metaphors derived from such terms as 'generation' and 'reproduction'. At the same time, she is quick to insist that such commentary does not constitute a criticism of Derrida: 'I am not necessarily faulting Derrida here. I am restraining the enthusiasm of readers like the two (woman) intellectuals in France who maintained in pedagogic discussion that Derrida "wrote like a woman"' (1984: 28).

8. For an extended discussion of the problems with Derrida's attempts to speak as a female subject, see Ellen K. Feder and Emily Zankin (1997).
9. In the French original this line reads: 'Si j'écrivais sur le cinéma, ce que m'intéresserait surtout serait son mode et son regime de *croyance*.' While 'écrivais' is not the grammatical subjunctive in French, which has fixed rules that rarely equate to the English grammatical subjunctive, Peggy Kamuf's translation accurately conveys the hypothetical meaning of Derrida's sentence here, since the English subjunctive captures Derrida's intention in the French: he is referring here to an action – writing about film – as conceived (rather than as fact), expressing thereby a contingent, hypothetical or prospective event. My thanks to Peggy Kamuf for her clarification in private correspondence on this point.
10. I take this word quite particularly from Artmour's description of elements of Derrida's thinking about sexual difference: 'One blind spot shows up in Derrida's vision of what lies beyond the current phallogocentric sexual economy. His projection of a vague multiplicity of sexual positions [. . .], like his exchange of masks to eternity, is too facile. It fails to recognize fully the reach of phallogocentrism and its tenacious grasp' (1997: 77 n. 21). I use 'facile' in its original meaning as 'straightforward, easy', 'simplistic', but without disguising the overtone of disparagement that arose in later use (see OED).
11. See, for instance: Marie-Claire Ropars-Wuilleumier (1980, 1981); Tom Conley (1991); Richard Dienst (1994); Gregory L. Ulmer (1985, 1989, 1994); and Peter Brunette and David Wills (1989). Such work is reinforced by comments in Derrida's own work: in his interview with Stiegler he notes that 'the way in which I had tried to define writing implied that it was already, as you noted, a teletechnology, with all that this entails of an original expropriation' (*EC* 37); in interview with Lewis and Payne he observes, 'I think that speech and image *are* in fact texts. They are writing. And therefore, the distinction was not between writing and speech, but between several types of text, several types of inscriptions, reproductions, traces' (*TGD* 62). For an excellent feminist critique of *Screen/Play*, see

Dianne Chisholm (1993). On Ropars, see Laura Oswald (1986). Philip Rosen (1981) usefully situates this body of work within post-1968 film theory on the politics of the sign.

12. See, for instance, Akira Mizuta Lippit (1990): 'To construct the premises of cinema within the confines of the grammatical, even the anagrammatical ("*cinema is an anagram of the real*"), is to dissipate the phenomenality of film into the recesses of an allegorical (literary) theory; it is to lose precisely that which initiates inquiry into the cinema; it is to lose, through substitution, the question saturating all film theory, "what is cinema?"' (1131).

13. The earliest example of such work is Peter Baker (1996), who uses Derrida's theories of violence in order to analyse *Fictions Letimimes* and *Pulp Fiction*. See also, for example: Ann Chisholm (2000), who uses Derrida's ideas about the supplement and the signature in a study of body doubling in film; Christopher D. Morris (2000), who uses Derrida's idea of the deferral of delivery in *The Post Card* to read Hitchcock's film as well as his fuller engagement with Hitchcock, informed by deconstruction, in *The Hanging Figure* (2002); Jonathan Burt (2006), who uses Derrida's thinking about the animal to address animal film imagery; Michele Zoey Élouard (2006), who employs 'the philosopher Jacques Derrida's [. . .] influential work on the metaphysics of presence to introduce and extend film theorist Laura Marks's [. . .] use of the metaphors of fetish and fossils with reference to documentary film' (48); Shannon Donaldson-McHugh and Don Moore (2006), who provide a reading of Van Sant's *Psycho* and its relationship to Hitchcock's 'original' in and through Derrida's idea of hauntology; Ray Chow (2009), who uses Derrida's idea of forgiveness to develop a reading of that idea in his work and in the film *Secret Sunshine*; Niven Kumar and Lucyna Swiatek (2012), who develop a reading of Haneke's films and terror guided by Derrida's idea of autoimmunity; Laura McMahon (2012b), who 'stages an encounter between the work of contemporary Belgian film-makers Jean-Pierre and Luc Dardenne and the thinking of the political elaborated by Jacques Derrida' (510); Laura McMahon (2012b), who uses Derrida's work on the animal in relation to Arnaud des Pallières' films; Eun-Jee Park (2012), who reads the Dardenne brothers' film *Rosetta* in the light of Derrida's concept of friendship; Carolyn D'Cruz and Glenn D'Cruz (2013), who use Derrida's ideas about identity and *différance*, and about hauntology, to read Hayne's Dylan film *I'm Not There*; Steven Marsh (2013), who uses Derrida's ideas about the postal in *The Post Card* to read *The Complete Letters: Filmed Correspondence*.

14. In addition to the examples they provide in footnote 41 (Cahill and Holland 2015b: 21), one might also add Louise Burchill's (2009) Derridean revisiting of the theories of Jean-Louis Baudry; as well as Laura Oswald (1986) and Akira Mizuta Lippit (1990) and their Derridean revisiting of the thought of Sergei Eisenstein.

15. The essays collected in Cahill and Holland (2015a), a double special issue of *Discourse* devoted to Derrida and cinema, constitute a landmark in contemporary work within this fourth category but none of them addresses feminist issues.

16. Cahill and Holland's literature survey opens with reference to work in the first category I have identified, but then usefully adds to the material given above a range of further texts and thinkers within film and media studies influenced by Derrida's thought. Their list ought also to be consulted (Cahill and Holland 2015b: 15).
17. The exchange in the film is in French. The English translation found in the subtitles is provided here.
18. A further iteration of this theme can be found in *Echographies of Television* (see esp. *EC* 117–20), in which Derrida discusses the scene in *Ghost Dance* cited above.
19. See, for instance, Burchill (2009) and Cahill and Holland (2015b).
20. From the above, it should be clear that I disagree on this point – 'Derrida's writing on cinema has not had the influence of other thinkers' (Weber 2015: 159) – because Derrida's writing on cinema was only ever subjunctive. Weber comes close to my position when he notes that Derrida's thoughts 'remain at a level of generality that does not really link up with the specific ways in which sound and image are organized in cinema. Which is not to say that it couldn't do so' (2015: 159).
21. See, for instance, Jean-Louis Baudry (1974–5). See Constance Penley (1985) for a feminist critique of apparatus theory as not 'a scientific description of film production, but a theory that itself perpetuates masculine desire' (Mandy Merck in Mayne 1991: 140).
22. See Bergstrom and Doane (1989) in their introduction to a special journal issue on 'The Spectatrix'.
23. My reflections here actualise the potential of Cahill and Holland's passing observation in 'Double Exposures', that Derrida's thinking in the *Cahiers* interview 'offers possible grounds for a response to a series of theoretical debates that emerged in the late 1960s through the 1970s in the journals *Cahiers du cinéma*, *Cinéthique*, and *Screen* and continue to haunt film theory. We are thinking in particular of the lines of inquiry concerning the basic effects of the cinematic apparatus, its subject effects, and theories to identification, including the consequent and important challenges of the presumed universal conditions of cinema and its idealized spectator by feminist scholars, critical race theorists, and historians of media technology such as Laura Mulvey, Manthia Diawara, and Anne Friedberg. Derrida's evocation of the grafted subject in cinema, consisting of both self and others, divided and supplemented by the technics of cinema in its multiple iterations, offers an approach that renegotiates both the fundamental relationships and the entanglements of apparatus and subject' (2015b: 14).
24. See Francesco Casetti (2015) for a reassessment of cinema in the context of the technological advances of the twenty-first century. See Ensslin et al. (2017) for analysis of the wider effects of the shift to small-screen narrative consumption. The CFP for Ensslin et al.'s special issue on 'Small Screen Fiction' – the issue itself is not in the public domain at the time of going to press – identifies the way in which small-screen narrative consumption can 'involve direct reader/viewer/player interaction, enabling highly idiosyncratic, individualized and

unique narrative experiences'. The CFP is available at: http://paradoxa.com/ (last accessed 25 September 2017).
25. See Chapter 5 for a fuller discussion of the punctum. See Mulvey (2006) for an extended reflection on the punctum in the postcinematic digital age, although not from an explicitly feminist perspective.
26. Close reading film is experiencing a current resurgence with a strong case for its continued importance being made by John Gibbs and Douglas Pye (2005). August 2010 saw the launch of *Movie: A Journal of Film Criticism*, a reboot of *Movie* (1962–2000), sharing its precursor's commitment to close reading, at http://www2.warwick.ac.uk/fac/arts/film/movie/ (last accessed 18 September 2017). The book series 'Palgrave Close Readings in Film and Television', edited by Gibbs and Pye and with books published since 2013, focuses on the detailed criticism of film. I share in Gibbs and Pye's belief that close reading and theory can mutually illuminate the text and reciprocally inform each other. Where I differ from Gibbs and Pye, and perhaps even more so from Clayton and Klevan (2011), is that I do not see an irreducible connection between close reading, analysis and interpretation on the one hand, and evaluation on the other.
27. For other assessments of the state of the field, see Gledhill and Williams (2000) and Bordwell and Carroll (1996).
28. Mulvey returns to these issues in *Death 24x a Second* in the context of the arresting power of contemporary digital viewing technologies. Rather than exiting from the categories of feminine=static/passive, masculine=kinetic/active, and exploring the power close attention offers the agential female spectator, however, she argues instead that these technologies serve to create 'a fragmented, even feminized, aesthetic of cinema' (Mulvey 2006: 180). Remaining bound by and within the limits of the psychoanalytic model, she concludes only that 'within the terms of the "Visual Pleasure and Narrative Cinema" model, the aesthetic pleasure of delayed cinema moves towards fetishistic scopophilia' (Mulvey 2006: 165).

CHAPTER TWO

Supplanting Spectrality

The film with which I begin the close readings of this book is the one perhaps most closely associated with deconstruction and film, since within it, as I have noted in Chapter 1, Derrida makes his now infamous comments on the nature of cinema. This film is Ken McMullen's *Ghost Dance* (1983) and these comments occur in an interview between Derrida and the actress Pascale Ogier fifteen minutes into the film. The interview lasts just under five and a half minutes. After it ends, Derrida never features visually in the film again, although he does recur in two voice-overs, one elaborating Nicolas Abraham and Mària Torok's theory of mourning, the other recounting his experiences during a trip to Prague. Despite the brevity of Derrida's role in the film, if one had never watched *Ghost Dance* and were informed only by the critical material surrounding the film, and the director's comments, it would be forgivable to surmise that the film is exclusively about ghosts and haunting, and that it is dominated by, and primarily stars, Derrida.[1] This is not the case.

In my engagement with *Ghost Dance* in this chapter I will also start with this scene. But I do so not, as previous commentary has done, in order to elaborate on its content – in particular, Derrida's thoughts on spectrality and film – and end discussion there. Rather, I want to propose that the spectral heuristic is only one interpretation of *Ghost Dance* and that an entirely other feminist interpretation of the film is possible. Such a hermeneutic can only be developed by paying attention to elements of the film beyond the Ogier–Derrida interview, in particular by attending to: the significance of the recurrent presence within the film's mise-en-scène, and as prop, of a knife; a crucial *trompe l'oeil* shot of Marx's grave that transitions the film from Part One to Part Two; and, the nature of the relationship between the leading female couple – the characters Marianne and Pascale – reflection on which is made possible through comparative analysis with the film's key cinematic rather than philosophic intertext, Jacques Rivette's *Céline et Julie vont en bateau: Phantom Ladies Over Paris* (1974). This approach to the film displaces the primacy of the Ogier–Derrida interview within its aesthetic fabric, and supplants the thematic focus on spectrality – linked as this is in the film with Derrida, the Academy and the masculine narcissism of mainstream cinema. In its place, the film opens up the feminist possibilities of female agency free from male control (in both cinema and life), possibilities that remain potential rather than actual, fantastical rather than realistic, in this male-directed film, but which we will see rendered real in the female-directed visual works which form the subject of the book's subsequent chapters.

I The Incidental Philosopher

In the interview, Ogier asks Derrida if he believes in ghosts, a question which produces his now famous statement that 'the cinema is the art of ghosts' and his equally famous but slightly different equation: 'cinema plus psychoanalysis equals the science of ghosts'.[2] In the previous chapter I briefly elaborated Derrida's ideas about spectrality – both in this interview and in other solicited comments about film – in order to acknowledge its importance to his thinking about cinema but also to argue that his ideas about cinema and singularity in the *Cahiers du cinéma* interview provide a more productive source for the development of a contemporary feminist deconstructive theory of film spectatorship and film critical practice. To move away from spectrality when discussing Derrida and film is a radical break with existing scholarship. It is one justified by those arguments I have already made, and by attention to the history of film theory which contextualises Derrida's statements as just another iteration of an association between film and the spectral which is as old as cinema itself. Louis-Georges Schwartz provides the best existing account of Derrida's relation to this history in 'Cinema and the Meaning of "Life"' (2006). In this essay, he moves from a wealth of evidence of responses to early film screenings which 'tend to link the new technology to questions of life, death, and mourning' (Schwartz 2006: 9) to Derrida's concept of cinema and spectrality. He argues that Derrida's reflections continue this tradition but with a deconstructive twist – for Derrida, cinema does not merely bring the dead back to life but radically destabilises our understanding of the very categories of 'life' and 'death', and of temporality:

> For Derrida, cinema does not merely ease mourning, help the bereaved to control it, or restore life to the living. Cinema spectralizes the world as forcefully as it enables survival. It introduces ghosts, neither living nor dead, into the world. (Schwartz 2006:16)[3]

Schwartz reaches this conclusion, of course, through an analysis of the Ogier–Derrida scene in *Ghost Dance* and Derrida's memories of the uncanniness of watching the scene some years later, after Ogier died.[4]

In line with all other existing commentary, Schwartz pays no attention to *Ghost Dance* beyond this scene – in fact, in his account, Ogier merely becomes the figure of Woman who functions in his text, as she does in so many of Derrida's, as *the* figure of deconstructive undecidability, 'the figure of the spectre' who 'makes possible the thinking of cinema' (Schwartz 2006: 14); the 'dead woman in a movie' who becomes 'a compact figure of some of Derrida's major later conceptual inventions' (Schwartz 2006: 14).[5] That Ogier does not exist in any sense here as an embodied woman who, at some point at least, had lived experiences is indicated by the constant slippage in the essay between reference to Ogier correctly as 'Ogier' (eight times) and incorrectly as 'Orgier' (also, eight times). The actress herself is so incidental to the discussion that it is not even imperative to get her name right. I want to turn the tables here and suggest that it is Derrida, not Ogier, who is incidental to *Ghost Dance*. In 'Back From the Future' (1995), McMullen asserts that 'Jacques Derrida is the film's intellectual core'. I want to assert that he is so not because of his theories of spectrality, but because of his incidentality to the film's emerging feminism. To make this argument, it is necessary to analyse closely how the body of the film represents him – rather than merely how he represents the medium in which he is taking a part – and to develop a new critical engagement with the film guided by attention to details of the film's texture, rather than merely by the verbal and intellectual content of the Ogier–Derrida interview.

The Ogier–Derrida interview takes place towards the end of Part One of the film, entitled 'Rituals of Rage Rituals of Desire', a part which itself could be divided into three distinct but connected sections: section 1 – Pascale's attempt to sell all her technology to the Salesman (Dominique Pinon), a section which ends with her first exchange with Marianne (Leonie Mellinger); section 2 – Pascale's encounter with her Professor (John Annette) and her dream of Derrida; and, section 3 – her first encounter with Derrida in the café and the subsequent interview.[6] Part One ends with a transitional scene focused on Marianne. In order to understand how the Ogier–Derrida interview is connected to the rest of the film, it is necessary to pay close attention to the two sections that precede it, and to the scene immediately afterwards, which transitions the film into Part Two on 'Myth'.

In Part One, section 1, Pascale approaches a table on which are arrayed eight items (Figure 2.1). She packs five of the items – technological objects – into her bag. Three items remain on the table. The identity of one of them is clear, since it is a large keyboard and we have already seen a close-up of her typing on it. The identity of the other two items is unclear at first, until she starts to record a message on one of them, which the viewer then realises is some sort of recording device. The final item is only taken up as she hits the button for the playback of her recording – its shape, the momentary reflection of light off its surface, and the clink of metal on the table as she lifts it,

Supplanting Spectrality

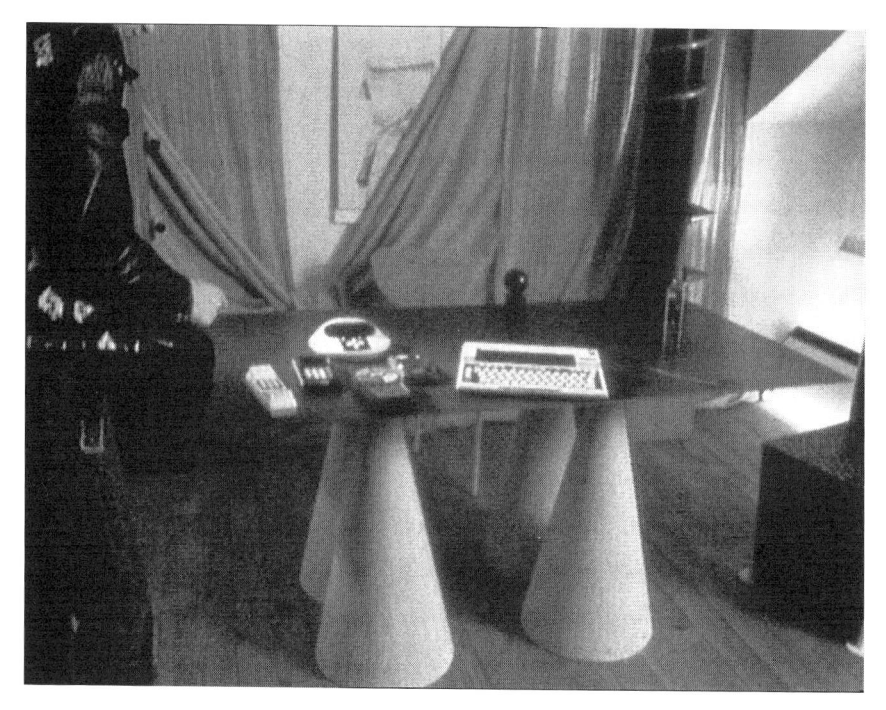

Figure 2.1 The ungrammatical knife.
Source: *Ghost Dance*, dir. Ken McMullen.

reveal that it is some sort of knife or blade. She holds it, considers it, and then takes it with her, along with the keyboard (Figure 2.2). The knife's presence on the table alongside otherwise technological objects is incongruous, an anomaly. It might even be construed as a visual 'ungrammaticality'. I take this term from Michael Riffaterre's *Semiotics of Poetry* (1978), a study I have found useful in previous work since it offers a powerful model of the way in which we read poetic texts.[7] I want to extend Riffaterre's work here to the process of reading film. Riffaterre wants to account for the way in which a poem can say one thing and mean another – in this instance, the way in which *Ghost Dance* is ostensibly about spectrality but actually means something else as well. Riffaterre argues that any text consists of a layer of representation which 'is distorted by a deviant grammar or lexicon (for instance, contradictory details)' (1978: 2). These 'ungrammaticalities', as Riffaterre calls them, alert the reader to the significance of the poem, that is, to 'what the poem is really about' (1978: 167 n. 3). While I am resistant to Riffaterre's implication that there is an 'authentic' meaning to which the ungrammaticalities can alert the reader, his theory provides an interesting way of thinking about anomalies in filmic texts, unexpected or surprising elements of the film's texture which

Figure 2.2 Pascale (Pascale Ogier) and the knife.
Source: *Ghost Dance*, dir. Ken McMullen.

rupture the narrative – be this the film's own narrative or, as is more the case with *Ghost Dance*, the narrative constructed for it by layers of criticism and interpretation – and send the reader off in a different interpretative direction.

Viewers may perceive these visual ungrammaticalities on their first or even subsequent linear encounter with a filmic text – what Riffaterre calls the *heuristic* level. Noticing them prompts a shift to a different level of viewing — the *retroactive* or *hermeneutic* – during which the viewer carries out a process of 'reviewing, revising, comparing backwards' (1978: 5–6); in essence, exactly the type of non-linear textual engagement now made possible by contemporary digital viewing technology and the distinct singularity of any viewer's engagement with a film on their own individual viewing platforms. This process uncovers the variations of the ungrammaticality throughout the text which in fact create a structure or matrix revealing a new meaning: 'the text, raised from the ashes of familiar description, is made into a novel and unique significance' (Riffaterre 1978: 12). The visual ungrammaticality of the knife prompts the feminist retroactive reading of *Ghost Dance* carried out here, offering the clue to an alternative feminist matrix of meaning and significance within the film. It does so also by pointing outwards, beyond *Ghost Dance*, connecting the film with one of the most significant early feminist avant-garde films, Maya Deren's short *Meshes of the Afternoon* (1943), in which a knife repeatedly recurs, also first appearing on a table. The recurrent knife makes a connection between these two films, drawing our attention to the presence in *Ghost Dance* of the feminist motifs of Deren's film, in particular the multiplied female lead and a thematic concern with male sexual violence and the cinematic representation of women.

It is easy to miss the knife and to focus instead on Pascale's act of recording and on the message she leaves: 'Fuck you. I'm sick of it. I'm selling everything. I'm off. Don't try to find me. As far as I'm concerned, you're a ghost.' Pascale's overt reference to ghosts is consolidated by the importance of the voice recorder to Derrida's understanding of spectrality. In *Archive Fever*, Derrida exposes the aporia that while we know that someone deceased will never speak again, in any case 'the phantom continues to speak' (*AF* 62), 'like the answering machine whose voice outlives its moment of recording' (*AF* 62). For Derrida, 'there would be neither history nor tradition nor culture without that possibility' (*AF* 62–3), the necessary possibility of a spectral response informed and mediated by technology, such as the device into which Pascale speaks. This is more than sufficient to initiate a heuristic response to the film that would follow the semantic chain of its visual, verbal and aural spectralities. But what if, instead, we follow the knife? To do so is to jump across the subsequent violent encounter with the electrical Salesman, to the first moment in which we see the two lead women together on screen. Pascale hands Marianne the knife and, holding it concealed in her inner breast pocket, she retraces Pascale's steps back to the Salesman, who we cannot now but think is going to meet a bloody end. Following the knife creates a new hermeneutic response to the film, one which attends to its concern with threatening male violence towards women and the possibility of united, even violent, female resistance. In this light, Pascale's subsequent encounters with her Professor, and then with Derrida, in the second two sections of Part One, take on a very different hue, just as the film itself moves from black and white to colour at the end of this first section.

In Part One, section 2, Pascale bumps into her American Professor (John Annette) in the street and is reprimanded for not having been to a tutorial for six months. The spectral heuristic again elides the woman – Pascale seems proud that it is her voice on the machine but the Professor does not recognise it as such, it is merely 'like a ghost in the machine'. But the feminist hermeneutic pays attention to Pascale's alienation from the University, manifest in her words, gestures, facial expressions and in the production of the soundtrack. Most obvious is her statement, 'I couldn't go there all the time. I can't stand sitting in that place. It's full of creeps down there.' She insists the

Professor is not one of them, and builds his male ego by spinning a yarn that in listening to the recordings of his lectures everywhere, she has made him into a kind of god. Apparently appeased, the Professor turns to the camera to discourse on his role as master in relation to Pascale as disciple. But this power relation is subverted by Pascale: she turns away from the Professor; rather than paying attention to him she rolls her eyes; echoing over his speech is her tape recording – 'Fuck you, I'm sick of it, I'm off' – the defiance of which makes her smile and gently nod. The implication is that the intended recipient of that message is not some ex-lover but the Professor who has been constantly ringing her, and the Academy he metonymically represents. What follows immediately afterwards is a cut to Derrida sitting in a café – a static camera shot that focuses on Derrida for thirty seconds. The Professor's voice fades out and is replaced by Hawaiian singing.[8] And an extra line is added to Pascale's message, one not included in the original recording: 'I'm heading to adventure.' These three elements – the shot of Derrida, the choral music and Pascale's voice-off – combine to align Derrida with Pascale's fantasy of the exotic, the mysterious, the promise of freedom, in opposition to the patriarchal restrictions of the Academy.[9] In this daydream, Derrida – the metonymic representation of deconstruction, that mode of enquiry which has sought to deconstruct the phallogocentrism of Western metaphysics and its institutionalisation in the Academy – represents for Pascale the possibility of escape. However, she is brought back to reality when the Professor finishes his monologue and literally manhandles her, dragging her out of shot. That this is a daydream, a fantasy, is confirmed by the fact that we learn in the subsequent café scene that she has lied to her Professor and has not in fact met Derrida before. When she does, the exchange is comically anticlimactic and self-parodic:

> JD: Briefly, Pascale, what's the idea behind your idea?
> PO: The idea behind my idea is that I have no idea.
> JD: Ah, I see. [English subtitles; in French in original]

From a feminist perspective, Derrida's importance to this film does not lie in the content of the Ogier–Derrida interview and his subsequent commentary on it. It is to be found instead in the way in which the opening of the film sets Derrida up as a metonym, a figure for female freedom from the patriarchal Academy. In making this argument, I am not unaware that I am replicating precisely the rendering figural of a real person that I have criticised in previous critical treatments of Ogier. But as I have noted in the Introduction and Chapter 1, this is also a classic deconstructive move and one which bears affinities with the dual-action of feminist critique and generation. To recall, in the interview 'Choreographies', Christie McDonald recounts Derrida's explanation in *Positions* that there are two phases of deconstruction. In the first the binary has to be reversed, in order to overturn the existing balance of power.[10] Only in the second phase might a new term come into play which is free entirely from the previously existing structures:

> In the first phase a reversal was to take place in which the opposed terms would be inverted. Thus woman, as a previously subordinate term, might become the dominant one in relation to man. Yet because such a scheme of reversal could only repeat the traditional scheme (in which the hierarchy of duality is always reconstituted), it alone could not effect any significant change. Change would only occur through the 'second' and more radical phase of deconstruction in which a 'new' concept would be forged simultaneously. (*C* 71)

To render Derrida the man, rather than Ogier the woman, figural is the phase one reversal. Phase two is a feminist move beyond the Ogier–Derrida pairing entirely to focus instead on what appears to be a new pairing – Pascale–Marianne – but one which, when examined carefully, is revealed to be anything but a binary relationship. In 'Choreographies', Derrida clarifies that phase two is not in fact temporal but spatial; it is not 'where a new concept follows an archaic one' (*C* 71) but rather a terrain marked 'by a transformation or general deformation of logic' (*C* 71). This deformation moves beyond the 'positional', beyond the idea of 'difference determined as opposition, whether or not dialectically' (*C* 71) and into new forms of relationality. With Pascale and Marianne, *Ghost Dance* begins to explore quite what such a female–female relationality might be, beyond the binary of Derrida–Ogier, man–woman. And Derrida is incidental to this terrain. By this, I do not mean irrelevant, not at all. I mean quite precisely, 'incidental'. Incidental images are those 'perceived by the eye as a consequence of visual impressions no longer present' (OED). In this sense, incidentality is a form of visual haunting. Derrida does not offer Pascale her feminist freedom – her daydream is indeed just a fantasy; she has to go elsewhere for that. But her encounters with him, just as mine have done, set her on her journey of self-discovery.[11] Derrida is a philosopher incidental to feminism; as McMullen's voice-over says, 'she met him many times [. . .]. But when she left she was never sure who she'd been speaking to. She was left with an afterimage that seemed to be drawing her own phantoms out of herself.'

II Feminist *Trompe L'Oeil*

In *Ghost Dance*, the transition from Part One to Part Two, 'Myth The Voice of Destruction The Voice of Deliverance', is marked by an incredibly clever *trompe l'oeil* shot. Against an outdoor soundtrack of birds singing, which tricks the viewer acoustically into thinking they are indeed outdoors, the shot pans down from the bust atop Marx's grave to an image of Marianne lying naked in a bed that appears to have been made *on* Marx's grave, between the railings (Figure 2.3). Although the outdoor soundtrack continues, the camera then pulls back as Marianne gets up, puts her top on and walks out of shot, to reveal with the expanded frame that we are not outside at all but rather that Marianne has been lying in a bed made up on the floor of a room in front of a *poster* of Marx's grave (Figure 2.4). The scene is followed by a black-out and sound-out which lasts for ten seconds before the birdsong plays back in, the surtitle of this part's title appears on screen and we enter a radically different section of the film. The black-out and sound-out clearly mark a shift, a change in the film's diegesis, but the *trompe l'oeil* which precedes them holds the key to the nature and meaning of this shift.

In a thought-provoking essay on the *trompe l'oeil* effect in Tod Browning's cinema, Hugh S. Manon identifies three key effects of the *trompe l'oeil* that are equally at work in this scene: the stalling of narrative; an exposure of the importance of the actor's body; and a self-referentiality that exposes the illusion of cinematic realism. I want to deal with each of these in turn in relation to this moment in *Ghost Dance*. In the first instance, the *trompe l'oeil* shot does indeed replicate 'the leisurely, self-directed pace necessary for a *trompe l'oeil* painting to have its effect' (Manon 2006: 61) – just as in Browning's use of the technique, in *Ghost Dance* the narrative is here allowed to 'momentarily "stall out"' (Manon 2006: 61). The *trompe l'oeil* thus functions as another visual ungrammaticality which prompts the viewer to pause and reflect – it activates the viewer, rendering her active rather than passive.[12] This is because rather than the visual track being structured 'as a secret-revealing revelation' (Manon 2006: 68) to which we passively respond, the *trompe l'oeil* destabilises our belief in what we are seeing. As a result, as Manon argues, 'our only recourse is a loop-like alternation: at one moment we pretend that the illusion is reality, and at the next we "step back" to appreciate the artifice of the illusion' (2006: 68). This oscillation between belief and disbelief is crucial to the *trompe l'oeil* effect; what is fundamental is that each time we watch this scene we still believe that Marianne is outdoors on the grave. The *trompe l'oeil*, in Manon's words, 'invites a remarkably self-directed form of enjoyment, permitting viewers to re-deceive themselves in the context of a revealed deception' (2006: 61); we are in control and we can choose to redeceive and undeceive ourselves in an endless alternation. As a visual ungrammaticality, the *trompe l'oeil* prompts a retroactive reading that reveals a significance beyond the surface meaning of the film – to diverge from Riffaterre, though, this is not the 'true' meaning but is rather an additional, alternative meaning

Figure 2.3 Marianne (Leonie Mellinger) on Marx's tomb.
Source: *Ghost Dance*, dir. Ken McMullen.

Figure 2.4 Exposure of the *trompe l'oeil*.
Source: *Ghost Dance*, dir. Ken McMullen.

that persists in unresolved oscillation with the surface meaning. The *trompe l'oeil* is 'a moment-by-moment injunction to imagine the truth of the representation or its opposite, without ever settling on either' (Manon 2006: 68).

To speak less theoretically, at this moment the *trompe l'oeil* exposes the spectral heuristic (with whom Marx is associated, even more so since *Ghost Dance* was in part the prompt for Derrida's extended work on spectrality and communism, *Specters of Marx*) as potentially fabricated – we are not seeing Marx's grave but only a representation of Marx's grave; the spectral heuristic is not real but merely an illusion.[13] In its place, we are offered the reality of the actor's body as she literally steps out of the spectral heuristic into a different realm. What is offered as the film's 'real' concern in place of the spectral is a diegesis centred around female embodiment. This is in stark contrast to the previous scene, in which Derrida's elaboration of spectrality is concerned exclusively with the voice.[14] But the exposure of the body is also, according to Manon, a further key effect of *trompe l'oeil* which, in Browning's cinema as here, 'reveals the undisguisable materiality of his actors' real bodies' (2006: 61). There is no need for Leonie Mellinger to be bare-breasted in this scene, but she is, and the unnecessary nakedness reminds us that this is Mellinger's body, as well as that of the character Marianne. Mellinger's body thus creates a similar effect to the *trompe l'oeil*, causing the reader to oscillate between the intra- and extra-diegetic; the body of the actor 'links the realm of representation concretely to "the self-evidence of the world" – directing viewers outside the realm of the story to consider the *hors-champ* of the film's production' (Manon 2006: 68). Mellinger's naked body, along with the obvious trickery of the *trompe l'oeil*, foregrounds *Ghost Dance*'s challenge to cinematic realism, rupturing the membrane between the film and the world.

It is important here that we recognise the *trompe l'oeil* as trickery, rather than merely deception; the latter is part of cinematic realism, the former exposes its manipulations. 'To deceive', says Manon, 'is not the same as to "trick," since deception genuinely desires the viewing subject's obliviousness, whereas all trickery doubles back on itself, gesturing beyond representation to indicate the source of the trick' (2006: 63). The viewer therefore consciously chooses to believe, to not believe, to believe again, to not believe again, in a movement that reifies Derrida's subjunctive speculations on cinema in the interview 'Cinema and its Ghosts':

> If I were to write about film, what would interest me above all is its mode and system of *belief*. There is an altogether singular mode of *believing* in cinema: a century ago, an unprecedented experience of belief was invented. It would be fascinating to analyze the system of *credit* in all the arts: how one believes a novel, certain moments of a theatrical representation, what is inscribed in painting and, of course, which is something else altogether, what film shows

and tells us. At the movies, you believe without believing, but this believing without believing remains a believing. (*CG* 27)

The *trompe l'oeil* reveals that this 'very strange phenomenon that is belief' (*CG* 37) has less to do with spectrality and everything to do with the rupturing of the cinematic illusion and the viewer's oscillation between belief and disbelief which renders cinematic spectatorship, whatever else it is, always also a continual process of self-reflection on the nature of cinematic representation itself.[15] Such a rupturing is of course part of the fabric of avant-garde or experimental films, such as *Ghost Dance*, that challenge 'Classical Hollywood's fetishization of a seamless realism' (Manon 2006: 68–9); but it is also effected, as I have argued in the previous chapter, by the empowered spectatorship of deconstructive film criticism which, in its sensitivity to the detail – here, to the visual ungrammaticality – actively ruptures the filmic membrane and creates the opening for new and original feminist interpretations, beyond even those ostensibly dictated by the film itself.[16]

In *Ghost Dance*, the *trompe l'oeil* takes us away from the realm of spectrality, ghosts and Marx and into a different realm, one of myth, symbolism and female intimacy. It is a realm of fantasy where the women, united, attempt to escape and at one point indeed flee an unspecified threat. I say unspecified but in fact there is a weight of evidence that associates the threat with phallic sexuality and female bodily penetration. In the myth which the male voice-over (Archie Poole) narrates, a woman is eaten alive from the inside out by rats who have 'ripped off her clothes and by the time she'd woke up it was too late. They had entered her body by every possible opening.' As they hide together, Pascale intimates that her defection from 'over there' is a result of discovering her teacher 'staring at a picture of a native Indian woman in a book called *La Vie Sexuelle des Sauvages*'. Later, a female voice-over (Barbara Coles) tells the story of another myth which again involves a woman being eaten from the inside, this time by a phallus that she has bitten off and swallowed:

> . . . she says she didn't put it in her mouth but I know she did, and when it was as far as it would go, she started to suck and suck. But when it remained dry she bit as hard as she could. That's how she swallowed it. And that's why she's always hungry, because the bit she swallowed ate everything else inside her to get its own back. So there she is empty and so hateful, waiting for the revenge that she knows is going to come. She's had it . . .

What is perhaps even more startling about this voice-over is that it occurs at the end of a scene in which the camera pivots to pan around the walls of a room in a disorienting shot, one that is made even more surprising by the fact that the audio recording of McMullen directing the scene is not deleted but persists along with the voice-over narrating the myth. This has the odd effect of aligning the male director's control and creation of cinematic space with the phallic threats from which the women are fleeing, and the male violence to which Pascale has already been quite clearly subject and which she recalls again a few moments later when she resists embracing the phallus: 'And suddenly I had this strong urge to put it in my mouth. But I didn't. Parce qu'il aurait éclaté ma tête. Et qu'il m'aurait étouffée. So I didn't.'

Marianne and Pascale are united in their attempts to escape the threat of male violence, which is linked in a chain of association with the Academy, with technology and with cinema. Against these stand female intimacy, myth and the primitive, and the murder of the figure of the male director. The latter takes place in another scene which has received no previous critical attention – one set in a dark cellar, in which George (Robbie Coltrane) attempts to rape Marianne at knife point while forcing Pascale to watch.[17] Positioning Marianne in front of a mirror, George threatens: 'You know what's going to happen, don't you. We're going to watch ourselves in the mirror. And you are going to watch us watching ourselves in the mirror [. . .] And we're going to watch you watching us watching ourselves.' George sets up a horrifying narcissistic mise-en-abyme of cinematic male sexual violence in which, as Laura Mulvey describes, the woman is doubly erased: both objectified on screen, and forced to adopt a position of masculine spectatorship which implicates her in the subjugation of her own sex. Pascale has been subject to male sexual violence throughout the film – the Salesman, the Professor, the Photocopier Man – but Marianne has always inhabited a position of power in relation to men: until now she has dominated George, and, remember, she may well have murdered the Salesman.[18] The knife from Part One in fact reappears here as George's weapon (Figure 2.5). Unlike Pascale, who is physically cowed by her male abusers, Marianne resists, fights back, and in fact kills George with no regret: Pascale is shocked she has killed him; Marianne responds, 'I wonder if there's anything here worth nicking.' It is possible to read this scene as one of female resistance to the male director, since George is in effect directing a scene here. This would offer a powerful feminist interpretation of the film in which the women are able to overcome the male domination to which they are subject within and by cinema. But such a reading is both compounded and complicated by the scene that follows.

The subsequent scene opens with a shot from one end of a long industrial room with striking internal architecture of pillars and roof beams creating the impression of a long tunnel. The floor of the room is flooded, reflecting back the beams, the pillars and the man standing at the centre of this industrial cage, obsessed with his own reflection (Figure 2.6).[19] Over the course of five minutes, the man performs a strange masturbatory dance, during which he

Supplanting Spectrality 53

Figure 2.5 Rape scene.
Source: *Ghost Dance*, dir. Ken McMullen.

writhes with his own image (Figure 2.7). The scene is a powerful evocation of the masculine self-obsession that characterises mainstream cinema and which has been subject to feminist critique in the cellar scene. Marianne and Pascale can be seen to the right, outside the frame of Brisley's performance, peering from behind a pillar. Their role as spectators is emphasised with a close-up of their watching faces, Marianne impassive, Pascale weeping. In this performative satire of the self-obsessed onanism of male mainstream cinematic production, women have been ejected entirely from the frame – their only option is to spectate from the sidelines, moved, or not, by what they see. This scene supplants the empowerment achieved in the resistance to the Director/George and repositions the women as passive spectators rather than active agents.

III Feminist Camp Artifice

Marianne and Pascale's different spectatorial responses to Brisley's performance – Pascale is moved to tears, Marianne is impassive – are metonymic of the different relationship these two characters have to the masculine realm.

Figure 2.6 Performance artist Stuart Brisley.
Source: *Ghost Dance*, dir. Ken McMullen.

Figure 2.7 Performance artist Stuart Brisley.
Source: *Ghost Dance*, dir. Ken McMullen.

Pascale is situated firmly within it, subject to the control, even violence, of the men who dominate it and the narratives and images they project; Marianne is situated outside of it, and thereby able, to some extent, to resist. Marianne frames the film, and she stalks through Part One of *Ghost Dance*, the part ostensibly dominated by the Ogier–Derrida couple. We see her when she receives the knife from Pascale in the electrical store, a scene which ends with her implied threat to the abusive Salesman. We see her strolling out of a metro station, hands in pockets, free, in a scene which places her in stark contrast to Pascale, cut as it is between the one in which the Professor seizes Pascale by the arm and our return to him frogmarching her across a road and into the café. It is to Marianne on the street that we return after the café scene and before the Ogier–Derrida interview, and she plays a leading role in the rest of the film.

In focusing exclusively on the Ogier–Derrida interview and the spectral heuristic of the film – aligned as it is with the masculine and with cinema – previous critical commentary has erased Marianne. Rather than attending to the relationship *between* the women, such commentary focuses exclusively on Pascale Ogier the actress, and her interview with Derrida, rather than on Pascale the character and her relationship with Marianne. In interview with McMullen, for instance, Jean-Max Causseu (2006) – the man responsible for the distribution of *Ghost Dance* in France – claims that 'the importance of *Ghost Dance* is the characters, two mythical ones'. Astonishingly, he is not referring here to the Marianne–Pascale couple, but rather to the Ogier–Derrida pairing, although quite how he perceives the latter to be 'mythical' is unclear: 'There is Derrida first of all, but also an actress who was very much loved in French cinema' (Causseu 2006). In Causseu's account of the importance of the film, Ogier is at least acknowledged, although not at first by name; Mellinger gets no mention at all; and the significance of the lead female couple is erased and supplanted by the Derrida–Ogier pair, despite their relatively brief amount of screen time.

Popular reception of the film proves less myopic; one reviewer, enigmatically called The Midnight Mollusc (2013), at least pays attention to the two female characters and their relationship to each other, even if only to criticise the film in this respect:

> For a film of such evidently academic/arthouse aspirations its portrayal of the two women is exuberantly insensitive. The French woman, named Pascal [sic], is a cartoon encapsulation of the vulnerable artiste: simultaneously troubled and enthralled by the introspection that motivates her vague journey for even more vague understanding. Meanwhile, the English woman represents a grounded force of logic, happy to chip in on the intellectual joy-ride, but essentially there to anchor Pascal [sic].[20]

The reviewer's interpretation of the respective roles of the two women is echoed in Mellinger's comments in the Mediabox DVD (2006) 'Special Features' interview with McMullen that she was 'the more earthy part of the two of us and Pascale was the one that was quite ethereal'. However, while the reviewer perceives the leading female couple as merely a 'pairing of national stereotypes' (The Midnight Mollusc 2013), Mellinger provides a different interpretation. She observes that she and Ogier 'got close during the filming. It was kind of a bizarre experience to be playing the same character' and again that they were 'playing one and the same character' and again later that she and Pascale were 'playing the same but different aspects of the same character' (Mellinger 2006). When I questioned Mellinger regarding these comments, she explained further that

> Ken made it clear to us (Pascale and I) that we were aspects of the same character. Perhaps one of us was the ghost of the other? I always thought that Pascale was my ghost as at the end of the movie I try to push her photo out to sea. However, in some scenes (like the one in the phone shop) I was more like her ghost, so I'm not sure . . . [21]

Mellinger interprets the female–female intimacy between the characters of Marianne and Pascale from the perspective of the spectral heuristic – 'Perhaps one of us was the ghost of the other?' – but a feminist hermeneutic suggests an alternative way of interpreting their relationship and its possibilities, for instance, if the leading female couple is viewed according to a butch-femme aesthetic.[22]

In 'Toward a Butch-Femme Aesthetic' (1988–9), Sue-Ellen Case begins her enquiries where Teresa de Lauretis ends hers in 'The Technology of Gender', with the argument that we cannot rethink the female subject if she is always and only perceived in relation to men – in a heterosexual context – rather than in relation to other women. Case proposes, therefore, the 'dynamic duo' of the butch-femme as 'the strong subject position' required by feminism, as the potential location of a politically empowered feminist subject. For Case, what is distinctive about the butch-femme couple is that they 'inhabit the subject position together [. . .] The two roles never appear as . . . discrete' (1988–9: 56):

> These are not split subjects, suffering the torments of dominant ideology. They are coupled ones who do not impale themselves on the poles of sexual difference or metaphysical values, but constantly seduce the sign system through flirtation and inconstancy into the slight fondle of artifice, replacing the Lacanian slash with a lesbian bar. (Case 1988–9: 57)

The rise of white middle-class heterosexual feminism forced the butch-femme duo along with lesbian bar culture and the working-class culture of which it was a part into the feminist closet. But this closeting, Case claims, has produced 'the discourse of camp' which, 'in combination with the butch-femme couple, may provide the liberation of the feminist subject' (1988–9: 59). According to Michael Bronski, homosexual camp 'is the re-imagining of the material world into ways and forms which transform and comment upon the original. It changes the "natural" and "normal" into style and artifice' (1984: 42). We can see this effect at work in *Ghost Dance* in the scene in which Pascale – playing the femme – is frightened by a rat in the shower. Marianne – playing the butch – comes to her rescue and the emergence of this dynamic prompts a transition from realism to surrealism (Figures 2.8 and 2.9). Through the butch-femme dynamic the couple escape from the masculine realist mode into the female realm of camp high artifice.

In 'Notes on "Camp"', Susan Sontag famously stated that 'it goes without saying that the Camp sensibility is disengaged, depoliticized – or at least apolitical' (1982a: 107), but later in interview with Robert Boyars and Maxine Bernstein for the magazine *Salmagundi* she qualifies this assertion, arguing that by ironising the sexes camp serves to depolarise them. It is for this reason that Sontag claims early sixties camp 'should probably be credited with a considerable if inadvertent role in the upsurge of feminist consciousness in the late 1960s' (1982b: 339). In *Guilty Pleasures* (1996), Pamela Robertson highlights the 'colloquial affiliation between lesbianism and camp' (3) in its 1920s origins – which Sontag elides – and asserts that since 'camp has an affinity with feminist discussions of gender construction, performance, and enactment', we can examine 'forms of camp as feminist practice' (6–7). In particular, it is camp's theatricality that helps to challenge 'certain stereotyped femininities – by exaggerating them, by putting them between quotation marks' (Sontag 1982b: 339). This insight into the feminist potential of camp is present in embryo in Sontag's original essay, where she first states that 'camp sees everything in quotation marks' (1982a: 109):

> It's not a lamp, but a 'lamp'; not a woman, but a 'woman.' To perceive Camp in objects and persons is to understand Being-as-Playing-a-Role. It is the farthest extension, in sensibility, of the metaphor of life as theater. (Sontag 1982a: 109)

To camp it up is to challenge realism and that mode's unquestioning representation of the 'norm', of what, for instance, it means to be a 'woman'. That this feminist political potential of camp artifice is present, at least in nascent form, in *Ghost Dance* is illuminated by comparison with its key filmic – rather than philosophical – influence: Jacques Rivette's *Céline et Julie vont en bateau: Phantom Ladies Over Paris* (1974).[23] The title of Rivette's film reveals immediate points of comparison with *Ghost Dance* – its French–English

Figure 2.8 Pascale (Pascale Ogier) and Marianne (Leonie Mellinger) keeping it real.
Source: *Ghost Dance*, dir. Ken McMullen.

Figure 2.9 Pascale (Pascale Ogier) and Marianne (Leonie Mellinger) camping it up.
Source: *Ghost Dance*, dir. Ken McMullen.

bilingualism, the leading female couple and the idea of spectrality. As we have seen, a concentration on Derrida and spectrality has skewed previous critical engagement with *Ghost Dance*, at the expense of attention to the leading female couple. This has not been the case with *Céline et Julie . . .* , where attention has very much been focused on the nature of Céline and Julie's relationship and the spaces created for women in and by the film.[24] *Céline et Julie . . .* reifies more persuasively than *Ghost Dance* the camp aesthetic, that is, the understanding of 'Being-as-Playing-a-Role'. The film is theatrical through and through, and in interview the actresses who play Céline and Julie – Juliet Berto and Dominique Labourier respectively – explain the dramaturgic origin of their characters:

> DL: we were [. . .] interested in creating characters that would emerge from our essential vocation as actresses. Very often we tend to forget that the profession of an actress is, above all, based on games, like children's games. So in *Céline et Julie . . .* we started off with the notion of amusing ourselves by creating interchangeable characters in many different forms in the style of a game. (Dasgupta 1975: 22)

Just as with Marianne and Pascale, Céline and Julie are a coupled subject, again evoking the butch-femme aesthetic, and they do indeed become an empowered feminist subject: they rescue a young girl from her potential fate in the film's masculine House of Cinema populated in the end only by agent-less mannequins. Their female–female intimacy, independent of the film's incidental men, offers up a space of feminist freedom. As Julia Lesage argues, 'the film progressively extends the process – begun by the women's movement – of redefining our notions of sexual structures and boundaries and of reconsidering our sense of "woman's place" within our image of society as a whole' (1981).

Through their camp artifice, both *Ghost Dance* and *Céline et Julie . . .* locate women's freedom and intimacy in spaces of play, of magic and myth.[25] 'Cast realism aside,' declares Case, 'its consequences for women are deadly' (1988–9: 71). Doing so might be empowering, but such a move also has its limitations. In *Ghost Dance* the removal of the women into a world of primitive myth contains within it both a troubling gesture of transcultural appropriation, and risks exoticising both the primitive and the female in an equivalent to Edward Said's idea of orientalism. This is a move which ostensibly empowers both the primitive and the female only by excluding them from the dominant discourses of cinema and culture.[26] That said, interpreting Marianne and Pascale's relationship according to a butch-femme aesthetic risks a similar reductionism. As Case notes, the derivation of an aesthetic model from embodied realities more often than not can only occur when those realities have been erased by the metaphorical appropriation: 'such symbols of a culture may only proliferate when a specific social reality has been obliterated and its identity has become the private property of the dominant class' (Case 1988–9: 63). Even more than this, the theoretical move results in an erasure of the body and of sexuality – 'the erotics are gone' (Case 1988–9: 63). Lesage makes a convincing case for the lesbianism of Céline and Julie's relationship, characterised in fact not by the fixed model of the butch-femme but by a more fluid, in fact almost dizzying, interchangeability of roles which we will encounter again in the photonovel *Right of Inspection* discussed in Chapter 5. Lesage (1981) argues that '*Celine and Julie* can be appropriated by anybody who wants to see it that way as a "lesbian" film not because of its depiction of sexual activity (none is seen) but because of the kind of intimacy between women it depicts'. For Lesage, to claim that the film's fantasy chimes with her own understanding of 'a continuum in women's sexual identity between heterosexual and lesbian' is of crucial import for her larger project of arguing for the importance of including lesbian experience within feminism. What remains problematic in *Ghost Dance*, what limits its liberatory potential, is the unconvincingness of the female–female intimacy between Mellinger and Ogier, the absence of a relationship truly free from orchestration or control by a male director, whether it be a lesbian relationship or other form of female intimacy. This is in strong contrast to the on-screen chemistry and creative freedom of Berto and Labourier, and is highlighted by comparing their reflections with comments made by Mellinger.

In interview with Gautam Dasgupta, Berto and Labourier agree that what was unique about working with Rivette was the freedom he gave them to create their characters and their characters' relationship: 'It was a most remarkable experience in that *we* were totally responsible for creating the characters of Céline and Julie' (Labourier in Dasgupta 1975: 22). Her character, Labourier explains, was 'a composition created by and within the limitations of my body, my voice, my head etc.' (Labourier in Dasgupta 1975: 22). Berto expands that for her, 'Céline [. . .] is a puppet that I can bring to life only within the boundaries of my own self' (Berto in Dasgupta 1975: 22). There is an irreducible relationship, then, between the embodied physicality of the actresses and the characters they create; while their acting is still a form of puppetry, *they* – not the director – are pulling the strings: 'As actresses and women in films dominated mostly by male criteria, we emerged as powerful individuals and creators in our own right' (Labourier in Dasgupta 1975: 23).[27] In contrast, in interview with McMullen, it seems that Mellinger found the lack of 'a clearly defined character' (Mellinger 2006) challenging – 'actors are by nature quite passive,' she observes, 'so an actor likes to be given a character'. This explains why, while 'there was room for improvisation within the script' (Mellinger 2006) of *Ghost Dance*, Ogier and Mellinger are not able to create and convey a powerful female intimacy on screen that might have opened up genuine sites of resistance to their cinematic control. We glimpse that freedom in *Céline et Julie . . .* , albeit, as noted, within the limitations of the domestic and the magical spheres. In *Ghost Dance*, there persists to the end a sense that the two women are controlled by, subject to, the film and its Director: from McMullen's voice-over before the Brisley scene, which is disturbingly possessive – 'They're going to see an image of their own struggle with their own persona. They'll be left with that. I'll leave them that at least' – to Pascale's enshrinement in celluloid in the stills at the end, to the futility of Marianne's attempts to cast the film off into the sea. *Ghost Dance* goes incredibly far in deconstructing women's place in cinema but it stops short of being able to realise fully the imaginative and political possibilities of feminist alternatives in cinema, in realism and in the real world; we must look elsewhere for those.

Hiding in the bowels of a derelict ship, Pascale tells Marianne,

> I studied with Jacques Derrida once. He taught me a lot about ghosts, but he couldn't teach me everything, 'cos there's things a man can't teach to a woman, right?

Let's come out of the fantastical shadows and see what real women can teach us.

Notes

1. Ken McMullen discusses *Ghost Dance* in 'Immortality and Cinema' (2012), focusing specifically on the Ogier–Derrida interview scene and noting that lectures around the world focus on just that scene in the film. Derrida himself recalls the scene in 'The Ghost Dance' (1989), an interview with Mark Lewis and Andrew Payne, and in conversation with Bernard Stiegler in *Echographies* (*EC* 117–20). Critical discussion of *Ghost Dance* that focuses exclusively on the Ogier–Derrida interview can be found, for instance, in Louise Burchill (2009) and Michael Bachmann (2008). One of the few engagements with the film that does not concentrate on the Ogier–Derrida interview is to be found in McMullen's 'Special Features' interview with philosopher Oscar Guardiola-Rivera, who reads the film from the perspective of a Columbian audience, for whom the most striking scene in the film is the one that takes place at the Père Lachaise Cemetery in Paris, in front of the Communards' Wall. 'In this scene', he says, 'the objects tell the story that those in power want to keep from us' (Guardiola-Rivera 2006); this is an example of potential resistance to State oppression that resonated with the Columbian audience.
2. The interview occurs in French in the film. The English translation provided in the subtitles is cited here and elsewhere.

3. Schwartz footnotes James Leo Cahill's observation to him that 'with the French use of the word "*séances*" to refer to public screenings, the rhetoric of early cinema already lurches toward Derrida's spectral concerns, as if his work were haunted by its own philological background' (Schwartz 2006: 25 n. 10). In 'Double Exposures', Cahill and Tom Holland note that Derrida's writings contribute to a long-standing association between cinema and spectrality: 'Media historians and theorists are well aware that ghosts have long been a primal element of the earliest experiences with photography, film and their conceptualizations: spirit photographers such as William Mumler, inventors such as Thomas Edison, and critics and theorists such as Maxim Gorky, Otto Rank, Siegfried Kracauer, Walter Benjamin, André Bazin, Roland Barthes, and more recently Jeffrey Sconce, Karen Beckman, Tom Gunning, Bliss Lim, Stefan Andriopoulos, and Murray Leeder, to name but a few, have all given serious consideration to the phantoms haunting technical reproducibility and optical media' (2015: 11). See a detailed list of further references in their accompanying footnote (Cahill and Holland 2015b: 19–20 n. 23).
4. See his conversation with Stiegler recorded in *Echographies* (*EC* 117–20).
5. The citations in this final clause are derived from the following line in Schwartz's text: 'Describing his experiences of seeing and hearing a dead woman in a movie occasions a compact figure of some of Derrida's major later conceptual inventions' (Schwartz 2006: 14). The phrasing here renders the intended meaning difficult to discern: it is not clear whether the 'description' is the 'figure' or whether the 'dead woman' herself is; in the absence of clarity it is possible to read the phrase as, at least, meaning both of these things, whether intentionally or not.
6. In order to distinguish clearly between the fictional and the real world, throughout I use 'Ogier' when referring to the actress and 'Pascale' when referring to the character she plays in *Ghost Dance* and whose first name she shares.
7. See Sarah Dillon (2007), especially Chapters 4 and 5.
8. While the majority of *Ghost Dance*'s score was composed by David Cunningham, Michael Giles and Jamie Muir, there is also the use of Hawaiian choral music sourced, as David Cunningham explained to me, from a found cassette: 'I think what you've identified on *Ghost Dance* is some Hawaiian music used in the scene with Derrida in Café Select – the only music in the film not recorded by us. A fragment of this music reappears later in a black and white shot of Pascale and Marianne wearing their "tribal" costumes. It's from a cassette that Jamie Muir found in an Oxfam shop which worked better than anything we had come up with for the Café Select scene. I don't think we were able to identify the actual recording' (private email correspondence).
9. I return below to the film's problematic exoticisation of the non-European.
10. Derrida's original comments can be found in *P* 41–2.
11. In 'The Philosopher Cameo' (2015), Trine Riel also pays attention to the nature of Derrida's relationship to the rest of the film, but her judgement is more severe than my argument regarding Derrida's incidentality. Via an engaging comparison

with Brice Parain's cameo in Jean-Luc Godard's *Vivre sa vie* (1962), she concludes that Parain (anonymous) functions to reveal Nana's character, whereas Derrida (clearly identified and identifiable) is positioned firmly outside of 'the film's affective realm' and therefore unable to effectively and affectively interact with any of the characters therein. He is, she says, 'impotent within the fictional narrative'. While Riel recognises that through their philosopher cameos both films 'activate a questioning of the philosopher figure in regard to his relevance and capacity outside of the academic structure', she curiously leaves unexamined the gender politics at play here. Her observations on the relationship between Ogier and Derrida could be more radical if explicitly gendered thus [insertions added]: *Ghost Dance* 'indirectly presents a dismissive characterisation of the [male] philosopher as a figure who, by his exclusion from the fictive realm, is symbolically removed from the sphere of the embodied, [female] gendered life, and thus ultimately useless when it comes to offering any guidance pertaining to everyday life and action'.

12. In causing the viewer to pause, the *trompe l'oeil* is in effect a stop mechanism to narrative progression: 'In encountering an instance of *trompe l'oeil*, the viewer pauses, in effect mentally "toying" with the self-evident falsity of the image' (Manon 2006: 61).

13. In 'An Organisation of Dreams' (2009), McMullen states that 'when *The Spectres of Marx* [sic] came out, he [Derrida] gave me the book on it, saying it had come out of *Ghost Dance*'.

14. Derrida's emphasis on a vocal rather than a corporeal spectrality frames his famous maxim in the interview with Ogier. The following two statements frame his pronouncement that 'cinema is the art of ghosts'. Before it: 'Since I've been asked to play myself in a film which is more or less improvised, I feel as if I'm letting a ghost speak for me. Curiously, instead of playing myself, without knowing it, I let a ghost ventriloquize my words, or play my role, which is even more amusing.' And after it: 'Therefore, if I'm a ghost, but believe I'm speaking with my own voice, it's precisely because I believe it's my own voice that I allow it to be taken over by another's voice. Not just any other voice, but that of my own ghosts. So ghosts do exist. And it's perhaps the ghosts who will answer you. Perhaps they already have.' Cinema is the art of a ghostly ventriloquism for Derrida, reified in *Ghost Dance*'s spectral soundtrack: both the overlaying and multiplicity of voices which speak over the image track, more often than not severed from any attachment to a diegetic body; and the film's musical score, created – as composer David Cunningham explains in the 'Special Features' interview with McMullen – by an early form of DIY sampling, a hauntological form of musical composition (on music and hauntology, see Simon Reynolds (2006) and (2011) and Mark Fisher (2013)). In an unpublished conference paper entitled 'Spectral Media in Ken McMullen's *Ghost Dance* (1983) and *Zina* (1985)', Tyson Stewart reads the soundtrack *as* spectral: '*Ghost Dance*'s rich soundtrack, comprised of voice-over, voice-off, dialogue, haunting music, discordant sound effects overlap and combine in ways that always emphasizes out of jointness [sic]'

(Stewart 1985: 3). Further information on the film's score is available at http://www.stalk.net/piano/piano502.htm (last accessed 18 September 2017).
15. Interestingly, in *Derrida Reframed* (2008: 16–17), K. Malcolm Richards mobilises *trompe l'oeil* to explain to the arts student the trickery of Derrida's deconstructive play, as reified in the 'a' in *différance*.
16. McMullen is quite open about his distaste for the Hollywood mode of cinematic production, valuing instead 'new texts exploding from the unconscious to challenge a cinema driven by anecdotal narratives, obsessive naturalism, a mystical star system, and a possessive production and distribution machinery – the opium of the twentieth-century mind' (McMullen, 'Back from the Future'). Interestingly, Manon notes that 'in his essay "The Myth of Total Cinema," André Bazin uses the idea of *trompe l'oeil* to distinguish the formative phase of cinema from its resolution in conventional realism' (Manon, 'Seeing Through' 75).
17. This scene seems to have somehow escaped the notice of previous commentators who are thus able to describe Coltrane as the film's 'funny man' (Jenkins, 'Edinburgh' 2) or as 'a droll, homely suitor who muses about improving his looks and is fascinated by weather reports' (Maslin, 'Review'), when in fact he is a violent rapist who is killed by Marianne in self-defence. Jenkins does at least recognise that George is killed but elides mention of the sexual violence in the scene: 'He is later killed by Marianne, after getting Pascale to watch himself and Marianne in front of a mirror' (Jenkins, 'Review' 45).
18. The Salesman and the Photocopier Man are linked by their verbal aggression towards Pascale, both using the faux-endearment 'Sweetheart' to belittle and threaten her. The Photocopier Man is in fact played by Coltrane, the same actor who plays George, a male character who also uses 'sweetheart' in the derogatory mode when addressing Marianne, thus linking him too into this chain of gender violence. When Pascale accuses the Photocopier Man of being a 'fucking voyeur', she anticipates the scene in the cellar with George.
19. The man is performance artist Stuart Brisley, with whom McMullen had collaborated previously on the experimental short film *Arbeit Macht Frei* (1973) and on the documentary *Being and Doing* (1984).
20. Another anonymous reviewer in *Time Out* recognises that the ghostly thematic takes place alongside the story of Pascale and Marianne, although s/he is at a loss as to how the two strands are connected: 'Quite how the thesis connects with the narrative – Ogier and Mellinger drifting around Paris and London and running into the bulky frame of Coltrane – remains a mythtery.'
21. From private email correspondence with the author.
22. To do so is to avoid reading the female–female intimacy in the film according to the logic of narcissism which, it has been shown, is firmly part of the masculine order in *Ghost Dance*. This move is in line with Julia Lesage's assertion that 'since Freud and more recently Christopher Lasch in his popular *Culture of Narcissism* pejoratively associate homosexuality with narcissism – and since that thesis has credence in the social sciences – we must be careful to delineate the ways that women's intimacy is of a profoundly different order than "narcissism"' (1981: n. 13).

23. *Céline et Julie vont en bateau* is the first film on the 'Ken McMullen's Films' website's list of comparable works to *Ghost Dance*. Other films included are *Thelma and Louise*, *Oh Lucky Man*, *Sans Soleil*, *Weekend* and *Viva Maria*. See https://kenmcmullenfilms.wordpress.com/ghost-dance/ (last accessed 18 September 2017). The film's connection to Rivette's work, as well as to the films of Jean-Luc Godard, is also noted, but not pursued, in Steven Jenkins' review of *Ghost Dance*.
24. See, for instance, Julia Lesage (1981), and recognition of this aspect of the film in general review, for instance in Brad Stevens' brief comparison with David Lynch's *Inland Empire* (2006): 'These masterpieces set out to liberate women from the narrative traps in which cinema has traditionally imprisoned them. Both Rivette and Lynch deconstruct the act of storytelling from an explicitly feminist perspective, showing their heroines negotiating, and ultimately escaping from, houses of fiction' (39). Rivette, he says, 'takes female solidarity as his starting point and ends by suggesting that the narrative is about to begin again' (Stevens 2008: 39).
25. *Céline et Julie* . . . also restricts it to the domestic realm, as Lesage notes: '*Céline et Julie* speaks to women's understanding of the structures, contradictions – including destructiveness, and liberating potential of personal intimacy in the domestic sphere. The film recognizes, through its witty depiction of Magic, that sphere's power, potentially subversive, potentially political. It also speaks about the hegemonic fear of women, which men translate personally and institutionally into open contempt' (1981). The film has less to say about female freedom and intimacy in other spheres, for instance the public sphere, or how such liberation might be represented in a realist mode.
26. Jenkins notes the troubling association between the female and the primitive in *Ghost Dance*: 'the predominant association of female characters with the eruption of repressed myths is a tricky area, leading perhaps into rather reactionary mysticism' (Jenkins 1984).
27. Lesage (1981) observes that 'the film gives a picture of women protagonists relating to each other or acting on their own, without men on their minds', and that 'due to Berto and Labourier's improvisation, the audience spends a long time looking at women in roles largely under their control'.

CHAPTER THREE

Feminist Countersignature

> THEO: Have you read *The Post Card* yet?
> MACEY: Yes, I didn't like it.
> THEO: Oh come on, Macey, you can do better than that. Why not?
> MACEY: Well, it's just heterosexist propaganda in which a male academic is unfaithful to his wife. It's the old clichéd story of male professor as seducer. It's so 1970s.
> THEO: That's unfair. Don't you think the relationship between Plato and Socrates is a little more complicated than that?
> MACEY: So it's a bromance too. Boys, boys and more boys. Just not interested. [Pause] Why should people continue to read *The Post Card*?
> (*Love in the Post*: *From Plato to Derrida*)[1]

This chapter moves from a film in which Derrida appeared and which inspired his work – you will recall his comment to director Ken McMullen that *Ghost Dance* in part prompted *Specters of Marx* – to a film which attempts to respond cinematically to a specific Derrida text. In *Love in the Post: From Plato to Derrida* (2014), filmmaker Joanna Callaghan engages in a feminist creative response to, and critique of, the epistolary 'Envois' section of Derrida's *The Post Card* (1987). In this chapter I will show how *Love in the Post* performs a specifically *feminist* countersignature of 'Envois', inserting women into structures of philosophic and other forms of inheritance-as-(in)fidelity, and exploring in practice the possibilities of a feminist film-philosophy. The central two sections of the chapter explore two aspects of the film's feminist philosophical work: in the first, I argue that the film generates an alternative concept of relationality and inheritance based not in an idea of (in)fidelity but in the idea of reproduction – both aesthetic and sexual – and the centrality of women to it; in the second, I explore how *Love in the Post* is able to materialise women in their embodied reality *and* perform the possibility of gender and sexual indeterminacy, of multiple possible signatories and addressees, a feat to which Derrida's 'Envois' only aspires. The chapter concludes that *Love in the Post* avoids an excess of fidelity to Derrida by this feminist countersignature, and by cinematically countersigning the idea of countersignature itself – a textual metaphor – by presenting an alternative cinematic way of figuring the relationship between film and philosophy.

Amid a challenging body of work, Derrida's *The Post Card* stands out as one of his more difficult texts: Benjamin Poore (2015) describes it as 'a gorgeous, if unreadable' book. Originally published in French in 1980 as *La carte postale: de Socrate à Freud et au-delà*, the English translation followed in 1987. The book consists of four essays: 'Envois', 'To Speculate – on "Freud"', 'Le facteur de la vérité' and 'Du tout'. 'Envois' is by far the longest piece, occupying roughly half of the book, and has received the most critical attention. This is not merely due to its length, but due to its tantalising hybridity: a combination of fact and fiction, philosophy and literature, 'Envois' consists of a series of letters written over a two-year period from 3 June 1977 to 30 August 1979. It is prefaced by a short introduction dated 7 September 1979, signed, ostensibly, by the author of the letters – 'Jacques Derrida'.[2] This 'Jacques Derrida' assumes 'without detour the responsibility for these *envois*' (*E* 6) but his signature is annotated with the following footnote:

> I regret that you [*tu*] do not very much trust my signature, on the pretext that we might be several. This is true, but I am not saying so in order to make myself more important by means of some supplementary authority. And even less in order to disquiet, I know what this costs. You are right, doubtless we are several, and I am not as alone as I sometimes say I am when the complaint escapes from me, or when I still put everything into seducing you. (*E* 6, n. 1)

This far from innocent footnote begins the game that is 'Envois' and sets up its key terms: 'Envois' is a text about the structural uncertainty of authorship and readership; it asserts the plurality of the signatory and addressee of these letters even as, at the same time, it undermines that assertion; it is a text addressed to 'you', the intimate *tu*, both the actual addressee of the letters and all the other singular readers who have and will encounter them; it is also, perhaps above all, a work of seduction. In 'Post/Card/Match/Book/"Envois"/Derrida' (1984), David Wills provides the best account yet of the story behind the letters: '*Envois* has its narrative structure, that of *The Thousand and One Nights*. It occurs in the stay of an execution, a delay in the arrival of a missive' (28). 'Jacques Derrida' is writing to defer or delay his lover's 'determination' (*détermination*) – it is never specified what this 'determination' is but one interpretation is that it is the lover's decision to end the love affair.[3] We can never be sure because, read as a literary text, 'Envois' falls within the genre of monologic epistolary fiction, that is, a text constructed of letters written by only one writer which therefore presents only one side of the correspondence.[4] Other than second-hand reports in 'Jacques Derrida's letters, we can therefore never know what his lover is actually thinking and feeling – she has no voice here, a point to which I will return below.[5]

If, as J. Hillis Miller asserts, 'Envois' is 'a cryptic, indecipherable text, out in the open, completely out in the open, but nobody is going to be able to figure it out' (2014: 176), how does one read it? One answer is: creatively. Wills' essay presents and performs one example of such a creative critical response:

> The kind of reading which I would advocate is one which, first of all, does not pretend to avoid the traps set by the paradoxes of *Envois*, but which, in the second place, exploits rather than seeks to resolve those paradoxes – which participates in the game, raises the stakes, and calls the bluff; perhaps even introduces a further trick which might divert the course of the play. Call it an attempt to hi-jack Derrida's hi-jinks. For if to read is *lire*, then a deconstructionist reading would be akin to *le délire* [the delirium], to which the author himself alludes (p. 106). (1984: 32)

Like the work of James Joyce – the literary figure who haunts 'Envois', as Derrida himself has avowed[6] – 'Envois' already itself accounts for its own excess, thereby usurping the location usually occupied by deconstructive criticism. As Wills explains,

> reading [. . .] since Derrida involves an attempt to unpack the paradoxes writing creates for itself; to unpack them, not in terms of the resolution of an enigma, as condensations of a truth that was never really lost, even if displaced, but rather to incite those paradoxes to exceed their own structural limits.
>
> In the case of *Envois*, even such an excess seems to be accounted for. (1984: 33)

The reader confronted with 'Envois' is in the same position as the signatory of 'Envois' when confronted with Joyce, that is, paralysed critically by the fact that anything he writes has always already been 'read and pillaged in advance' (*NW* 151): 'He has read all of us – and plundered us, that one' (*E* 148), says 'Jacques Derrida' of Joyce. A creative critical piece must respond to 'Envois' by finding a new location for deconstructive criticism in the excess of its *own* creativity, not in the already occupied space of the text's own potential excess.[7] Even at the end of his own playful response, however, Wills still feels that Derrida has got one over on him, that he has been duped 'into discoursing at length on things that *Envois* never did anything but make patently obvious' (1984: 36).

If responding to 'Envois' creatively in its own medium – writing – is a kind of madness, shifting medium – for instance, responding creatively in and through film – might seem to be an even more delirious move. In fact though, a shift of medium – from the written word to film – opens up new possibilities and opportunities, the new medium itself automatically offering a space of excess not already accounted for by 'Envois' in advance. For although Derrida's text contains repeated references to film, its own medium of writing is a material structural limit 'Envois' is unable, or unwilling, to exceed.[8] 'Jacques Derrida' understands the love affair not just as a correspondence, but also as a sort of film for screening only in their 'small private cinema' (*E* 179). But by presenting only the script, 'Jacques Derrida' does away with the material support of the rolls of celluloid (moving and still images) that document their relationship – in fact, he is all for burning 'the films and the photos' (*E* 179): 'I am burning all the supports and am keeping only several purely verbal sequences' (*E* 187). He wishes to dissociate 'film' from its material medium, empty it of its physical and visual connotations, and play only with what is left, 'the word film' (*E* 179) and its verbal – in both senses of that word – resonances. He retains the word film in order to think about the way their relationship is 'filmed' (*filmé*), that is, covered with a thin layer or coating. This 'filming' obscures rather than reveals the reality of their embodied physical interaction and erases its visual documentation. To film, here, is not to record embodied relationality visually, but, quite the opposite, to veil or cover with and through words. To film, for 'Jacques Derrida', is not to reveal, but to conceal.

Why? Why does filming in its cinematic rather than veiling sense pose such a threat to 'Jacques Derrida'? I suggest it does so because the visual and the embodied pose a challenge to the undecidability of signatory and addressee to which 'Envois' is dedicated and which it attempts to perform; an undecidability which, if maintained and believed, opens the text to the gendered and sexual multiplicity which Derrida so often claims is effected in and by his writing. How would it be possible to *watch* this love affair unfold without its participants becoming embodied and therefore becoming to some extent fixed in their gendered singularity? Would any cinematic response to 'Envois' destroy 'Jacques Derrida''s claim that 'we are several' and in doing so expose his assertions of gendered and sexual fluidity as nothing but fantasy? What would the consequences be of a film giving not just voice but body to the addressee, and/or of embodying the signatory as irreducibly female? It seems that 'Jacques Derrida' fears the answers to these questions, hence his eagerness to destroy the visual accompaniment to 'Envois'. But I want to turn my attention here to the visual in order to explore the answers to these questions and more. My focus is not the real or fictional rolls of film and photographs that 'Jacques Derrida' destroys, but the visual works produced by Callaghan.

I Female Infidelity

From 2003 to 2014, Callaghan undertook a project entitled *Ontological Narratives*, the aim of which was to explore through practice-based research how one might adapt 'a philosophical text into a film in order to perform and re-inscribe the philosophical problems presented by that text' (Callaghan 2012). The results of the project are three short films and a feature. The first short, *Thrownness* (2004), responds to Martin Heidegger's thought, the second, *A Mind's Eye* (2008), to Plato's. The third and fourth films are both inspired by Derrida's 'Envois': the mesmerising short, *DO NOT READ THIS* (2012), and the feature, *Love in the Post*. *Love in the Post* is accompanied by five short work-in-progress research films – *Deconstructive Film*, *Adaptation*, *Postal*, *Letters*, *Love* – and five filmed interviews with key Derrida scholars, parts of which are used in the feature film. (The interviews are preserved in full on the *Love in the Post* website and transcribed in the accompanying book, *Love in the Post: From Derrida to Plato – The Screenplay and Commentary* (2014).) Callaghan's body of work represents a major contribution to the study of film and philosophy in general, and deconstruction and film in particular, one which, as she notes, brings 'an understanding of creative practice almost entirely absent from the current philosophical discourse on film' (Callaghan 2010). Her work also prompts a reconsideration of what we might understand film-philosophy to be. There exists a body of work committed to thinking through the possibilities of film as philosophy in action, but it is carried out primarily by theorists rather than practitioners, and primarily by men.[9] There is also a growing body of films which present cinematic portraits of philosophers and their work, but, as Callaghan notes in the 'Research Context' section of her article for *Screenworks* on *A Mind's Eye*, 'all these seek to illustrate philosophy rather than use film as a medium for the production or interrogation of knowledge itself' (Callaghan 2010).[10] In contrast, Callaghan's practice-led research leads to works of film-philosophy which both produce and interrogate knowledge, and prompt the viewer and critic to reflect on the practices through which film might do so.[11] In addition, as the epigraph to this chapter taken from *Love in the Post* makes clear, Callaghan is a female filmmaker thinking through the possibilities of a feminist response to Derrida's work in particular, and, more broadly, providing a much-needed feminist perspective on the possibilities and actualities of film-philosophy.

In reflection on her practice, Callaghan observes that

> In approaching a film based on a source text, the question that arises is one of fidelity – whether to adapt or not. [. . .] For a book such as *The Post Card*, part epistolary novel, part essays, part 'end of literature', what kind of approach could be faithful to Derrida's text and, more widely, to his project? In some ways Derrida provides the answer over and over again in *The Post Card*. (2014: 58)

In fact, Derrida provides the answer over and over again throughout his work, since, as I touched on in the Introduction, Derrida's understanding of fidelity differs from the traditional interpretation of this notion. As Callaghan notes, in conventional adaptation studies, 'fidelity criticism depends precisely on there being a single, final, correct meaning to which the filmmaker adheres or otherwise violates or tampers with' (2014: 59).[12] In contrast, for Derrida to be faithful means to betray. From the perspective of deconstruction, fidelity to a text means not absolute adherence to it but rather relentless questioning of it, what Derrida calls 'the countersignature'. For instance, in 'The Night Watch (over the book of himself)' (2001), Derrida's preface to Jacques Trilling's book on Joyce and matricide, Derrida praises Trilling's work for its 'countersigning and contravening at once, faithfully, unfaithfully. Unfaithful: how can one not be unfaithful, always unfaithful, in the name of a more intense fidelity?' (NW 96).[13] How, then, does Callaghan's work, in particular Love in the Post, countersign 'Envois'?

Love in the Post mimics 'Envois''s generic hybridity by interweaving documentary interviews with leading Derrida scholars with a complex fictional narrative involving three main characters: scholar Theo Marks (Leigh Kelly), his wife Sophie (Birgit Ludwig), and a filmmaker called Joanna (Lucinda Lloyd). Theo's storyline revolves around his life and work as an academic, and his discovery of love letters hidden in the leg of his desk which reveal that his wife has had a long and serious love affair. Sophie's storyline focuses on two different but comparable situations of intimate communication: a performance piece in front of an audience in which she delivers sections from 'Envois'; and her therapy sessions in which we see her working through her emotions in relation to Theo and the affair. Joanna's storyline is highly self-reflexive since she is making a film inspired by *The Post Card*, with Theo one of the academics she interviews. All the elements of the film therefore interconnect: Joanna interviews Theo; Theo is aligned with the real Derrida scholars interviewed in the documentary footage; Joanna is in Sophie's audience, as is Martin McQuillan, co-writer of Callaghan's film and interviewer of the real Derrida scholars; Sophie is citing from *The Post Card*, which some of the real Derrida scholars also do. Callaghan plays with this interconnection between narrative and documentary, purposely teasing the viewer by permeating the boundary between the two strands. For instance, ten minutes into the film we see a man reading from *The Post Card* in a recording booth. He is captioned in the same way as the academics who have already been interviewed and who will also read from the book: first we see on screen the date of the passage he is reading – '9th September 1977'; then we see his name and institutional affiliation – 'Charles Leavis, University of Wessex'. This man is therefore aligned with the real Derrida scholars who appear in the film but both Charles Leavis and the University of Wessex are fictional, they are a character and an institution from the narrative strand of the film. Whereas it had at first appeared to be part of the documentary strand of *Love in the Post*, it is now apparent that this studio recording must be for Joanna's film-within-the-film. To complicate things further, though, Charles is being played by Robert Rowland Smith, renowned in academic circles as the author of *Derrida and Autobiography* (2008), a book which remains the seminal study on this topic. Smith therefore could well have been interviewed, in his own persona, along with J. Hillis Miller, Samuel Weber and the rest of the real Derrida scholars. To tease the viewer even more, Smith is reading the section of 'Envois' in which 'Jacques Derrida' parodies academics' desire to distinguish conclusively between 'the authentic and the simulacrum' (*E* 89). With such hi-jinks, Callaghan's film reproduces Derrida's game-playing in 'Envois'. Both texts exploit but also challenge generic boundaries, for instance between documentary and narrative, fact and fiction, philosophy and art.

Callaghan's cinematic hi-jinks are characteristic of the film's humour and ironic distance from its philosophical subject matter. Such distance is crucial to the film's ability to countersign Derrida's text effectively. For with too much proximity comes too much fidelity; the greatest danger in Derridean circles is that deconstruction will die for too much love of its master. Callaghan gently probes this topic in one of her research films, 'Love', in which she asks attendees at the 2010 Derrida Today conference in London a deceptively simple question: 'Why love Derrida?' Of the answers given, two stand out. While an encounter with Derrida might well make the earth move – as Elissa Marder says, 'The world tilts in a different way, reading with Derrida' – there is a risk in falling too heavily for him: as Stephen Barker wryly observes, 'I would say there's way too much loving Derrida going on.' Even at the outset of the project, it seems Callaghan was conscious of the dangers of too much proximity, of an excess of fidelity. In 'Reflections' she confesses:

> As another act of rebellion, I didn't read *The Post Card* until after a long time into the project. This might seem outrageous, but it was a genuine attempt to consider the book from a distinct location. To be free to ask any kind of question (including those I was warned against asking) in order to listen to how others spoke about the text. That would be my entry point, the speaking about the text that had 'grown up' around it. (2014: 61)

Callaghan's film is therefore to some extent as much about how *The Post Card* has been received – a kind of ethnographic venture into the Derrida tribe – as it is a response to the work itself. Having Derrida scholar and co-writer of the film, Martin McQuillan, as her guide in this world allows Callaghan to preserve the distance which enables her observations, to still make the film despite avowing that after interviewing the conference attendees: 'I understood very little of what they said' (Callaghan 2014: 62). Callaghan in fact goes so far as to assert that naivety in relation to one's subject matter is possibly essential to all filmmaking, and most definitely to philosophical filmmaking:

> A naïve view or let's call it one free of prejudice, perhaps even innocent, is an essential prerequisite of making a 'philosophical film'. I would even say that perhaps all filmmakers are in some sense naïve. For me, this has been a strength. It allowed me to enter what is a very small and closed world of Derridean thought and attempt to open it out (or prise it open). (2014: 92)

Such a position ensures that the filmmaker is not what 'Jacques Derrida' in 'Envois' calls 'the *bad* reader' (*E* 4), one who is too impatient and who determines or predestines his or her reading in advance. Callaghan avoids this danger, which is one of the reasons why she, along with any *good* reader, is 'constantly surprised' by what happens in the work she produces, work which, as a result, exceeds her own ability to understand it, even on reflection (Callaghan 2014: 66).

Callaghan does have a very clear sense, however, of what she is aiming to achieve in her filmmaking practice. She wishes, in her own words, 'to perform the production of knowledge within film, moving beyond illustration or representation and engaging with problems of representation and communication at the level of the film's own ontology' (Callaghan 2016). Both documentary *and* narrative, fact *and* fiction, are integral to this cinematic knowledge production; both play a role in *Love in the Post*, as do the interconnections between them. I will turn to a fuller consideration of the documentary form in the next chapter; here I want to focus on narrative, taking my lead from Callaghan herself who comments that in making *Love in the Post* one of the guiding research questions was 'What role can narrative play in developing a coherent vision of a philosophical concept?' (Callaghan 2016). As a philosopher's literary experiment, 'Envois' might well be understood to be guided by the same question. *Love in the Post* is most purely narrative in its final scenes, which move away from the intercutting with the documentary interviews and the self-referential scenes with Joanna in the production suite, and resemble most closely the ending to a conventional narrative feature film. I want to look at this ending in order to propose that *Love in the Post* performs a specifically feminist countersignature of 'Envois', one which causes us to reinterpret both that text's philosophy and its story.

At the end of the film, Theo travels to Oxford to deliver his invited lecture on 'Envois', deconstruction and infidelity. In it, he summarises the deconstructive theory of (in)fidelity:

> When Derrida deconstructs Heidegger or Plato he betrays the thing he loves. [. . .] Deconstruction *is* infidelity. It *is* the betrayal of the loved one. But in the best possible way. I would like to think of the whole of philosophy as a history of serial betrayal, of pupils who betray their masters. Hegel who betrayed Kant, Marx who betrayed Hegel, Nietzsche who betrayed everyone, Heidegger who betrayed Nietzsche, Derrida who betrayed Heidegger. Everyone justifying their betrayal as a certain kind of faithfulness, the act of least violence.

Theo seems to accept the structural necessity of (in)fidelity, even within his own marriage: 'I would go as far as to say that there can be no future without infidelity, no social bond and no politics without it . . . [pause] . . . And no relationship either.' The image montage that accompanies the lecture's soundtrack aligns Theo's acceptance of the philosophical theory with personal catharsis and resolution: while he speaks, shots of the lecture are intercut with other scenes, most significantly a shot of Sophie lying on a couch (this time the one at their house) cradling her pregnant stomach, and footage of Theo burning the love letters he has found. The past is being erased; their relationship and family are starting afresh.

Theo accepts Derrida's philosophical theory of (in)fidelity, despite the fact that he confesses at the opening of the lecture that he has had a strong negative emotional reaction to the narrative of 'Envois':

> You know, I consider 'Envois' to be a truly awful text. So bad I can hardly bear to read it. There is nothing more commonplace than infidelity within marriage, nothing more devastating either.

The effect of discovering his wife's betrayal seems to have caused Theo to share a glimpse of his student Macey's view, that 'Envois' is simply 'the old clichéd story of male professor as seducer'. But Theo's outrage at his wife's affair is compromised by the fact that he himself has had an affair with a blonde and beautiful young female student, one he is quite prepared to continue when she visits him during the film, were she willing. In the face of Theo's anger at Sophie, his friend Ben tentatively observes, 'Don't like to mention Penelope . . .'; Theo insists, 'That was different, that wasn't even in the same league as this.' The question the film poses is, why not? Why is female infidelity so shocking and outrageous, while male infidelity is so commonplace that despite the devastation it causes it is not just accepted but in fact forms the structural basis for an understanding of the history of Western philosophy? In answer, and perhaps counterintuitively at first, *Love in the Post* suggests not that male infidelity might be considered shocking and outrageous, but rather that female infidelity might also be considered as commonplace, with women thus able to take their own places within inheritance structures of faithful betrayal, rather than merely facilitating them from without.

Love in the Post countersigns 'Envois' then by foregrounding women in their embodied reality as active participants, for better or worse, in chains of betrayal. For Theo's lecture is in fact part of a montage of shots constituting the film's dénouement which in their visual reverberations strongly imply that Sophie's affair has been with Joanna. For example, the dénouement of the film begins at a party in a warehouse. Joanna receives the last in a series of recorded-delivery letters that she has been signing for but leaving unopened throughout the course of the film. This time, however, she signs for the letter and steps outside the party onto a riverside walkway where she opens it. As she reads its contents, she smiles, looks up, and seems both relieved and satisfied – as if something has finally come to an end. The film then cuts to Sophie on the therapist's couch, who is holding back tears but exuding a similar aura of relief at an uncomfortably suspended situation having been resolved. Sophie then gives voice to her decision to let go of her love affair and return to her husband: 'Je retournerai à la maison, trouver mes enfants, je retrouverai ma vie, avec Theo [I will go back home, back to my family. I will get back my life with Theo].' Theo's lecture follows, after which there is a cut back to Joanna who, now free, flings her letter into the water. We then get almost parallel shots of Joanna, and of Sophie and Theo reunited (Figures 3.1 and 3.2).

This visual montage offers a narrative explanation for the letters Joanna has been receiving but leaving unopened throughout the film: they are from Sophie, who is reluctant to accept Joanna's ending of their love affair. The final letter, which we see Joanna open, must be communicating to Joanna what Sophie tells the therapist in the next scene – that she loves Theo and is returning to him. Joanna's visible relief is at being released, at her ex-lover having accepted her decision; Sophie's visible relief is in being able to finally give up the affair. Unlike 'Envois', then, *Love in the Post* is not all 'boys, boys and more boys' (Macey would now be interested). Rather, a woman betrays a man with another woman, only to be betrayed in turn by the woman with whom she has been unfaithful. Here, the female manifests not just as 'Woman', an empty signifier, the undecidable figure who makes possible the masculine structure of inheritance by betrayal. Rather, 'Woman' has been replaced by embodied women who themselves commit acts of betrayal with each other, as well as with men. To claim that women can betray too, that we can participate in the structural necessity of (in)fidelity rather than merely enable its exclusive masculinity, might not at first seem to be a feminist gesture. But Callaghan's film is here performing what Penelope Deutscher argues Derrida is himself unable to do, that is, the insertion of women into societal bonds

Figure 3.1 Filmmaker Joanna (Lucinda Lloyd) released.
Source: *Love in the Post*, dir. Joanna Callaghan.

Figure 3.2 Sophie (Birgit Ludwig) and Theo (Leigh Kelly) reunited.
Source: *Love in the Post*, dir. Joanna Callaghan.

such as friendship or hospitality and an exploration of the consequences of doing so.

In 'Derrida's Impossible Genealogies' (2005), addressing Derrida's relationship with feminism, Deutscher focuses on Derrida's analysis of the tradition of fraternity in *The Politics of Friendship* and his argument that its conceptual basis for political association depends on an exclusion of 'the feminine or heterosexuality, friendship between women or friendship between men and women' (*PF* 277), not to mention friendship or sexuality between women. Derrida's analysis exposes the way in which political association, as well as the history of metaphysical philosophy, depends upon the 'exclusion of the feminine' (*PF* 279). Deutscher goes on to identify Derrida's writing on hospitality as a particular locus of investigation of the role of women in facilitating, while at the same time being excluded from, social bonds between men. In *Of Hospitality* (2000), for instance, Derrida proposes the idea of an impossible unconditional hospitality, a radical openness to the other without preconception or expectation – the kind of unconditional hospitality to a text ideally necessary, for instance, to avoid the predetermination of bad reading. Unconditional hospitality is impossible, but its impossible possibility traces conditional hospitality and causes us to reflect on the conditions always attached to it. Unconditional hospitality would be a radical openness to the other, no matter its sex, gender, race or even species; conditional hospitality determines who is welcome from these categories in advance, a predetermination which historically excludes the homosexual, the female, the non-White, the non-human animal and more. As Deutscher summarises:

> Conditionality is figured in our supposition of the humanity of the foreign, just as it is figured in our supposition of their sex. A possible unconditionality is figured in our (impossible) willingness not to predetermine their humanity, just as it is figured in our willingness to be open to all permutations of the stranger as male, or as female. And the 'we' doing the anticipating, must, of course be figured as potentially female, just as it might be male. (Deutscher 2005: para. 19)

In drawing attention to the need to rethink the subject positions of both host and guest, master/mistress and heir/heiress, as potentially male or female, Derrida seems to open up the question of the consequences of inserting sexual difference within structures of hospitality or inheritance. But Deutscher argues that Derrida opens up the question only to close it down; the question of sexual difference is introduced not in order to actually think through the consequences if the host and guest were indeed, for example, to be female, but in order to think through the still irreducibly masculine structure of conditional hospitality. As Deutscher so convincingly argues: 'The place of women and men's receptivity to women, becomes the marker of the dilemmas of hospitality (conditional and impossibly unconditional) with which men negotiate' (Deutscher 2005: para. 21). While Derrida draws attention to the fact that women have traditionally facilitated hospitality among men, in his own theorisation he recasts Woman in the same role; his attention to sexual difference only functions in order to facilitate his own analysis of hospitality with the result that, as Deutscher argues, 'even with his welcome "feminist" stress on the necessary place of women as the condition of hospitality between men, [. . .] Derrida isn't quite able to interrupt the tendency to figure women as the condition of the latter' (Deutscher 2005: para. 22). Whereas Derrida's work does not think through hospitality, inheritance or, for that matter, infidelity *between women*, *Love in the Post* does. Sophie betrays her husband with another woman; Joanna betrays Sophie by ending their love affair; female–female infidelity.

II Adaptation as Reproduction

Derrida's work on hospitality opens up a host of feminist questions regarding female–female personal, social and political interaction, but Derrida never actually situates women in these roles in order to develop answers to these questions.[14] *Love in the Post* does. For instance, it exposes the fact that if women are really inserted into these structures, they may, just as equally as men, be terrible hosts, or unfaithful lovers: as Deutscher says, 'the terrible might occur between women' (Deutscher 2005: para. 26). But more powerfully, the film's reinsertion of women enables it to move beyond a critique of Derrida's thought into its own philosophical generation of ideas. Derrida's formula of faithful betrayal encodes the essential deconstructive idea that continuance ought necessarily be iterative rather than merely repetitive; that is, each repetition must also be inherently different. But as we have seen, philosophically, the idea of faithful betrayal is traditionally a masculine structure that excludes women. In contrast, *Love in the Post* inserts women into this structure and in doing so generates an alternative conception of relationality based in the idea of reproduction – both aesthetic and sexual – and the centrality of women to it.

Pregnant bodies abound in the film – the actresses that play Sophie, Lucy (the receptionist at the film production company, played by Jessica Boyde) and the therapist (Frauke Requardt) were all pregnant at the time of filming. This was a conscious decision on Callaghan's part, a challenge to the fact that pregnant women are so visibly absent from film, except when their pregnancy is the focus of the storyline: 'Imagine the day that I can make a film which is "stuffed" full of pregnancies' (Callaghan 2014: 74).[15] The pervasion of the film by pregnant bodies and the unborn children they contain, as well as an actual child – five-year-old Byron – cinematically reproduces 'Envois''s obsession with the child and with children, but it does so to different effect. The film is therefore functioning as an 'adaptation' of 'Envois', but in a quite specific sense. In 'On the Origin of Adaptations' (2007), Gary Bortolotti and Linda Hutcheon propose that in place of traditional fidelity criticism we think about adaptation by homology with evolutionary biology. In this homology, 'stories, in a manner parallel to genes, replicate; the adaptations of both evolve with changing environments' (Bortolotti and Hutcheon 2007: 444). Criticism becomes not a process of studying fidelity but one of studying 'lineages of descent' in order to think about 'how a specific narrative changes over time' (Bortolotti and Hutcheon 2007: 445). Bortolotti and Hutcheon here gesture towards a memetic theory of adaptation, in which the story or, in this instance, philosophical idea is the meme. Memes are passed on through vehicles, be they philosophical texts, novels, films, poems, graphic novels, computer games or any other medium capable of carrying them.[16] In this homology, an 'adaptation' can be understood as a different phenotypic expression of the memes that are contained in the source vehicle. Here, *Love in the Post* is a different phenotypic expression of the memes carried by 'Envois'. But in the transmission from one vehicle to another, the meme (story or idea) also of course *adapts*, that is, it changes. The success of sexual and aesthetic reproduction is absolutely dependent on such mutation – in Derrida's language, on iteration rather than repetition – and this biological understanding of reproduction as mutational replication, rather than as mimesis, is how I am using the term here on in.[17] Bortolotti and Hutcheon's interest is in changes or mutations that occur in relation to a different cultural environment; for instance, the way in which Baz Luhrmann changes *Romeo and Juliet* for a contemporary audience. Such an approach is productive for thinking about how different elements of stories are relevant to the different times in which they might be told. But Bortolotti and Hutcheon miss an opportunity here to think about adaptation to a different environment in terms of the effect of movement from one *medium* to another. Adaptation criticism in this sense, and as performed here, is a critical practice that pays attention to the way in which narrative or philosophical memes (stories or ideas) are adapted to and by new vehicles (media) of their expression.

In this sense, we can see that in the vehicle of *Love in the Post* the memes of pregnancy and the child are encoded positively within a new feminist foregrounding of reproduction. But in the vehicle of 'Envois', the same meme, that of the child, threatens the singularity of the signatory's love affair (with himself). As so many male writers have done before him, 'Jacques Derrida' figures his own creative productions *as* children, lending a reproductive capacity to masculine chains of interaction, for instance from Socrates to Plato to Derrida: 'The two impostors' program is to have a child by me, them too. And let it be made in the dorsum' (*E* 24). But the figure of the child here, and elsewhere in Derrida's work, is a monstrous generality, another figure for

Figure 3.3 Martin McQuillan and playground.
Source: *Love in the Post*, dir. Joanna Callaghan.

Figure 3.4 Joanna (Lucinda Lloyd) reproducing portrait.
Source: *Love in the Post*, dir. Joanna Callaghan.

the radical alterity that defines the structural limits of masculine conditional hospitality.[18] The Child, together with the Woman, takes its place in the chain of impossible undecidable figures which facilitate Derrida's deconstruction. They stand behind his philosophy, an exclusion ironically reproduced in *Love in the Post*, in which philosopher Martin McQuillan's contributions are

Figure 3.5 Lucy (Jessica Boyde) reproducing poster.
Source: *Love in the Post*, dir. Joanna Callaghan.

Figure 3.6 Lucy (Jessica Boyde) reproducing portrait.
Source: *Love in the Post*, dir. Joanna Callaghan.

filmed in a bay window, behind which, in the distance, we watch a children's playground (Figure 3.3).

In contrast, in *Love in the Post* women are essential to cultural and intellectual transmission, functioning as key players in chains of aesthetic reproduction. It is not just that the director of the film-within-the-film, as well as of the film itself, is a woman. More so, this idea is encoded in the film's mise-en-scène, in which the actresses are repeatedly positioned so as to reproduce an image of a woman behind them. For instance, when we first see Joanna in the film studio, she is sitting in a wooden rocking chair. Behind her is an ornate frame containing the portrait of a woman. The woman is sitting with her arms cradled across her stomach in a position which evokes that of a pregnant woman. Joanna, sitting in front of her, plays with her nails in a way that means her arm positions reproduce those of the woman in the portrait (Figure 3.4). Further on in the film, we see Lucy, who is actually pregnant, holding her stomach in a reproduction of the position of the woman featured in a poster on the noticeboard behind her (Figure 3.5), and again a little later holding her cup of tea in such a way that she reproduces the portrait that was first viewed behind Joanna (Figure 3.6). Extending these female chains of reproduction even further, the painting is itself a reproduction, a film prop for another film.[19] Girls, girls and more girls . . . 'Everything begins', as 'Jacques Derrida' observes, 'with reproduction' (*E* 63).

III Phenomenal Film

Love in the Post's feminist countersignature produces a critique of the philosophical content of 'Envois', and generates a new theoretical concept of continuance not as (in)fidelity but as reproduction. But the film also provides the possibility for a new interpretation of 'Envois''s narrative content and form. For Sophie's reluctance to release Joanna, reified in the constantly sent but unread letters, clarifies the story of 'Envois'. It emphasises that, similarly, 'Jacques Derrida' cannot let go of the lover who has already determined to leave him, who has quite possibly, by the end of the letters, already left him. The film thus exposes the fact that 'Envois' stages a tension between theory and reality, between generality and singularity. It does so in the form of the undecidable genre of the work – philosophy or literature, fact or fiction – but also in the work's story: for in his continuing attachment to this aborted love affair, 'Jacques Derrida' betrays Derrida's own deconstructive theory of (in)fidelity and is, instead, 'monstrously faithful' (*E* 243).[20] 'Jacques Derrida' explains that 'it is somewhat in order to "banalize" the cipher of the unique tragedy that I prefer cards, one hundred cards or reproductions in the same envelope, rather than a single "true" letter' (*E* 11). The single letter is too singular, too specific, and also too final – it would constitute an acceptance of the determination of his lover and of the pain of actual betrayal. 'Envois' is not about 'Jacques Derrida''s infidelity – if the assumption is that this love affair is an extramarital one – 'Envois' is about 'Jacques Derrida''s struggle to accept having himself been betrayed by his lover's determination to leave him.

This is the radically different understanding of the text opened up by *Love in the Post* – exactly the response to it in fact that Catharine Malabou says is needed: '*The Post Card*? Radicalise it. Find what seems to be the most radical point in it' (2014: 165). For her, this is 'the possibility of total destruction' (Malabou 2014: 165); for me, and perhaps for Callaghan, it is 'Envois''s staging of the tension between the comforting abstraction of the general theory and the painful reality of the singular experience, between philosophy and the phenomenological experience film is able to convey and create.

If this is how *Love in the Post* recasts 'Envois', then the context of 'Jacques Derrida''s theoretical insistence that the signatory and the addressee are undecidable changes. It is no longer (just) part of Derrida's deconstruction of the metaphysics of identity and his theory of adestination, that is, that the possibility of a letter not arriving is necessary to the possibility of it ever arriving; that the open circulation of the post puts into question the singularity of both sender and receiver. Nor is it (only) the radical challenge to sexual and gender essentialism or determinism that 'Jacques Derrida' repeatedly claims it is.[21] Rather, it is (also) 'Jacques Derrida''s defence mechanism; if neither he nor his lover are singular individuals, then she can cause him no pain and he can feel no pain:

> Understand me, when I write, right here, on these innumerable post cards, I annihilate not only what I am saying but also the unique addressee, and every destination. I kill you, I annul you at my fingertips, wrapped around my finger. (*E* 33)

To 'lose the identity of the, as they say, sender, the emitter' (*E* 112) is to inure oneself to harm; 'Jacques Derrida' is vulnerable when he enters into the singularity of love: 'no one better than I will have known how, or rather will have loved to destine, uniquely. This is the disaster on the basis of which I love you, uniquely' (*E* 112). The potential multiplicity of 'Jacques Derrida' and of the addressee is a protective fiction against the dangerous vulnerability of one unique being's monstrously faithful love for another unique being:

> others will believe that we are four, and they might indeed be right. But whatever the number decided upon, it is you whom I love uniquely, to you that, without even deciding upon it, I always will be faithful. (*E* 243)

Whereas for the fictional character 'Jacques Derrida' the pretence of generality is a protection from the pain of singularity, for the philosopher Jacques Derrida the literary form enables the playful disguising, but not serious disavowal, of philosophical authority. Interestingly, this argument is made by Christine van Boheemen-Saaf when she analyses the shift from philosophical to literary form at the end of Derrida's 'The Night Watch'. This ending recalls 'Envois' in form and content: like 'Envois' it puts into question the identity of the signatory, appearing 'to present a personal confession of the speaker' although at the same time, due to the move into dialogic or polylogic form, 'there is no guarantee that that speaker is Derrida' (Boheemen-Saaf 2013: 195). As Boheemen-Saaf argues, at the end of 'The Night Watch', 'the signature becomes spectral. The statement appears histrionic, play-acting, pretending to conclude in the name of Derrida, while deferring to a dramatic alter ego or secret sharer' (Boheemen-Saaf 2013: 195). Boheemen-Saaf does not interpret this as a serious questioning of philosophy's masculine authority, but rather as a disingenuous gesture that merely disguises philosophy's arrogation of literature: 'What we see happen here, at the moment when the text must conclude and make its point, is philosophy's coy gesture of hiding itself in the guise of (post)modernist literature, spectralizing its own discursive authority' (Boheemen-Saaf 2013: 195).[22] Likewise, in 'Envois', Derrida adopts a literary form, taking advantage of literature's playful potential in order to justify the signatory's repeated claims to be unsettling the identity of signatory and addressee and, in doing so, challenging sexual and gender norms. But in fact 'Envois' is a philosophical text as structurally dependent as any other in the metaphysical tradition on the exclusion of Woman, reproducing the arrogant 'dissymmetry of "authority"' of which 'Jacques Derrida' criticises another male letter writer in 'Envois': 'Simply he is writing, it is he who destines (he thinks), and the other is placed on stage by a letter the rest of which is supposed to bear witness. The other does not answer, is not published' (*E* 96).

'Jacques Derrida' knows he is playing a risky game here. He asks directly:

> Who *will prove* that the sender is the same man, or woman? And the male or female addressee? Or that they are *not* identical? To themselves, male or female, first of all? That they do or do not form a couple? Or several couples? Or a crowd? Where would the principle of identification be? (*E* 234)

But in asking these questions he reveals his misunderstanding of literature: literature is not about proof, it is about persuasion. Persuading your reader of the sexual or gendered indeterminacy of your narrator is not a matter of evidence, nor is the burden of proof on the reader. Rather, it is a matter of style, rhetoric and, crucially, belief. There is no question that one *believes* that the narrator of Jeanette Winterson's *Written on the Body* is undecidably both male and female, gay and straight, single and multiple, for example, in a way in which one never *believes* 'Envois''s 'Jacques Derrida''s claims to be so. This is a question of style and of literary skill, but it is also a question of form. 'Jacques Derrida''s claims are undermined by his undisguised connection to the real Derrida, evidenced by the events recounted in 'Envois' that are verifiably 'true', Derrida's own experiences; and they are undermined by the choice of the monologic rather than a dialogic or polylogic epistolary form. As a result,

'Envois' remains a narcissistic work by a male philosopher in which Woman, silenced and excluded, features only to facilitate the masculine discourse.

'Jacques Derrida' anticipates that he will receive criticism for publishing in the monologic form:

> if because I love them too much I am not publishing *your* letters (which by all rights belong to me), I will be accused of erasing you, of stifling you, of keeping you silent. If I do publish them, they will accuse me of appropriating for myself, of stealing, of violating, of keeping the initiative, of exploiting the body of the woman, always the pimp, right? (*E* 231)

But there seems no awareness here of the possibility of joint authorship, of the possibility that the woman could assume responsibility for her own correspondence, her own voice. Unless, of course, there is no 'body of the woman' here at all, and the fear is not of violating the rights of a real woman but of being unable to adequately imagine himself into a female body and mind in order to creatively write a female character, as well as his own. 'Jacques Derrida''s literary fear of his inability to imagine himself a woman parallels (recalling Deutscher's criticism above) his philosophical inability to think through the position of real women. The result in 'Envois' is that his correspondent becomes an empty figure. It makes no difference, in fact, whether she is even real: 'I ask myself occasionally quite simply if you exist and if you have the slightest notion of it' (*E* 29). It does not matter, for she exists only to facilitate his writing: 'And then you no longer exist, you are dead, like the dead woman in my game, and my literature becomes possible' (*E* 29).

While 'Envois' lays claim to a gender and sexual undecidability it however cannot, or will not, perform, *Love in the Post* – perhaps counterintuitively, since it has real gendered bodies to contend with – proves more persuasive. In doing so, it demonstrates that 'Jacques Derrida''s fear of film is unfounded. *Love in the Post* is at the same time able to materialise women in their embodied reality *and* perform the possibility of gender and sexual indeterminacy, of multiple possible signatories and addressees. For example, while the visual associations created by the closing montage suggest that the love affair has been between two women, an earlier scene in which Theo takes the letters to a handwriting expert refers consistently to the lover as a man. And when Sophie is in therapy she confesses her affair to her therapist as a heterosexual one: 'I realised I was doing the same gestures and it felt awkward because it's not the same man.' The conflicting implications of different scenes create in the film an irresolvable undecidability about the gender of the lover and therefore sexuality of the love affair. This undecidability manifests itself most profoundly in the scenes in which Sophie delivers extracts of 'Envois' to an intimate live audience.

These scenes were filmed at Dorich House Museum, former home and exhibition space of the Russian sculptor Nora Gordine, which now 'operates as an international centre to promote women creative practitioners'.[23] As the website draws attention to, Dorich House 'is an exceptional example of a modern studio house created by and for a female artist'. The setting therefore emphasises and celebrates female creativity and authority, as does the power of Sophie's delivery, which gives an emotional intensity to the letters absent, in comparison, from the scenes in which academics read from the text.[24] An embodied woman, performing in front of material reproductions of women by a woman (Gordine's bronze casts), in a space created for and by a woman (Dorich House), Sophie appropriates and conveys the words of a male signatory, 'Jacques Derrida'. In doing so, she multiplies and multigenders the addresser of 'Envois'; the viewer feels that these words come from Sophie as much as (or perhaps even more than) they come from 'Jacques Derrida'. The film also gives Sophie an audience; her addressees, male and female, literally materialise on screen in a series of shots that self-consciously evoke film's power to give embodied form to immaterial characters, concepts and ideas (Figures 3.7, 3.8 and 3.9). With a purposeful lack of continuity editing, the sequence moves from a wide shot, to a medium shot, to a wide shot; whereas the chairs are empty in the opening wide shot, they are filled with people on the return to it, with no bridging shot denoting a shift in time that would have allowed the people to take up their seats. There is a surreal uncanniness to this moment as the film materialises Sophie's audience, men and women who are, in this instance, the highly visible multiple recipients of the letters.

For Callaghan (2016), film is a form of 'phenomenological inquiry' that takes place through the embodiedness of its human actors, and its director as agent, but also through a self-reflexive relationship with the medium which consciously manipulates and explores how film, both 'process and outcome' (Callaghan 2016), can be used. *Love in the Post* plays with the 'possibilities appropriate to itself (and only to itself)' (Callaghan 2016), possibilities which can probe the relationship, and the differences, between philosophical and phenomenal experience. In Callaghan's Heideggerean words, film can make 'apparent the "hiddenness" involved in the "ontological difference" between "being" and "beings"' (Callaghan 2016). Crucial for Callaghan in the movement from philosophy to film is film's power to acknowledge 'the subjectivity of the lifeworld in the transformation of text to image' (Callaghan 2016). *Love in the Post*, just as it materialises Sophie's audience, literally brings 'Envois' to life. It emphasises, as does Callaghan's own research process, the 'intuitive, embodied responses to the content researched' (Callaghan 2016). The result is a reification of the difference between philosophical and cinematic thinking,

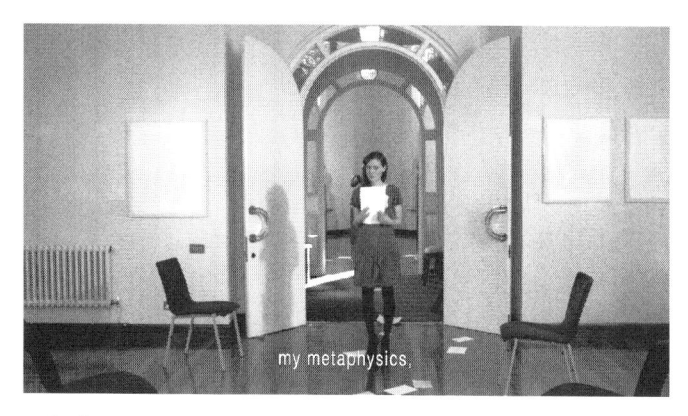

Figure 3.7 Sophie (Birgit Ludwig), wide shot without audience.
Source: *Love in the Post*, dir. Joanna Callaghan.

Figure 3.8 Sophie (Birgit Ludwig), medium shot.
Source: *Love in the Post*, dir. Joanna Callaghan.

Figure 3.9 Sophie (Birgit Ludwig), wide shot with audience.
Source: *Love in the Post*, dir. Joanna Callaghan.

towards which Catherine Malabou gestures in interview with McQuillan and Callaghan. 'There is of course,' she says, 'a frontier between the visual and the intellectual, the philosophical' and, recalling Gilles Deleuze, she locates this frontier in film's ability to produce affect: 'he [Deleuze] says that it is at the level of the production of affects, that the film is able to produce knowledge through affect, more than philosophy'.[25] That this is exactly what *Love in the Post* achieves is evidenced in the post-screening reactions collected after the premiere of the film at Somerset House in London in March 2014: one audience member says that the film makes an esoteric subject 'come alive'; another is moved to observe that 'film has its own way of presenting a truth'. Another contributor notes that 'what the film does is establishing [sic] the connection between the intellectual and the emotional in a really clever way'.[26] Through the phenomenal power of its cinematic medium, *Love in the Post* makes explicit what Weber detects only the implication of in 'Envois': 'a reassessment of the relation between thinking and feeling' (2014: 192). Interestingly, in the interview 'Cinema and Its Ghosts' (2015), Derrida observes that cinema produces in him 'an emotion that is completely different from that of reading, which imprints a more present and active memory in me' (*CG* 24), but since for him cinema is 'a way of forgetting work' (*CG* 24), for him 'cinematic emotion cannot [. . .] take the form of knowledge' (*CG* 24). In contrast, Callaghan's work demonstrates that in cinema emotion can produce knowledge, can in fact be knowledgeable, and knowledge can produce emotion, can in fact be emotional. While for Derrida, cinematic emotion 'must not be work, knowledge, or even memory' (*CG* 24), it is Callaghan's contention, and my own, that cinema can be all of these things, and more.

IV Dorsal Philosophy

At the end of their part in the film, Sophie and Theo, reunited, embrace in a position which explicitly recalls the position of Plato and Socrates in the image on the post cards on which 'Jacques Derrida' writes 'Envois': Plato is behind Socrates, Theo is behind Sophie. In each image, the dorsal embrace denotes an acceptance of (in)fidelity as constitutive of philosophical and personal relationality. At the climax of the love story, then, Sophie and Theo's positioning returns us to philosophy, or rather to a palimpsestuous superimposition of the philosophical and the personal which colours the viewer's interpretation of the final scene in the film. The film ends with a close-up of Joanna sitting, staring thoughtfully ahead, with light flickering over her face. According to the personal interpretation, this is a continuation of the shot of her throwing away the letter – she is sitting reflecting on the final conclusion of her love affair. But the image is accompanied by a voice off from Derrida, speaking in French, which translates as:

> I believe that when you read someone, that when you inhabit or let yourself be inhabited by the text of an author – which is a sort of correspondence – well the relationship between the author and yourself is inevitably a phantomatic relationship.

Reinforced by the philosophic echoes in Theo and Sophie's embrace, this voice off changes the interpretation of Joanna's final scene. It seems that the flickering is from a cinema screen and that the voice off is coming from the image on the screen. In this case, it might be deduced that Joanna is watching further footage of Derrida in interview, footage she has been using in creating her own film. According to this interpretation, as we watch the end of *Love in the Post*, we are watching Joanna watching the end of her own film; and we are seeing her relief but also sadness at being finally done with Derrida, being free of his phantomatic hold. Suddenly it occurs to the viewer that the letters Joanna has been receiving throughout the film are not from Sophie but from Derrida, or, more precisely, from both Sophie and Derrida, again reifying Derrida's assertion of the multiplicity of the signatory. Joanna has resisted reading them just as Callaghan for so long resisted reading *The Post Card* in order to preserve her independence, but when her film is finished (the party can be interpreted as a celebration of its completion) she is able to read his final letter and be free of him. This is an entirely plausible interpretation of the end of the film, until we get a reverse shot which reveals that the flickering light is not from a screen, but from a fire. With this revelation, the film returns us to the personal, to the love story narrative, with the image of the fire recalling the flames Theo has used to destroy Sophie's lover's letters and purge the past. But the letter-burning scene is itself taken from 'Envois' – 'and in a suburb that I did not know, where I chose to wind up, I burned everything, slowly, at the side of a road' (*E* 33) – which takes us back to Derrida and philosophy . . .

In a similar way to the functioning of the *trompe l'oeil* in *Ghost Dance*, analysed in the previous chapter, this final shot/reverse shot metonymically represents the dependence of the film's affect on an 'endless oscillation' (Manon 2006: 61–2) between coexistent possibilities: in Hugh S. Manon's analysis of *trompe l'oeil* this is between truth and its denial; in *Love in the Post* it is between film and philosophy, fiction and fact, narrative and documentary. It is perhaps no surprise that at this point *Love in the Post* replicates an effect also found in *Ghost Dance*, since Derrida's voice off in this closing sequence comes from a lost reel of the interview with Derrida that director Ken McMullen recorded for *Ghost Dance*.²⁷ Derrida therefore does not just communicate with Joanna and with Callaghan in his letters and in the written-text 'Envois', but also cinematically, through the *Ghost Dance* interview footage. His phantomatic relationship with both directors (imagined and real) is both textual and, as befits his own theorisation of film's spectrality in that interview, cinematic.²⁸

Derrida haunts *Love in the Post* in its narrative, in its ideas, in his actual presence but, most cinematically, he haunts the film in its colour palette. In the *Ghost Dance* interview footage Derrida is wearing a blue shirt and a red cravat. Blues and reds saturate *Love in the Post*: the red carpet in Dorich House; Sophie's blue dress; Joanna's blue scarf; one of the audience member's red hair; the blue carpet and red curtains in Theo's office; Joanna's red jacket and blue tights when interviewing Theo; the blue rug and red curtains in the therapist's office; Sophie's blue bracelet at breakfast; Sophie and Theo's blue chairs; the light from Theo's laptop bathing him in blue at his desk; Theo's red jumper . . . I could go on. Drawing attention to such fine detail of the film's colour palette responds to Callaghan's own appeal that her viewers, many of whom she knows will be scholars of literature and of philosophy, 'watch the film with the same dedication with which you read (and I know many of you are very good readers)' (2014: 58). She advises 'multiple viewings', and urges 'a sensitivity to a different kind of language than that to which some of you as text-based scholars may be accustomed' (Callaghan 2014: 58). Colour is one such language, and the prevalence of blues and reds across the film cinematically links the film both with Derrida (via his clothing in the *Ghost Dance* interview) and with his predominant philosophical concern in 'Envois', that of the post. For blue and red are of course the colours that border British airmail envelopes, envelopes such as those in which Sophie's lover posts his/her own *envois*.

A film so saturated by Derrida might fall foul of the risk that Jonathan Lahey Dronsfield discusses in relation to David Barison and Daniel Ross' 'adaptation' of Heidegger's lectures on Hölderlin, *The Ister* (2004), in which an excess of fidelity leaves the film merely 'a companionable "accompaniment" to Heidegger's text' (2014: 222). We have already seen how, in its feminist cinematic countersignature to 'Envois', *Love in the Post* escapes this trap. But in closing I want to suggest that the film goes even further than this, by cinematically countersigning the very idea of countersignature itself. For thinking about the relationship between one text and another, or a film and a philosophical text, as a 'countersignature' is a textual metaphor. It is one Callaghan (2012) adopts in her written comments on the film: 'The story we are creating is not strictly that of *The Post Card*, but functions as a counter signature to the text.' But the film itself cinematically generates an alternative way of figuring the relationship between film and philosophy; one inspired by 'Envois', but moving beyond its textual terms.

Love in the Post's refiguration of the relationship between film and philosophy responds to 'Jacques Derrida''s interest in 'Envois' in the figural conceptual potential of the post card. In particular, 'Jacques Derrida' is fascinated by the recto and verso and the relationship between image and text, front and back:

> What I prefer, about post cards, is that one does not know what is in front or is in back, here or there, near or far, the Plato or the Socrates, recto or verso. Nor what is the most important, the picture or the text, and in the text the message or the caption, or the address. (*E* 13)

The particular post card 'Jacques Derrida' focuses on reifies this play further in that it inverts the received wisdom about the usual order of precedence between Plato and Socrates. In a dizzying mise-en-abyme, the image on this specific post card thus reproduces the uncertainty the post card in general reifies about priority and succession. It is no surprise then that 'Jacques Derrida' declares that here 'reversibility unleashes itself, goes mad' (*E* 13). *Love in the Post* embraces this madness and spatialises it, architecturally representing philosophy as *behind* film. On each side, the 'signatories' are so multiple that the idea of the countersignature loses its hold and is replaced by a three-dimensional architectural representation of how one discourse stands behind another.

This can be seen through close analysis of the mise-en-scène of two comparable scenes in the film, bearing in mind one of Callaghan's other key research questions: 'What role does mise en scene play in developing a coherent vision of these [philosophical] concepts?' (Callaghan 2010). I want to compare the mise-en-scène of the first scene in the film's narrative strand with the mise-en-scène of the first scene in the film's documentary strand – compare the still in Figure 3.7 with the still in Figure 3.10. In both images, the camera position and camera work is the same – we have a stationary camera with a wide front shot. Both shots contain one figure, reading against a backdrop. Sophie is standing in front of two receding arches, framed symmetrically by the double doors and the two chairs. Behind her, through both arches, is a sculpture. In the comparable shot, Marian Hobson is seated also in front, although slightly to screen left of, an arch, also with a sculpture behind her, but this time the sculpture is before, not through and behind, the arch. In addition, while the shot of Sophie is carefully balanced and centred, Hobson is off-centre, and the backdrop is of a building covered with scaffolding and barriers. It is as if in Hobson's shot we are privy to the backstage of a theatre, glimpsing the material support that holds up the curated façade that we see the front of in Sophie's shot. The parallelism of the shots invites a comparison between them; their slight differences tell a specific story – in the documentary shot we have gone through the arches behind Sophie and are looking back at, looking

Figure 3.10 Marian Hobson reading from Derrida's 'Envois'.
Source: *Love in the Post*, dir. Joanna Callaghan.

at the back of, her shot. Philosophy, we might say, is behind the film, offering it material support. This is a new, spatial and visual way of thinking about the relationship between film and philosophy in particular, and adaptation in general. The positioning of the sculpture is crucial here: it is through the arch in Sophie's shot, but before the arch in Hobson's shot. Its position informs us that we are on different sides here; if we were to walk past Hobson, past the scaffolding, past the sculpture, and through the arch we would be in the narrative world of the film. In 'Envois', 'Jacques Derrida' conceives of film as that which is 'behind', that which he is trying to gain access to: 'I am watching you sleep, trying to get under your eyelids (where there is something like a film)' (*E* 90). But *Love in the Post* is located *in* that 'under' or, rather, 'behind', reversing the order of priority; here, philosophy is behind the film, we gain access to it *through* the film, in a quite spatial sense. *Love in the Post* replaces the text-based idea of the countersignature with a film-based idea of the material support and a spatial understanding of philosophy as *behind* film, as film as that *through* which we can access philosophy.

'Envois'/philosophy: boys, boys and more boys, behind which are women and children.

Love in the Post/film: girls, girls and more girls, together with their children, behind which is philosophy.

Notes

1. The full screenplay for *Love in the Post* is available in Callaghan and McQuillan's *Love in the Post: From Plato to Derrida – The Screenplay and Commentary* (2014), but the printed version differs to the delivery in the film. All citations here are transcribed from the film's audio and/or subtitles.
2. 'Jacques Derrida', in inverted commas, will be used throughout to refer to the signatory of the letters, to differentiate him from Derrida the actual man and philosopher. As Martin McQuillan observes, 'critical commentary on "Envois" has correctly already chosen to accept the possibility that the "I" of the "Envois" is not reducible to "Derrida" and that in fact such a suspension of referentiality in which we occupy the self-contradictory simultaneity of truth and falsehood is the basis by which we approach all literature and fiction' (2014: 98). See McQuillan (2014) for an extended discussion of how to read 'Envois' non-biographically.
3. 'Jacques Derrida' makes reference to his addressee's 'determination' repeatedly throughout 'Envois', for instance (*E* 40, 125, 126, 227).
4. Other examples of monologic epistolary fictions include Goethe's *Die Leiden des jungen Werthers* (*The Sorrows of Young Werther*) (1774), *The Letters of a Portuguese Nun* (1890) and, more recently, Stephen Chbosky's *The Perks of Being a Wallflower* (1999).
5. I say 'she' because despite the fact that, as Martin McQuillan notes in interview in *Love in the Post*, 'the French pronouns are very difficult to follow and are slippery', due to the constraints of the French language the addressee does eventually become gendered as female. I follow Wills here: 'In the writing she becomes sooner or later unavoidably feminine, such are the demands of the French language, namely, that a gender be chosen sooner or later. Hence I shall refer to her as "she"' (1984: 19).
6. In 'Two Words for Joyce' (1984), Derrida states that '*La Carte postale* is haunted by Joyce, whose funerary statue stands at the centre of the *Envois* (the visit to the cemetery in Zurich). This haunting invades the book, a shadow on every page, whence the resentment, sincere and acted, always mimed, of the signatory' (*TW* 150). Derrida goes on to detail some of the connections between Joyce and 'Envois' (see *TW* 150–2). In her engagement with '*La Veilleuse* (" . . . au livre de lui-même")', Derrida's preface to Jacques Trilling's *James Joyce ou l'écriture matricide* (2001), Christine van Boheemen-Saaf suggests the 'struggle between spirit and matter' in Derrida's preface is 'best addressed by means of a scrutiny of Derrida's own stylistic practice – reading him as if he were Joyce' (2013: 194).
7. For further examples of, and reflection on, creative critical responses to Derrida's life and work, see 'Imagining Derrida', a special issue of *Derrida Today*, edited by myself and John Schad (2017).
8. Fascinatingly, another early response to *The Post Card* recognised exactly this paradox and possibility. In 'The Post-Age', his review of *La carte postale* for *Diacritics* in 1981, Gregory Ulmer argues that '"Envois" is a book in the process of becoming a (film or video) *script*' (56).

9. See Rupert Read and Jerry Goodenough (2005), Murray Smith and Thomas E. Wartenberg (2006), Daniel Frampton (2007), Thomas E. Wartenberg (2007), Stephen Mulhall (2008), John Mullarkey (2009), Aaron Smuts (2009), Robert Sinnerbrink (2011), Gregory Flaxman, Robert Sinnerbrink and Lisa Trahair (2016), and Bernd Herzogenrath (2017).
10. These include Derek Jarman's *Wittgenstein* (1993), Richard Linklater's *Waking Life* (2001), Michael Dibb's *Edward Said: The Last Interview* (2004), Astra Taylor's *Zizek!* (2005), *Examined Life* (2008), Sophie Fiennes' *The Pervert's Guide to the Cinema* (2006), Michel Gondry's *Is the Man Who is Tall Happy?* (2010), Tao Ruspoli's *Being in the World* (2010) and Margarethe von Trotta's *Hannah Arendt* (2012).
11. Callaghan situates her work in the context of practice-led research such as Gary Hill's installations *Plato's Cave* (1992) and *Remarks on Colour* (1994), Victor Burgin's *Nietzsche in Paris* (2000), Ross and Barison's *The Ister* (2007) and the work of Benoît Maire who, Callaghan (2012) explains, 'uses philosophical texts and ideas as a point of departure for his performances, painting and videos'. More widely, on philosophy as performance see Bowie (2015) and Cull Ó Maoilearca and Lagaay (2014).
12. See, for example, Brian McFarlane's summary of this position in *Novel to Film* (1994).
13. For more on the countersignature, see Derrida's 'Countersignature' (2004) and an excellent elaboration of the concept in Leslie Hill (2010: 274–324). See also the Introduction to Derek Attridge (1992) and – on Derrida, Joyce and the countersignature – see John D. Caputo (1997: 189–98).
14. For Deutscher such questions include: 'what will be the hospitality between the woman guest and the woman host? Can women anticipate female guests and hosts? What are the conditions of their being able to do so? Does feminism engage with a problematics, not just of conditional, but (of course) of impossible, unconditional hospitality?' (2005: para. 22).
15. It is so unusual to see multiple pregnant actresses in one film that one wonders what the collective noun is for a group of pregnant women – there is none, officially. One ironically apt suggestion on the internet is derived from the collective noun for gnus – how does an *implausibility* of pregnant women sound?
16. According to the OED definition, a meme is 'an element of culture that may be considered to be passed on by non-genetic means, esp. imitation'. The concept was first proposed by Richard Dawkins in *The Selfish Gene* (1976) and was taken up and elaborated by Susan Blackmore in *The Meme Machine* (1999). Blackmore develops her theory of the meme out of the foundational principles of evolution, and by loose analogy with biological evolution. In biological evolution, genes are what Richard Dawkins terms 'replicators', a replicator being 'anything of which copies are made' and the organisms and groups of organisms that carry them and pass them on are 'vehicles', a vehicle being 'the entity that interacts with the environment' (Blackmore 1999: 5). 'Meme' is the new noun that Dawkins

coins in *The Selfish Gene* for a new replicator 'that conveys the idea of a unit of cultural transmission' (1976: 192). 'Memes are stored in human brains (or books or inventions)', the 'vehicles' of meme theory, 'and passed on by imitation' (Blackmore 1999: 6).

17. For a useful collection of citations from Derrida on 'iteration' and its allosemes, see Smith (1995: 99–100). See also Derrida's *Speech and Phenomena* (1973) for an extended theorisation of iterability.
18. For detailed discussion of the figure of birth as it appears across Derrida's work, see Samir Haddad (2013), Stephen Thomson (2012) and Penelope Deutscher (2013).
19. In private correspondence, Callaghan explained that 'the painting behind Joanna is at Sands Film studios [. . .] We chose locations that were "dressed" already and that we could then situate scenes in. I don't know the name of the painting but as Sands specialises in period costumes it will be a copy of some artist they used as a prop in a set.' She says that the mirroring of the painting was 'wonderful', 'one of the magical moments in the film'.
20. Samuel Weber gestures towards this interpretation in his interview for *Love in the Post*: 'I think the postal principle at that point was one way that Derrida was trying to think this difficult connection of singularity and generality. In other words, how do you establish communication, commonality, on the basis of an experience that remains to some extent irreducibly singular' (Weber 2014: 191). Indeed, as I discuss in Chapter 1, it is 'precisely this problem that always fascinated Derrida [. . .]' (Weber 2014: 191).
21. 'Jacques Derrida' repeatedly implies that neither 'he' nor his addressee are of one singular gender or one singular sexual orientation. See, for instance, *E* 50, 53, 60, 70, 79, 112, 143–4, 145, 155, 176, 179, 229, 234.
22. Wills makes a similar observation regarding 'the paradox of authorship explicitly raised in *Envois*, the fact that hand-in-hand with claims to ultimate control exist statements of authorial abrogation (surely another more subtle form of manipulation)' (1984: 32).
23. Description available at https://www.dorichhousemuseum.org.uk/ (last accessed 18 September 2017).
24. Callaghan's short research film *Letters*, as the introduction on the 'Research' pages of the *Love in the Post* website explains, 'cuts together a series of readings of letters from *The Post Card* by academics attending *Derrida Today* in 2010. The act of reading aloud the letters publicly, [sic] became a feature of the final film, in which Sophie, [sic] recounts the letters as a performance to a public audience', available at: http://loveinthepost.co.uk/research-in-progress/ (last accessed 18 September 2017).
25. On cinema and affect, see in particular Deleuze (2005), as well as work inspired by Deleuze's theory, including Marks (2000 and 2002) and Brinkema (2014).
26. The post-screening reactions are available at https://vimeo.com/113471895 (last accessed 18 September 2017).

27. Callaghan tells the story of this lost footage in 'Reflections' (Callaghan 2014: 91).
28. The spectrality of writing, reading and cinema is the explicit focus of another of Callaghan's films inspired by Derrida's work, the mesmerising short film *DO NOT READ THIS* (2012).

CHAPTER FOUR

Auto/biography

Whereas the previous chapter considered a cinematic response to one of Derrida's texts, 'Envois', this chapter develops out of an analysis of a film which responds to Derrida's life and work more broadly, Kirby Dick and Amy Ziering Kofman's *Derrida* (2002).[1] The larger question that drove the previous chapter concerned how a feminist film adapts philosophy, while also itself performing a specifically cinematic form of thinking. In this chapter, the broader concern is primarily with the life, rather than the work: how does film perform biography and autobiography, and in doing so, how does it cinematically redefine how we might understand both of those concepts? More specifically, how does film perform auto/biography in the face of Derrida's deconstruction of those concepts? And how might feminist film theory and practice inform, and be informed by, an exploration of the answers to such questions?

This chapter begins by placing *Derrida* within a cinematic rather than a philosophical context: that is, within the context of Dick and Ziering Kofman's wider oeuvre, and within the history of feminist documentary filmmaking, of which their wider work is a part. Contextualising *Derrida* in such a way challenges claims in existing critical commentary that the film is unique and original in its techniques, for instance, Nicholas Royle's celebration of it as 'a strange and singular adventure film, seeking new and different ways of thinking and experiencing film' (2015: 128), or Eric D. Snider's (2002) claim that the film is 'vividly achieving new ground in documentaries'. Situating *Derrida* in the history of feminist experimental filmmaking dispels the myth of originality around its cinematic techniques, but it also dispels any belief in the originality of Derrida's theories of biography. For feminism has always necessarily understood *its* realism *against* the traditional notions of biography and identity as Derrida portrays them, since such notions have always already excluded women and our representation. The second part of the chapter moves from a concern with biography to a concern with autobiography, and from the phase of feminist critique to that of feminist generative thought. Through a comparative analysis of *Derrida* and Safaa Fathy's *D'Ailleurs, Derrida* (1999), I develop a theory of *quer* cinematic autobiography, from the German cognate of 'queer', *quer*, which, when used to describe a glance, means 'directed sideways'. I argue that in documentary cinema, in particular that which is biographical or autobiographical in nature, the *quer* glance (directed sideways) is the most effective technique for establishing intimacy, avoiding narcissism, and simultaneously both protecting and revealing the self. I provide a close reading of Michelle Citron's *Daughter Rite* (1978) and Sarah Polley's *Stories We Tell* (2012) as examples of this particular form of *quer* autobiography. What becomes clear is that film as a medium deconstructs autobiography, aligning cinema with Derrida's work without subordinating it to it. In closing, I turn to another example of Derrida's autobiographical writing – not 'Envois', but 'Circumfession' – in order to propose that Derrida's deconstructive autobiographical practice, although written on the page, might be considered in some sense cinematic, but also in order to expose the limits in any analogy between 'Circumfession' and the feminist autobiographical cinematic tradition.

I Biography, or, the Realist Paradox

Early on in *Derrida*, the audience is presented with footage of Jacques Derrida at an academic conference on biography at New York University. In the short excerpt from Derrida's lecture presented in the film, he cautions against biography, its assumption of authority and its dangerous ability to fix a philosopher's life in a single, stabilised image, sometimes for as long as centuries after publication, or at least until another 'authoritative' biography comes along to challenge it. In contrast, he argues that close textual engagement with a philosopher's work is far more revealing biographically than any attention to the life could be:

> That's why I would say that sometimes the one who reads a text by a philosopher, even for instance just one tiny paragraph, and interprets it in a rigorous, inventive and powerfully deciphering fashion, is more of a real biographer than the one who knows the whole story. (Kofman 2005: 59)

More than this, Derrida states that biography is structurally excluded by traditional philosophy; to include biography within philosophy would be to contaminate it with anecdote and render it no longer, in fact, philosophy. In a wonderful moment of performative irony, however, Derrida illustrates – and therefore according to metaphysical logic *compromises* – his own philosophical argument *with* an anecdote:

> You remember Heidegger's statement about Aristotle . . . Heidegger once was asked 'What was the life of Aristotle?' What could we answer to the question 'what was Aristotle's life?' Well the answer is very simple, 'Aristotle

was a philosopher' and the answer holds in one sentence: 'He was born, he thought, and he died.' And all the rest is pure anecdote. (Kofman 2005: 61)

With this playful move, Derrida is both proving his point and situating deconstructive thought as different from traditional philosophy in this respect: deconstruction is unlike metaphysics because it is capable of including the life as well as the thought, without destroying the latter by the inclusion of the former.[2] This hospitality to the other of philosophy is (just) one of the reasons why deconstruction was received with such hostility by analytic philosophy, and why it has always gained a more welcome reception in literary studies. It is also why Derrida is able to be far more experimental with the form of his philosophical texts, often including within them autobiographical detail, as we have seen in the previous chapter in discussion of 'Envois' and as I will explore again below in engagement with 'Circumfession'.

Cut between Derrida's two comments above, Dick and Ziering Kofman place footage from the Laguna Beach House in California in which Ziering Kofman is helping Derrida choose the right jacket for his upcoming interview: they both like the blue jacket but Derrida is concerned that it does not go with his black trousers; Ziering Kofman reassures him that they will not film his bottom half and asks him, apologising for the trouble, if he might try the jacket on so she can see what it looks like. With this intercut the filmmakers are creating the same effect with their editing methods that Derrida achieves in his writing – adopting an ironic performativity that both explicates but undermines the work's aims. *Derrida*'s task is to attempt a cinematic biography of Jacques Derrida, but at its very opening it signals to its audience the impossibility of such an exercise: including details of the mundane life of the man (choosing what clothes to wear) brings us no closer to actually knowing him; biography is not authoritative but inventive – it always fabricates its subject and only reveals him partially (here, just his top half); and rigorous close textual attention to the philosopher's writing remains most effectively performed *in* writing, not through images – the citations of Derrida's texts which regularly intrude into the film's soundtrack remain uninterrogated, neither rigorously, inventively nor powerfully deciphered.[3] Faced with these challenges, what Dick and Ziering Kofman appear to produce is a film about the difficulty of making a documentary film about Jacques Derrida – a meta-documentary about the impossibility of biography. In doing so, while they might not be philosophically engaging with the *content* of Derrida's thought, they do attempt to replicate its *method* cinematically.

Such formal mimicry is not unusual in response to Derrida's work in general, and in relation to work in the field of deconstruction and biography in particular. For instance, in his preface to *Derrida and Autobiography* (1995), Robert Smith explains that his stylistic and structural choices 'put into practice the tonal variety that takes what is theoretical in Derrida beyond theory' (viii). By taking the risk, as Derrida does himself, of combining 'both more and less academic registers', Smith hopes to ensure that his book is not 'deaf to its own statements' (1995: viii). In contrast, Benoît Peeters, Derrida's 'authoritative' biographer (at least for the moment) feels the need to end his introduction by noting his decision *not* to performatively emulate Derrida's style: 'I have sought, in the final analysis, to write not so much a Derridean biography as a biography of Derrida' (2012: 6). Peeters' biography of Derrida is as straight as biographies come, its methodology untouched by Derrida's own thought on the subject. The only explanation Peeters offers for this is his decision that 'mimicry, in this respect as in many others, does not seem the best way of serving him [Derrida] today' (2012: 6). The allure of the authoritative biography, of fixing the image of a man (so often a man), his life and work, remains too strong for Derrida's thought to (yet) deconstruct, even when he himself is the subject. Geoffrey Bennington was therefore prescient in 1996 when he decided to 'hazard a guess that one of the last genres of academic or quasi-academic writing to be affected by deconstruction is the genre of biography' (2008: 423).[4]

While Peeters' biography refuses the way in which Derrida's life as a philosopher (which means of course his work) ought to 'dictate a biography to come' (Bennington 2008: 405), the filmmakers of *Derrida* attempt to respond to that dictate by formal experimentation with the documentary mode. In 'Making Derrida', Ziering Kofman explains:

> My interest was primarily in Derrida's work, and, as such, I was not interested in producing something along the conventional narrative lines meted by the standard grammar of Western documentaries; a narrative grammar whose ideological implications Derrida's writing had, if nothing else, effectively taken to task for the past some four plus decades. (Ziering Kofman 2005: 23–4)

Ziering Kofman wanted to make a film which honoured Derrida's thought as well as testifying to its power and significance; the best way to do that, she believed, was to 'cinematically mime' (Ziering Kofman 2005: 27) the structures of Derrida's own arguments in the film's editing. So, just as Derrida's texts tend not to be linear but to weave together multiple levels of argument and insight, so too does the film's composition aim to function like a fugue, introducing and repeating a number of key themes, following no narrative storyline but instead building to a complex pattern.[5] Key to this method, in the examples Ziering Kofman gives, is the juxtaposition of shots in order to add new meaning to each, for instance the contrast of verité footage of Derrida joking about his own narcissism with a voice-over quoting Derrida on narcissism; Derrida telling a journalist that anyone who links his work with TV sitcoms would do better to 'turn off the TV and read' followed by Derrida himself watching TV; or Derrida's discussion of the eyes and the hands being followed by a shot of his portrait in a gallery. With respect to this latter, Ziering Kofman argues that 'a cut which at first might have read as an incidental or textbook graphic match cut (based on relationships of contingency or accident) now points as well, more directly, to issues of spectatorship and specularity' (2005: 28).

In addition to the editorial juxtapositions intended to instigate thought, the film also aspires to *be* Derridean in its repeated reflexivity. In 'Deconstructive Film', Joanna Callaghan interviews Derrida scholars about what would make or be a deconstructive film, and their answers repeatedly point to the necessary presence of reflexivity, that is, that a deconstructive film would necessarily interrogate its own mode and genre: 'It would break with expectations about genre' (Peggy Kamuf); 'It would exhibit its own artificiality, its own means, its own mechanisms' (Geoffrey Bennington); 'Thinking of the books, the literary works that Derrida was interested in, it would obviously be something that would take the formulae, the conventions of film, to some point where they questioned themselves or questioned the art of filmmaking' (Derek Attridge). *Derrida* certainly meets these requirements, incorporating as it does: repeated shots that include the directors, camera crew, sound men and so on in the frame; regular use of the technique of shooting into mirrors; and Derrida's own comments on the artificiality of the situation and the lack of realism captured by cinema verité.[6] But such techniques are common to a host of other films. Examples contributors give to Callaghan of deconstructive film directors include: Michael Moore, Chris Marker, Jonas Mekas, Federico Fellini, Jean-Luc Godard, Werner Herzog, Terrence Malick, Ron Howard, Mikhail Kalatozov, Jean Cocteau (all men). In fact, John Phillips reveals the problem when he observes that 'I actually think that you can begin to think what would a deconstructive film look like by answering, "like any film that we can see today"' (*Deconstructive Film*).

Thought-provoking editing, using multiple cameras, blending formats, employing reflexivity (verbal and visual) to foreground its own status as artifice – none of these techniques is new to filmmaking with *Derrida* and none is even particularly experimental. Even in cinema verité (as opposed to direct cinema), for instance, the director was always already a participant in the work.[7] The problem is that *Derrida* is not experimental enough – there is so much more that could have been done in order to push the form and produce a film that effectively performed Derrida's thought, including his thought on biography. Dick and Ziering Kofman admit as much when they acknowledge in interview that during the editing:

> At several points we had a much more abstract film. More like an experimental film, which we pulled back from because we wanted the film to be something that could reach a wide audience and not be just something that might, at best, show in museums on occasion. (Macy et al. 2005: 133)

While such experimentalism could have remained primarily within the documentary mode, it is fascinating to speculate how fiction might also have been used. One could, for instance, compare *Derrida* to *The Kidnapping of Michel Houellebecq* (2014), another 'biographical' film about another French intellectual superstar but one which, through its 'fictional' scenario, provides far greater intimacy with Houellebecq than *Derrida* ever achieves with its subject. Or what might the film have looked like if it had taken up the film scenario Richard Rand comes up with when asked how he would imagine making a film on Derrida, one which is so thought-provoking I cite it in full here:

> I would let the movie be about a woman, who would be the figure of Jacques Derrida, simply because Jacques Derrida is a man. She would be a passionate woman, and the film would cover much of the lifespan of this heroine. Let us allow that she has many lovers. They would all fall in love with her, and she would maintain a relationship with each, such that each would feel completely singled out. This would continue over the years: some relationships would simply end; some would weave in and out. To make this an interesting movie, there would have to be a principle of fidelity holding the thing together. (One of the lovers might be me, but I do not see myself as the one to whom my heroine would be the most faithful.)
>
> The ending would have to be ever so slightly tendentious. It would end up that one man counts more than any other man, and when it happens you would know that it happens. The allegorical take would be that my heroine is capable of infinite attention to a variety of partners yet one is more singular and to him she'd be more faithful. Let the title be the name of the heroine. That's how I would do it – and I think justice could be done, in a funny way, even in Hollywood. And perhaps Vanessa Redgrave could play Jacques Derrida. (Rand cited in Dick 2005: 43–4)

But Dick and Ziering Kofman restrict the experimental possibilities of *Derrida* in order to reach a wider market – their artistic expression is compromised by their distribution ambitions. So when they say that 'what was interesting and challenging about the film is that there was no model' (*DOD* 116), this is not in fact true. There is a whole history of experimental documentary filmmaking prior to *Derrida* that challenges the traditional grammar of the form and adapts that form to suit its subject matter. In particular, many of the techniques used in Derrida can be found in feminist experimental documentary filmmaking, as well as, often, effective integration of fiction into the documentary mode.

One might think, for instance, about *Grey Gardens* (1975), directed by Ellen Hovde, Albert Maysles, David Maysles and Muffie Meyer, in which, just like Derrida, the two female subjects would not ignore the camera as they were supposed to do, thus forcing the filmmakers to adapt their methods and their form in response to their subjects. As Jay Ruby observes, 'the filmmakers were allowing the circumstances of the shooting to dictate the form of the film, which consequently revealed the process and producer' (2005: 43). In the same way, Derrida's constant observations on the presence and effect of the camera dictated that Dick and Ziering Kofman weave elements of reflexivity into the film, revealing producer, process and product; this was not their original intention, as Ziering Kofman notes:

> To me, it seemed like that self-reflexive angle had already been fairly well played out and mined in film since the 60s and there was no need to revisit that issue again at this time. [. . .] However, once we started working with the material it became increasingly apparent that the self-referential angle would have to be addressed in some way since Derrida could not help but call attention to and reference the filmmaking process at any and all given opportunities. (Ziering Kofman 2005: 32)

Or one might consider Michelle Citron's *Daughter Rite* and its technique of repeating clips of home movie footage on a loop. This technique mimes cinematically the continued haunting of the women by their childhood, the repetition compulsions passed down from mother to daughter, and the way in which trauma is replayed visually. Here is a precedent for one sequence in particular in the early experimental editing that did not make the final cut for *Derrida* but which is included in the 'Deleted Scenes' section of the ICA Projects 2005 *Derrida* DVD. The sequence plays with footage of Derrida's wife Marguerite putting on her coat, shutting the hall cupboard door, picking up her bag, passing the camera to kiss Derrida goodbye, passing the camera again, going down the hall and leaving the house. It is mundane footage that is included without alteration and with little affect in the final film. But the 'Deleted Scenes' sequence is deeply moving – there is no new footage here, but the material is manipulated in post-production editing, with elements being repeated and then slowed down, and Derrida's thoughts on mourning overlaid:

> The work of mourning doesn't wait for the death to occur, there is a work of mourning at work as soon as there is some experience, as soon as we refer to something, to the object, as soon as we speak, of course because we idealise

and we incorporate as we interrogate, so the work of mourning is not some specific experience that we could experience, at some point, after the death of someone, it is always already at work in the experience, which means that there is no origin.

The combination of words and manipulated images performs Derrida's argument here – that mourning does not take place after death but is always already with us in our present relationships, never more so perhaps, as Schopenhauer (2004) noted, than when we say goodbye to a loved one every day: 'Every parting gives a foretaste of death.' But the film does more than just perform this idea; by its manipulation of the image it creates the *affect* of the experience Derrida is describing. That is, the viewer feels real grief when in slow motion Marguerite glances back, smiles and closes the door (Figure 4.1). The more experimental editing here produces a strong affective response, one which is not created by the final cut of the film. The same argument holds for the first sequence in the deleted scenes, in which segments of Derrida speaking over a black screen alternate with glimpses of him in which he then exits out of shot, or the camera pans away, or he is caught leaving a

Figure 4.1. Derrida's wife Marguerite leaving their home in Paris.
Source: 'Deleted Scenes', *Derrida*, dir. Kirby Dick and Amy Ziering Kofman.

room, or the camera crew are literally chasing him. This sequence, entitled 'Chasing Derrida: The Autobiography of the Other', effectively evokes the film's self-awareness of the impossibility of catching Derrida the man on and with film, and the disjunction between that attempt and the very real ability of film to reproduce the thought of the man simply by broadcasting his speech without an associated image. Again, this highly experimental sequence achieves these effects more economically and successfully than the final cut.

Another example of how experimental the film could have been can be found in the deleted scene which cheekily mimics the split-page structure of Derrida's collaboration with Bennington in *Jacques Derrida*. In that work, Bennington's systematisation of Derrida's philosophical thought on the top half of the page is constantly interrupted, ruptured and intruded upon by Derrida's deeply personal and autobiographical text, 'Circumfession', which occupies the bottom of the page. Film of course is more able to effectively employ a split screen than the page, since we are able to view both elements of the screen simultaneously in a way in which it is not possible to read both the top and bottom texts simultaneously in *Jacques Derrida*. Here, then, Dick and Ziering Kofman are able to employ a cinematic technique that mimics Derrida's own experiments but is in fact better suited to the task. In this sequence Bennington, sitting next to Derrida at the Biography Conference, talks about deconstruction's challenge to biography in the top half of the split screen, while in the bottom half a handheld camera makes its way around Derrida's house until it finds him at his desk (Figure 4.2). The effect is humorous but also entirely effective in performing through a uniquely effective visual technique the incompatible aims of representing a philosopher's work and his life. This sequence reifies Ziering Kofman's ambition for the film 'to perform or work through both thematically and structurally some of the topics Derrida's work interrogates' while at the same time negotiating 'the problem of introducing Derrida as a biographical subject to audiences' (2005: 28). But again it seems this sequence was too experimental to make the final cut.

In his *Sight and Sound* review of the film, Michael Witt (2003) notes that *Derrida* is 'reminiscent at times of the forms and strategies of the self-reflexive political cinema of the 1970s', but locating it specifically in relation to feminist experimental documentary filmmaking of that period helps to shed further light on why Dick and Ziering Kofman may have retreated from the more experimental form. Giving the film this historical context situates *Derrida* – with its final cut versus its experimental deleted scenes – fascinatingly within a key debate in the history of feminist documentary film theory and practice: that of the viability or validity of realism versus experimentalism in challenging patriarchal forms and structures of control in both society and in cinema. The so-called realist debates raged primarily in the

Figure 4.2 Split screen: Derrida and Geoffrey Bennington above; Derrida's apartment below. Source: 'Deleted Scenes', *Derrida*, dir. Kirby Dick and Amy Ziering Kofman.

late 1970s and early 1980s but continued well into the 1990s and beyond, with feminist thinkers contributing to both sides. While Claire Johnston and Eileen McGarry argued against cinema verité as adequate to the creation of a feminist counter cinema, others, such as Jane Gaines, Julia Lesage and, more recently, Alexandra Juhasz, have come to the defence of realism as a necessary aesthetic for repressed groups, critiquing antirealism and recognising, as Dick and Ziering Kofman could also be said to, 'the necessity of working with audiences to create a public for more difficult or complicated works' (Walker and Waldman 1999: 12).[8]

While *Derrida* does not reveal Dick and Ziering Kofman to be feminist filmmakers, the majority of their other films do. In particular, their two most successful collaborations after *Derrida* are overtly feminist activist documentaries intended to effect political and social change: *The Invisible War* (2012) and *The Hunting Ground* (2015) both expose epidemics of sexual assault and rape, the first in the Military, the second in US Higher Education Institutions. These two films fall firmly into the feminist realist tradition; they are committed documentaries that, as Julianne Burton defines this genre, 'us[e] the film medium to expose and combat the culture of invisibility and inaudibility'

(1990: 78).⁹ As such, their realist aesthetic befits their political aims in that it ensures the films reach their intended audience and locates their power in their *use* rather than their *form*. Such indeed is Juhasz's argument in defence of realism: 'the feminist realist debate missed the most critical point of all: the impact and power of these films and videos comes more from their *use* than from their *form*. These films are first, but not merely, forms of political action' (1994: 188). The form of these films, then, is not to be judged (merely) aesthetically but in terms of how fit for purpose that form is for the use that film is intended to be put to, and the audience it is intended to reach in order to achieve its aims. As Lesage argues:

> And if the feminist film-makers deliberately used a traditional 'realist' documentary structure, it is because they saw making these films as an urgent public act and wished to enter the 16mm circuit of education films especially through libraries, schools, churches, unions, and YMCAs to bring feminist analysis to many women it might otherwise never reach. (1986: 15)

Similarly, Dick comments in an interview about *The Hunting Ground* that 'the film was actually made for two audiences: moviegoers who turn out for documentaries and also policymakers. The documentary had to speak in such a way that *both* could receive the message' (Dick in West and West 2012: 13). This meant, as Dick continues, carefully modulating the film's tone, especially avoiding polemic and outright hostility to the Military or to policymakers, but it also no doubt determined the choice of the realist mode given its political efficacy. That such a choice paid off is demonstrated by the fact that the film could claim to have changed policy. As Dick notes, 'I think we were successful because we know that the documentary has made a huge impact in Washington. It's been seen at the highest levels of the Pentagon – Secretary Panetta has seen it – and we know that the film has played a major role in the most significant change in the last five years' (Dick in West and West 2012: 13). Without claiming a direct causal relationship, the dramatic end titles of the film suggest one: 'On April 14, 2012, Secretary of Defense Leon Panetta watched this film' fades out to be followed by 'Two days later,' to which is then added, 'he took the decision to prosecute away from unit commanders'. This was a radical military policy change when it comes to who has responsibility for the decision to prosecute sexual assault. The film therefore exhibits what Juhasz defines as 'the political efficacy of realism', that is, 'the power to convince, document, move to anger and action, and the ability to take control of identity and identification within systems of representation so as to move towards personal and collective action' (1994: 176–7). As Lesage argues regarding many early feminist documentaries, but entirely appropriately also for Dick and Ziering Kofman's works, both 'the stance of the people filmed [and] the stance of the film as a whole reflects a commitment to changing the public sphere as well; and for this reason, these film-makers have used an accessible documentary form' (1986: 22).

Derrida, then, appears anomalous in Dick and Ziering Kofman's oeuvre. It is neither feminist, nor political, nor realist, although it falls short of being effectively experimental. In their commentary on the film, both Dick and Ziering Kofman stress repeatedly how important it was for them that the film's style befit its content, that is, that the film *be* Derridean.[10] But, as we have seen, they compromise the film's ability to achieve that aim by shying away from real experimentation in order to reach a wider audience. *Derrida* therefore ought to be a film in which form is determined by content, but it ends up being a film in which form is determined by intended use. In that sense, then, it is in fact consistent with Dick and Ziering Kofman's clear commitment to this determination of practice in their other work.

But there is a further reason why *Derrida* appears to sit oddly in their oeuvre: French theory, such as deconstruction, played a key role in devaluing and in many cases rejecting early realist activist feminist documentary, the tradition to which Dick and Ziering Kofman's other work in fact belongs.[11] However, continued theoretical defences of realist feminist documentary, as well as continued production of such works, reveals that Derrida's theories pose less of a problem for cinematic realism, for documentary and for biography than might have first appeared.[12] In fact, Derrida and *Derrida* are only saying what feminist filmmakers have always already known, and what anyone who appears in front or behind a camera understands: that the camera mediates between audience and subject; that filming is never an innocent act; that the camera affects self-presentation and interaction; that the image never bears an absolutely indexical relationship to reality; that editing multiplies all these truths infinitely. But feminist filmmaking does not, as a result, feel the need to abandon the realist mode – biography does not need to be '*fractal*', as Bennington puts it, in order to 'escape the totalising and teleological commitments which inhabit the genre from the start' (2008: 423). This is not least because no one believed in that totalising teleology in the first place – for biographers have *always* known that they are only ever presenting one version of a person's life, or why else would they always feel the need to claim that theirs was the authoritative version? To do so implicitly acknowledges that other versions are possible. But more than this, feminism has always necessarily understood *its* realism *against* the traditional notions of biography and identity as Derrida portrays them, since such traditional notions have always already excluded women and our representation. Instead, feminist realism *is* 'specifically about *constructing* our own identities' (Juhasz 1994: 186) in a society that has usually done this for us. Feminist realism always already embraces the realist paradox, acknowledging that identity and reality are 'always constructed, [. . .] neither fixed nor essential' but that they need 'to be present nevertheless' (Juhasz 1994: 189).[13] In this sense, all feminist film, all feminist biography, might well already be considered deconstructive; or, to put it differently, on this point at least, deconstruction is only telling us what we already know, illuminating a truth with which we have always already been contending.

II *Quer* Autobiography (directed sideways)

i Obstructive Piety

In 'Deconstructive Film', Stephen Barker declares that *Derrida* is 'not a film on Derrida, it's a film on deconstruction', but it might also be thought of as an autobiographical film. Understood as the autobiography of Amy Ziering Kofman, *Derrida* is a cinematic exploration of a female student's feelings about her illustrious male professor and his work.[14] Although Derrida's constant reflexivity regarding the act of filming avowedly forced Dick and Ziering Kofman into incorporating such reflexivity into the film – including positioning Ziering Kofman as the figure of the filmmaker – the *effect* of that reflexivity, as Jay Ruby argues of all cinematic reflexivity, is 'to reveal that films, whether they are labeled fiction, documentary, or art – are created, structured, articulations of the filmmaker and not authentic, truthful, objective records' (2005: 454–5). Reflexivity is the most obvious method of highlighting that truth, and, as the driver of the film's reflexivity, Derrida of course does not fail to draw attention to it within the film and in discussion of it: at one point he observes to Ziering Kofman that 'it will be your autobiography, and your signature, in a certain way' (Kofman 2005: 105); in one of the deleted scenes he insists that 'I am not the main subject or the main author of your film'; and in a Q&A after the film's theatrical opening at Film Forum in New York, Derrida observes:

> I had to accept the experience of knowing that this film would become an archive, and that it would, in fact, be signed by the filmmakers. That they would have a hundred hours of – how do you say this? – footage, from which they would keep only one and a half hours, and that ultimately this selection would of course be their selection; the film would be their work and I had no real initiative in it, no initiative. So I knew from the beginning that I would be exposed to their own autobiographical signature; that this would be their autobiography. (*DOD* 113)

Talking with journalist Rhonda Lieberman for her piece on *Derrida* in *Artforum*, Derrida reiterates this point: 'I consider this film to be a work signed by Amy Kofman. OK? So that's why I said that to some extent it's also a portrait of her' (2002: 36). In *Derrida*, the film's self-reflexivity reveals this to be a film about Ziering Kofman's feelings about Derrida, but so too do the soundtrack and the score.

The film's soundtrack is punctured repeatedly by Ziering Kofman's voice-overs in which she earnestly reads passages from Derrida's writings. These voice-overs have an interesting history in the making of the film: they were Dick's idea, not Ziering Kofman's, and after two years of Ziering Kofman avoiding choosing the quotations, Dick eventually chose them for her. In a revealing passage in 'Making Derrida', Ziering Kofman firstly explains that this avoidance was because of 'an informed sense that it was impossible to extract pieces of Derrida's writing from their context without doing the work a tremendous disservice and injustice' (2005: 30). She could not select the quotations, according to this logic, because of the complexity and interwoven nature of Derrida's arguments. However, Dick *was* able to excerpt some quotations successfully. Therefore, by the end of the paragraph another explanation has to be offered for why he could do so and she could not: the reason proffered is that as a non-academic, Dick was able to read the texts differently to her, and was freed 'from some of the more reverential institutional preconceptions that haunted and to some degree paralyzed me [Ziering Kofman] when I approached Derrida's written works' (2005: 30). Ziering Kofman reveals here, consciously or not, the nature of her feelings about Derrida – she reveres him. But we are not intimate with that which we revere – it is necessarily at a distance from us, worshipped, held aloft, (often) divine. Far from inhabiting and appropriating Derrida's words in the voice-over – as a professional actor would have been able to do – Ziering Kofman always sounds like she is reading someone else's words, carefully and slowly pronouncing them as though they are scripture.[15] Ziering Kofman is not echoing Derrida, and in doing so 'speaking in her own name, by repeating the words of others' (Derrida in *Derrida*, cited in Lieberman 2002: 36); rather, she is reciting Derrida's words without ever inhabiting them. The fact that she is not a professional actor, the reverence in which she holds the texts and their author, and the fact that she did not even select the quotations (Dick did), mean that she never makes these words her own. Both Ziering Kofman and, as a result, the film's audience are, as Lieberman observes, 'alienated by the film's piety' (2002: 36). In the film, Derrida attempts to read Echo as an empowered figure, despite being condemned to repeat the words of others, but Ziering Kofman's performance as Echo to Derrida's Narcissus does not reify such a reading. Instead, as Lieberman notes, 'the film repeats the stereotype of the male Narcissus Echoed by his reverent female amanuensis (literally mouthing his *écriture*)' (2002: 36).

Ryuichi Sakamato's score also contributes to making the film an autobiographical representation of Ziering Kofman's feelings about Derrida. Sakamato was Ziering Kofman's choice from a range of composers the Hollywood editor and filmmaker Curtiss Clayton had suggested to her and Dick: after listening to his work, she tells Dick that Sakamato 'was the right match' (*DOD* 112). Sakamato's score reifies Ziering Kofman's reverence and her sense of Derrida as beyond her knowledge or grasp – it is minimalist, haunting, even chilling, acoustically painting Derrida as ethereal, distant, as that which cannot be known. It could not be more different to the soundtrack for *D'Ailleurs, Derrida* (1999), Safaa Fathy's film on Derrida, which provides a productive point of comparison. Whereas *Derrida* is the autobiography of a student's reverence for her professor, *D'Ailleurs, Derrida* is co-signed by artistic and intellectual collaborators and friends – Fathy and Derrida – as in fact is the book that accompanies it: *Tourner les mots: Au bord d'un film* (2000). (Derrida notably makes no contribution to the book accompanying *Derrida*, other than in the transcribed Q&A.) Whereas the score for *Derrida* distances the viewer from the film and from the man, performing Ziering Kofman's own sense of removal from Derrida, the Arabo-Andalusian music that plays across *D'Ailleurs, Derrida* draws the viewer into the film with warmth and intimacy.[16] Unlike Sakamato's score, the music in *D'Ailleurs, Derrida* is both intra- and extra-diegetic; in this sense, we the audience *share* it with Derrida, and share in his enjoyment of it, in particular in the scenes in which he grooves to the music playing on the car stereo while driving. Derrida is at ease in *D'Ailleurs, Derrida* in a way we rarely glimpse in the final cut of *Derrida*: Fathy and the camera appear not to interrogate him but to accompany him (hence the many scenes in which he is filmed walking and exploring; by comparison, in *Derrida* when Derrida is walking the camera is usually chasing him); and although Derrida does point up the artificiality of the filming endeavour in *D'Ailleurs, Derrida*, Fathy does not choose to allow such comments to dominate the final cut of the film. Peggy Kamuf (2010: 110–12) analyses one such self-referential moment in *D'Ailleurs, Derrida*, recorded on the first day of filming, in which, similarly to his comments in *Derrida*, Derrida observes that the film will be authored by Fathy: 'a text that *you* are going to write and sign' (translation of the film's French by Kamuf 2010: 111). Interestingly, while the making of the film was, according to Derrida and Fathy, 'an ongoing and at times explosive struggle between the two of them' (Kamuf 2010: 115), importantly, Fathy asserts herself in that struggle – 'the filmmaker had repeatedly to tell her subject that he did not see, he could not see, was unable to see' (Kamuf 2010: 115) – rather than being dominated and subdued by Derrida. This leads to an intimate cinematic portrait of Derrida and his work, reflective of Fathy's confidence in her relationship to (her) film and to (her) subject; as she says, 'the time-space is [. . .] free, open, giving, and its energy is sustained by the vital double bind between the self and the other' (Fathy 2008). In comparison, *Derrida*'s assertion of the impossibility of such a portrait reveals itself as a reflection of Ziering Kofman's own relationship to Derrida, rather than evidence of the structural impossibility of such an enterprise.[17]

While *Derrida* is punctuated by repeated moments of reflexivity which point up the artificiality of Derrida's encounter with the camera, but in doing so prevent the intimacy that the camera might facilitate between viewer and subject, *D'Ailleurs, Derrida* is punctuated by repeated shots of Derrida glancing sideways at the camera (Figures 4.3, 4.4 and 4.5). With such shots, Derrida acknowledges the camera's presence but he does so visually, not verbally. The effect is not to draw attention to the camera as a potential barrier between those behind it and viewing the film, and its subject. Rather, these glances break the fourth wall, looking *through* the camera at us, mischievously welcoming us to take part *along with him* in this cinematic game. These moments are queer, not in a sexual or gendered sense, but in the visual sense: while the etymology of the English 'queer' is uncertain, the *Oxford English Dictionary* suggests that it is derived from or perhaps cognate with the German *quer* which, when used to describe a glance means 'directed sideways'. It is through a sideways look, a *quer* glance, that Derrida draws us into intimacy with him and the filming process; any attempt to view Derrida head-on meets with resistance. Derrida's desire to reveal himself only *quer*-ly is confirmed by his preference for photographs of him, when he eventually allowed them, to be taken in profile. Front-on, Derrida is unwilling to reveal himself – 'No', as he says to Ziering Kofman when she asks directly, 'Could you characterise any traumatic breaks in your own life?' (Kofman 2005: 109). Derrida's refusal to respond to such blunt demands for intimate exposure – we find the same resistance when Ziering Kofman asks him and Marguerite about their relationship – are not, however, unique to Derrida alone. Rather, I want to suggest that in documentary cinema, in particular that which is biographical or autobiographical in nature, the *quer* glance (directed sideways) is the most effective technique for establishing intimacy, avoiding narcissism and simultaneously both protecting and revealing the self. This mode is characteristic of feminist autobiographical cinema, as well as being, as I explore at the end of this chapter, the technique that Derrida himself uses in his autobiographical text 'Circumfession', which could in fact be read, as unlikely as this might at first seem, as part of that tradition. Before I turn to 'Circumfession', however, I want to develop this theory of *quer* auto/biography through a close analysis of its specific techniques and their effects in two feminist autobiographical films: Michelle Citron's

Auto/biography

Figure 4.3 Derrida's sideways glances (1).
Source: *D'Ailleurs, Derrida*, dir. Safaa Fathy.

Figure 4.4 Derrida's sideways glances (2).
Source: *D'Ailleurs, Derrida*, dir. Safaa Fathy.

Figure 4.5 Derrida's sideways glances (3).
Source: *D'Ailleurs, Derrida*, dir. Safaa Fathy.

Daughter Rite, already mentioned above, and its contemporary heir, Sarah Polley's *Stories We Tell*.

ii 'We all being everyone but you'

Derrida did not want to make *Derrida*. In fact, he wrote a postcard to Ziering Kofman saying no to her request to make him the subject of a film, but his handwriting was so bad that she could not decipher it. She decided it must be a 'yes' – who would say 'no' on a postcard? – and proceeded to secure funding.[18] Similarly, Sarah Polley did not want to make *Stories We Tell*, but her hand was forced by a phone call she received from a journalist while she was dressed as a Neanderthal woman filming on the set of *Mr Nobody*. The journalist had discovered that her biological father was in fact Canadian film producer Harry Gulkin, with whom her mother had had an affair, and he wanted to run the story. Polley had made the discovery herself some months earlier, but had not yet told her Dad, Michael Polley. Aware that the story was going to come out, one way or another, Polley took control. She secured a promise from the journalist to hold the story and set about making a film which would be her way of telling it to the world – the story of her journey to find out about her mother, who died when she was eleven, and of her discovery in the process that Gulkin was her biological father.

In 'Fleeing from Documentary', Michelle Citron observes, 'the question arises, what compels a filmmaker or videomaker to create an autobiographical work' (1999: 280). For Polley, the initial compulsion came from an external source; what becomes of interest is how she made a film she did not want to make. Or, to put it differently, what cinematic techniques does she use in an autobiographical work that both reveal but also protect a self that is deeply ambivalent about self-exposure? Such ambivalence leads to complex, as well of course as reflexive, filmmaking. As Polley says in interview:

> I think it really helps to be totally mortified that you're making this film in the first place. You're constantly looking at it, wondering what you'd say if you were reviewing it. 'It's the most narcissistic, self-indulgent piece of crap.' Strangely, I think it was a healthy way to check in on how stupid I thought the film was. And still, I have questions about why I made it, and what it means that it's out there. (Polley in Dowd 2013)[19]

In a genre which, as Smith notes, is 'all about such immeasurable self-involvement' (1995: 52), how does one avoid narcissism? Polley does so by making a *quer* autobiography, employing a number of techniques which reveal herself only through glances directed sideways.

Stories We Tell is a generic hybrid – it is far from a 'straight' autobiography. In fact, reviewers have defined the film as many, many things: a documentary, a genre-bending documentary, a hybrid documentary, a metadocumentary, a self-portrait, an autobiography, a cine-memoir, a family memoir, an extended family portrait, a homage/vigil/tribute to a dead mother, a biography, a multi-narrator cinematic personal essay, a choral work.[20] The genre into which *Stories We Tell* perhaps most comfortably fits is one identified by Ruby (1977) as emerging in the 1970s as a result of the revolution in film technology which took place from the mid-1960s onwards. With the development of lightweight cameras and portable sync sound equipment, documentarians were able to have more intimate access to, in fact participation in, people's lives. One of the consequences of this, Ruby argues, is the violation in the 1970s of the previous distinction between documentaries – films about people *other* to yourself – and personal art films – previously, the genre you worked in if you wanted to make films about you, your family, or your immediate environment. A new nonfiction genre emerged – *personal* documentaries. Some examples Ruby gives of such films are Jerome Hill's *Film Portrait* (1972) and Jeff Kreines' *The Plaint of Steve Kreines as Recorded by His Younger Brother Jeff*, but he also mentions two films by female filmmakers which explore female liberation, sexuality, the work-life balance and the filmmaker's relationship with her mother: Miriam Weinstein's *Living with Peter* (1973) and Amalie Rothschild's *Nana, Mom, and Me* (1974). Such films often, like *Stories We Tell*, explore the daughter's relationship with her mother, and in general are characterised by formal experimentation and the interweaving of different modes – direct interview, home-movies, old photographs. Even more experimental is the interweaving of fact and fiction, of documentary and narrative film, creating fictional (at least in part) personal documentaries. Of this type, Michelle Citron's *Daughter Rite* is perhaps the most well-known example; *Stories We Tell* could be considered its heir.[21]

Daughter Rite is a fictional personal documentary which interweaves a first-person narration playing out over loops of old home-movie footage with talking-head interviews with two sisters – Maggie and Stephanie – and cinema verité footage of the sisters, for instance, making a salad, sorting through records, rifling through their mother's things. First-time viewers of *Daughter Rite*, then and now, easily believe that the first-person narrator is Citron, talking about her own mother, and that Maggie and Stephanie are real sisters being interviewed. In fact, the first-person narration is voiced by an actress, and Maggie and Stephanie are also actresses performing in both scripted and improvised scenes. The only 'real' material in the film is the home-movie footage of Citron and her sister which was shot by her father, but the way in which the footage is manipulated in the editing, with abrupt cutting and repetitive looping, denaturalises this 'real' element of the film. Overall, the 'real' elements of the film appear the most mediated, and the most mediated appear in fact as the most 'real'. The voice-over script and the interviews with the sisters do contain accurate autobiographical details from Citron's life, but they are also created from interviews Citron carried out with thirty-five daughters. The film is therefore both autobiographical and biographical, tells singular and collective stories, interweaves fact and fiction, and functions in both documentary and narrative modes.[22] All of these techniques enable Citron to both reveal and conceal herself: 'I could make an autobiographical film, while at the same time denying its autobiographical nature' (1999: 277) – the audience glimpses her, but only sideways.

Given Polley's similar need to also both reveal and conceal herself, it is no surprise that many of the same techniques, and more, are to be found in *Stories We Tell*: the film combines old Super 8 home-movie footage, some real, some re-enacted with actors; voice-over – from Michael Polley, as well as emails read aloud by their authors, Gulkin and Polley; talking-head interviews; and, a technique not explicitly present in *Daughter Rite*, reflexivity, in the form of footage of the filming of the interviews and of the re-created Super 8 scenes, including Polley directing the actors.[23] Whereas Polley builds the reveal that some of the Super 8 footage is constructed, not real, into the diegesis of her film, the constructed nature of Citron's film is only revealed extra-diegetically in the final credits, which identify the scenes with Maggie and Stephanie as 'character improvisations' (providing the names of the actresses who played each character, 'Penelope Victor as Maggie, Anne Wilford as Stephanie') and which identify the narrator as Jerri Hancock. The only clue that the scenes which appear to be cinema verité are in fact scripted or improvised occurs in the brilliantly comic extended salad-making scene in a small detail of the mise-en-scène: a pot of yoghurt on the table has a label which reads, ironically, 'NO ARTIFICIAL ANYTHING'. *Stories We Tell* also consists of more standard documentary techniques absent from Citron's film, for instance clips from a black-and-white audition tape of Diane, footage of photographs and newspaper clippings, and extracts from other films. All of these elements combine to create, as Polley intended, a film in which one story is told from many different perspectives but, more than this, they combine to create a film which functions according to the *quer* autobiographical logic of the sideways glance.

Polley does not speak directly in the film; in *Stories We Tell*, the voice-overs, like Citron's, both reveal and conceal the filmmaker. In *Daughter Rite*, this is achieved by giving the 'I' to an actor and weaving into that 'I''s narration stories that both are, and are not, her own; in *Stories We Tell* it is achieved by giving the primary voice-over to her father, in which Polley then features only in the third person and, very interestingly, sometimes in the second person. When the 'I' of the filmmaker does speak in voice-over in *Stories We Tell*, Polley is not doing so directly, but rather creates a temporal and modal buffer by reading emails she wrote in the past. Polley's voice is therefore not immediately present, avoiding the narcissism that such a presence risks, but she is continually evoked in the 'she's and the 'you's of Michael's voice-over, the comments of the interviewees, and in the cited emails. The second- and third-person pronouns of the soundtrack evoke Polley acoustically, they summon her presence and present her story, without her speaking. But Polley is strongly *visually* present in the film, and a repeated pattern of a second- or third-person address to Polley followed by a cut to a sideways shot of her metonymically represents the mediated access we have to her. I use the term 'third-person address' quite intentionally here, precisely because of the strangeness of the term, given that the third person is usually used in the absence of the pronoun's subject. The fact that the storytellers are talking about 'her/she' – Polley – in her presence reinforces the film's *quer* autobiographical effect.

This pattern first begins when the question of her paternity becomes prominent half an hour into the film; her brother Mark tells her that he started to believe the family joke about Michael not being her biological father and that 'we' all had a discussion about whether or not to talk to Polley about it seriously: 'We all being everyone but you.' *We* all being everyone but *you*. *We* are present visually and acoustically in the film – 'we' being her four older siblings and Michael, all of whom are interviewed. *You* is Polley herself, separate from that 'we', both cut off from but also revealed by the story 'we' are telling and that a different 'we' are hearing. Polley recurs twice more in Mark's account here, as a 'you' and a 'her': 'And I think Johnny said I had a big mouth and that I was probably going to tell you or something, and I was saying, "I think we *should* tell her".' The image track then cuts to a medium close-up profile shot of Polley at the mixing console in the recording studio, on 'her' (Figure 4.6). We (the audience) only have acoustic access to her (Polley) through her storytellers ('we') who are retelling to her ('you' and us) what she has already told them, and visual access through sideways glances.

This pattern occurs again when Michael narrates Polley's story but makes it clear that 'what happens next is what I can remember of Sarah's relating the event'. Polley experiences events which she relates to Michael, who writes down what he remembers of her narration for his family and then reads it for us while he is being filmed, and Polley is filmed, sideways on, listening to him. Such mediated access to Polley, to the 'I' of the filmmaker, is at its most intense as the story builds to the climactic revelation of her parentage. Her siblings, like Michael, tell 'you' Polley, behind the camera, what she told them

Figure 4.6 Sarah Polley at the mixing console.
Source: *Stories We Tell*, dir. Sarah Polley.

of the events they are now telling her but of which they themselves had no direct experience: 'You asked him the question', says Mark; John even checks that he is remembering it right: 'I think those were the exact words you said to me on the phone, weren't they?' The siblings and Gulkin both oscillate between referring to Polley as 'you' and as 'she', their grammar interrupted and shifted by the presence of the filmmaker behind the camera.

Since Michael is not being interviewed but rather recording his written words, he is able to maintain the third person in relation to Polley despite her presence. But a significant shift in his own pronouns occurs when he narrates the day Polley receives the results of the DNA paternity test. Until this point Michael's narration has taken place in the third person for all characters, himself included, but at this moment he shifts into the first-person 'I':

> On Monday, January 22 2007, Sarah's life changed forever. She opened the registered letter and read the results. It recorded that Harry Gulkin was Sarah Polley's biological father, and that the test results were 99% certain. [. . .] I won't even try to guess what her thoughts were as she digested that stunning discovery.

It is as if the enormity of the discovery, and its consequences for his own sense of himself and his relationship to the woman he thought was his daughter, are so great that they rupture the distance he has thus far maintained between himself and the story he is telling – he collapses into the intimacy of the first person from here on in. But Polley does not. Instead, we get again only the

Figure 4.7 Six-second pause on Sarah Polley.
Source: *Stories We Tell*, dir. Sarah Polley.

sideways glance – another profile shot of her which begins after Michael's 'were' and continues for six seconds as her new stepmother's voice-over begins (Figure 4.7). This pattern – Michael narrating a highly emotional moment followed by the camera's sideways glance at Polley – recurs three times after this. Polley is listening to Michael because she is directing him – lest we forget this, we occasionally see her ask him to retake a line. But these sideways glances are not (or not just) part of the film's self-reflection on the filmmaking process – they are also reaction shots. Polley is at once distanced, director of the film, *and* intimately affected by the story being told, the subject, in fact, of its diegesis. Polley therefore tells her *quer* autobiography – and both reveals and conceals herself in it – through others telling her story to her ('you') and through a recurrent visual technique of sideways glances at her which remind us that she is simultaneously both the film's director and its diegetic subject.

While attention to shots is not unusual in film criticism, such detailed attention to pronouns in close engagement with a film might seem to be a very literary critical concern, but it is pertinent to *Stories We Tell* for two reasons. First, this is a very *literary* film. It is built out of images but driven by verbal and written stories: Michael and Harry's written versions of events; written emails; and oral recollections. Second, when a perceptive interviewer raised the issue of pronouns with Polley, her response was revealing:

> JT: The text your father reads aloud, the one woven throughout the film, begins in the third person and ends in the first, which somehow reflects the

film's structure. It also reminded me of Bob Dylan's 'Tangled up in Blue,' another work dealing with painful memories and marital malaise. In the earlier, demo version of the song, Dylan shifts between –

SP: – between first and third person. He switches perspectives in the verse about loading cargo onto a truck. Another is the one about chopping down trees. It's my favourite song. I know both versions extremely well. I've always been obsessed with that earlier version that no one seems to know. Cameron Crowe gave it to me. I'd never heard it before then. No one's ever brought that up with me before. It's an enormous source of inspiration. (Teodoro 2013: 55)

Polley is a filmmaker to whom words as well as images matter, so critical preconceptions about the type of close attention one might pay to film – for instance, the need to prioritise its medium specific properties over its literary elements – need to be put aside in order to write productively on her work.[24] Paying attention to the pronouns in *Stories We Tell*, as well as to the shots they work in collaboration with, reveals the way in which the 'I' of the filmmaker, Polley, is repeatedly evoked by the film's 'you's and 'she's but also shielded and protected by them. The sideways glances at Polley which occur regularly throughout the film reify in the cinematography the mediated logic of this *quer* autobiography, situating Polley in her own way, just as Derrida wishes to situate himself in *Derrida*, always 'on the edge of an impossible confidence' (Kofman 2005: 79).

As Michael settles down at the beginning of the film for his mammoth recording session, he observes with characteristic wry humour:

MICHAEL: I hope you'll explain to me some time what all this is that you're trying to do, two cameras and me recording it, visually, and . . .
POLLEY: What about it?
MICHAEL: I mean it's not the normal way of doing it, is it?

Polley's *Stories We Tell* is not the 'normal' way of doing documentary, but it is a hugely effective and affective way of doing *quer* cinematic autobiography.

iii The Mediated 'I'

In 'Eye for I: Making and Unmaking Autobiography in Film' (1980), Elizabeth Bruss posits that film as a medium is incompatible with autobiography as we have traditionally understood it:

Film upsets each of the parameters – 'truth-value,' 'act-value,' and 'identity-value' – that we commonly associate with the autobiographical act to such an extent that even deliberate attempts to re-create the genre in cinematic terms are subtly subverted. (1980: 301)

While the logic of her argument and many of her assumptions in this essay are problematic, sometimes even confused and confusing, what Bruss importantly concludes is not that cinematic autobiography is therefore impossible, but that cinema always already deconstructs what we understand autobiography to be. In particular, cinema structurally challenges the unity of the 'I' upon which traditional conceptions of autobiography have depended. Film cannot easily construct a first-person position; it is a collaborative enterprise; and it reifies the question of the true or staged nature of the events being recalled or represented. As a result, film compromises the idea that there is a pre-existing independent singular subject to which autobiographical discourse then simply gives voice and whose experiences it represents. Film confronts us with the reality of the constructed nature of identity, not just on screen, but on the page as well. Bruss concludes:

> one potential effect of film is to 'deconstruct' the autobiographical preoccupation with capturing the self on paper, demonstrating the delusion of a subjectivity trying to be 'through and through present to itself' in the very writing that is the mark of its own absence. The ideal of self-possession – the reifying desire for mastery over an essential self – might then give way to both an identity that could not be possessed and a more playful and disenchanted autobiographical quest. (1980: 317)

The *queer* cinematic autobiographies I have discussed above, including *Daughter Rite* and *Stories We Tell*, are examples of how this 'disenchanted autobiographical quest' might manifest itself, in self-awareness, in reflexivity, in the evocation of the singular through the multiple (and vice versa), in the interweaving of fact and fiction, in pronominal play in both image and soundtrack.

Film, as a medium, deconstructs autobiography. It is no surprise, then, that Bruss' conclusion above is preceded by a citation from Derrida. She chooses to splice extracts from 'Signature, Event, Context' (1977) which summarise Derrida's argument that writing functions in the absence of the signatory, cutting off the trace from the intentionality behind it. Later in his work, however, Derrida comments directly on autobiography, his deconstructive critique echoing philosophically what we already know from film:

> the 'I' does not exist, it is not present to itself until what involves [*engage*] it in this way [occurs], and which is not it. There is not a constituted subject which commits [*engage*] itself to writing at a given moment for such or such a reason. It exists through it [writing], given [*donné*] by the other: born [*né*] as we bizarrely said earlier, born [*né*] through being given [*donné*], delivered, offered and betrayed all at one and the same time. (*ACM* 279)

If Derrida's deconstructive theoretical arguments challenge traditional understandings of autobiography in the same way cinema does, I want to propose in closing that Derrida's deconstructive autobiographical practice, although written on the page, might be considered in some sense cinematic.[25] Even more than this, 'Circumfession' might, to a limited extent, be productively situated within the tradition of feminist autobiographical film.

In discussion of *Derrida* above, I have already suggested that the divided page in Bennington and Derrida's co-signed book, *Jacques Derrida*, is a cinematic technique – the literary equivalent of the split screen. But Derrida's autobiographical text – which occupies the lower half of the page/screen – also employs a number of other cinematic techniques found in the films under consideration in this chapter. Despite being written in the first person, Derrida's autobiography still attempts to mediate access to the 'I' and it does so in a similar way to Citron's *Daughter Rite*. Derrida does not – *cannot*, given the literary medium – use an actor to speak the 'I' but he does self-consciously remind the reader that it would be a mistake to consider the 'I' as self-identical or irreducibly singular:

> [. . .] *everything would be said in the first person, I, I, I and from one sentence to the next, even within the same sentence, it would never be the same I, whence the unreadability, unless there is a code, for example the tense of the verb, or another feature, grammatical or not, to guide the writing and allow the attentive or hard-working reader to reconstitute the scenography of narrators* [. . .] (*CM* 291)

In this passage, Derrida does not just *assert* the multiplicity of the 'I' but he metaphorically conjures the dramatic possibility reified in *Daughter Rite* – that the 'I' might be inhabited by multiple voices. The attentive reader can see in his text a 'scenography of narrators'. This term relates to theatre rather than cinema: 'scenography' (*la scénographie*) is the theatrical equivalent of mise-en-scène, both terms denoting all of the elements that contribute to establishing an atmosphere and mood for a theatrical or cinematic presentation. But in using the term, Derrida is drawing the visual and the performative into his written text; it is also an expression, 'the scenography of narrators', that might well describe the storytellers in *Stories We Tell*.

Derrida mediates access to any singular 'I', then, by enlisting the performative possibilities of theatre (shared by film) to multiply the identity of the 'I'. But there is a further mediating technique at play in the form of the passage above, for it is actually a quotation within Derrida's text (as is evident from the quotation marks and the italic font), a citation taken, we are told, from notebooks Derrida wrote from 27 December 1976 onwards (*CM* 69). Just as Polley only speaks in the first person in *Stories We Tell* by citing herself (her own emails), so here Derrida mediates the 'I' by multiplying the 'I' of the body text with the 'I' of the notebooks, from which he cites repeatedly throughout 'Circumfession'. And these are not the only citations in the work – he also inserts long, untranslated passages from Augustine's *Confessions*. In doing so, he protects himself through close engagement with, even mutual identification with, the other:

> Even when speaking of the most intimate thing [. . .] it is better to know that an exegesis is going on, that you carry its diversion, its outline, and its memory inscribed within the culture of your body. (*ACM* 284)

But in the end, he admits, such mediating techniques do not entirely protect him, for autobiography, even in its most mediated and *queer* forms, is always in the end an almost violently self-exposing endeavour: 'above all do not believe that I am quoting any more than G., no, I am tearing off my skin, like I always do, I unmask and *de-skin* myself while sagely reading others like an angel' (*CM* 240).

Derrida's use of mediating techniques that we have already encountered in cinematic autobiography enable him to produce a deconstructive autobiography *within* the written form without merely changing genre entirely into fiction, the ultimate form of mediation. The use of such techniques renders 'Circumfession' not just deconstructive, then, but cinematic, with the challenge the latter poses to traditional autobiography being medium-specific, not dependent on the insights of deconstruction. Is it, though, as I have suggested above, also possible to read 'Circumfession' as a feminist cinematic autobiography? The answer is both yes and no. Yes, like *Daughter Rite* and *Stories We Tell*, 'Circumfession' is motivated by the autobiographer's relationship to her/his mother – not a philosophical figure of the mother but a very real, visceral, embodied mother (often dead or dying or in old age). As Derrida says in *D'Ailleurs, Derrida*, '"Circumfession" is a kind of vigil, of watch, of vigil, of wake, if you like, for my mother'. And Derrida shares with Citron and Polley a guilt or concern about the ethics of creating art out of that relationship. Derrida says that he feels 'really guilty for publishing her end, in exhibiting her last breaths and, still worse, for purposes that some might judge to be literary' (*CM* 36–7); Citron comments that she made her next film, *Mother Right*, 'to assuage my guilt over *Daughter Rite*' (1999: 278). Derrida therefore breaks in this text with the masculine philosophical tradition which, as Andrew Parker argues in *The Theorist's Mother*, has 'systematically *failed* to think about the mother' (Marder in Marder and Parker 2013). His text is a vigil for the mother as she lies dying rather than yet another masculine attempt at textual matricide.[26] That said, Derrida is not able to resist even in this autobiographical, embodied, visceral text, the persistent logic of his philosophical thought in which the feminine – whether it be the Woman or the Mother – becomes figured as that which is absolutely other. While 'Circumfession' might probe the depths of his mother's bedsores, in the conventional philosophical gesture, the maternal is still abstractly figured as 'absolute knowledge' (*CM* 46), 'this figure of absolute survival' (*CM* 51).

This intrusion of a conventional philosophic figuration sits oddly in a text which otherwise works well to achieve its intended aim – to rupture, challenge and destabilise the 'authoritative' programmatic presentation of Derrida's philosophical scheme which Bennington presents in the text above. While this intention resonates with Derrida's repeated insistence that deconstruction is not a philosophical system, the structure of *Jacques Derrida* also emulates that of feminist autobiographies: a personal 'I', at the same time both singular and multiple, challenges the monologic account of that 'I' by an authoritative masculine figure. For feminist autobiographers, this is the account of themselves in particular, and women in general, given by patriarchal culture; for Derrida, it is the reductive systematisation of his work presented by Bennington: 'you have the whole of this circumfession, the sieving of the singular events that can dismantle G.'s theologic program' (*CM* 305). But there is one hugely significant difference – in *Jacques Derrida*, Bennington and Derrida are complicit in this game. 'The book presupposes a contract', we are told at its opening: Bennington is aware from the outset of the futility of his attempt at a systematisation of Derrida's thought; Derrida's text is precisely intended to escape 'the proposed systematization, surprising it' (*JD* 1). And all this was commissioned by a publisher. There is no balance of power being weighed here, this is all done 'on the basis of a friendly bet (challenge, outbidding, or raising of the stakes)' (*JD* 1). But for feminist autobiography there is no contract, no friendly bet with the other – real power and inequity is at stake. As Citron argues:

> The autobiographical act is historically significant for women, and all others, who have traditionally lacked either a voice or a public forum for their speaking [. . .]. It is in this sense that the autobiographical act is a political act, something we risk losing sight of when women's autobiography is labeled confessional. (1999: 272)

This is of course exactly how 'Circumfession' *is* labelled. Derrida adopts this label, inhabits it, even, perhaps, disrupts it, but in the end 'Circumfession' is a philosophical act – a deconstructive autobiographical challenge to traditional philosophy's structural exclusion of the personal, its 'will to truth' (Smith 1995: 8). In contrast, for feminist filmmakers, auto/biography is always a political act, precarious and contingent, both singular and general.

Notes

1. For clarity, I will refer to Amy as Ziering Kofman throughout, despite the fact that in later work she drops 'Kofman', since I am primarily discussing *Derrida* in which she retains 'Kofman'.

2. See Robert Smith (1995: esp. pp. 8–19) for a good account of the relationship between philosophy and biography. Smith elucidates the argument that philosophy is always structurally determined, and therefore destabilised, by its attempted exclusion of the contingent.
 3. See Chapter 3 for a discussion of the work of filmmaker Joanna Callaghan, whose oeuvre demonstrates how it *is* possible to engage rigorously and inventively with philosophical texts and ideas cinematically.
 4. Bennington's essay 'A Life in Philosophy' was written for the conference 'Thinking Lives: The Philosophy of Biography and the Biography of Philosophers', at which Dick and Ziering filmed Derrida's lecture in October 1996. It remains a useful Derridean analysis of the relationship between philosophy and biography and might be read as an a priori critique of Peeters' work: 'It is of course to be expected that Derrida will some day be the subject of biographical writing, and there is nothing to prevent this being of the most traditional kind, according to the ontological supplement as I have outlined it [. . .]. But this type of complacent and recuperative writing would at some point have to encounter the fact that Derrida's work should at least have disturbed its presuppositions' (Bennington 2008: 423).
 5. Ziering Kofman uses the metaphor of the fugue to describe the structure of the work in 'Making *Derrida*': 'Somewhere in the middle of this editing process, I came up with the idea of thinking about the structure of the film in terms of a musical metaphor. Since our film had no storyline or dramatic narrative per se, I thought it might be of help to think about structuring it the way a fugue is structured – that is, with themes that are introduced and repeated, but, in their repetition, augment, weave, complicate and compete with one another – producing a steady and ever more rich and complex build that would not necessarily resolve into some neat and unifying fashion. With this metaphor in mind, the film began to fall more quickly into place' (2005: 26).
 6. Perhaps most well-known of these occurrences in the film is Derrida's line – 'So, this is what you call cinéma-verité [sic]? Everything is false. Well, almost everything' (Kofman 2005: 67) – and his explanation that, for example, he does not usually get dressed to work at home (who does?). Derrida repeatedly highlights 'the completely artificial character of this situation' (Kofman 2005: 65).
 7. Erik Barnouw provides clarification of the difference between US direct cinema and French *cinéma-vérité*: 'The direct cinema documentarist took his camera to a situation of tension and waited hopefully for a crisis; the Rouch version of *cinéma-vérité* tried to precipitate one. The direct cinema artist aspired to invisibility; the Rouch *cinéma-vérité* artist was often an avowed participant. The direct cinema artist played the role of uninvolved bystander; the *cinéma-vérité* artist espoused that of provocateur' (1974: 254–5). Janet Walker and Diane Waldman further contextualise Barnouw's distinction in their 'Introduction' to *Feminism and Documentary* (1999: 30, n. 32).
 8. Walker and Waldman's introduction to *Feminism and Documentary* provides a comprehensive analysis of the feminist realist debate (1999: esp. pp. 6–13).

For key primary texts, see: Claire Johnston (1973); Eileen McGarry (1975); Jane Gaines (1984); Julia Lesage (1986); and Alexandra Juhasz (1994).
9. Although Dick and Ziering Kofman differ from committed documentary filmmakers in that, as far as the viewer knows, they are not part of the community they are helping to speak out.
10. See, for example, Ziering Kofman (2005: 28), Dick (2005: 38, 44), and both Ziering Kofman and Dick (in *DOD* 115, 116) and Macy et al. (2005: 128–30).
11. See, for instance, Juhasz's personal analysis of this conflict: 'As a feminist, AIDS activist, media scholar and videomaker, it disturbs me that the theory I respect and use is often at odds with the media I make and watch. This essay attempts to reconcile the contradictions between my practical experience as a teacher, maker, spectator and scholar of political documentary by women and the critical and theoretical knowledge I have amassed in my academic work' (1994: 176).
12. Just a few contemporary heirs to early feminist political documentaries include *Live Nude Girls Unite!* (2000), *The Business of Being Born* (2008), *No Woman No Cry* (2010), *Misrepresentation* (2011), *Dark Girls* (2011), *It's a Girl* (2012), *Half the Sky* (2012), *After Tiller* (2013), *Buying Sex* (2013) and *The Punk Singer* (2013), as well, of course, as Dick and Ziering Kofman's own films. For a history of women's documentary filmmaking up until its date of original publication in 1981, see Patricia Erens (1988).
13. As Juhasz notes, embracing this tension is imperative for political filmmaking: 'The tension between theory and practice seems most tense for theorists. People making political art are more than capable of simultaneously understanding that while reality is constructed through discourse, it is also lived in ways that need to change for many individuals' (Juhasz 1994: 188–9). As Walker and Waldman summarise, 'feminism's political grounding has mitigated any facile reduction of documentary to its fictive properties by retaining the paradox of the "reality fiction" as a *paradox*, and moreover, as a paradox in which there is much at stake' (1999: 11–12).
14. My focus on only one half of the directorial duo here – Ziering Kofman rather than Dick – is justified by the fact that the film's conception and drive was Ziering Kofman's, a former graduate student of Derrida's. Ziering Kofman brought Dick on board for his documentary-making experience, not because of his connection with the subject or subject matter. Thus, despite Dick's involvement, the film's vision and ambition remain signed primarily by Ziering Kofman.
15. The filmmakers did make 'numerous attempts to secure a professional voice to read aloud the excerpts from Derrida's written work in the film' (Ziering Kofman 2005: 32–3). Birgit Ludwig's performances (as the character Sophie) of excerpts from 'Envois' in *Love in the Post* demonstrate how a professional actor *can* inhabit Derrida's written work in affective ways; see Chapter 3 for further discussion of this point.
16. Peeters identifies the music as such in *Derrida* (489), as does Kamuf (2010: 108).
17. It is beyond the scope and intention of this chapter to develop a more detailed comparative analysis of *Derrida* and *D'Ailleurs, Derrida*, but the reader might

well follow the advice on the University of California, Irvine's Hydra Humanities site entry for *D'Ailleurs, Derrida*, which, after summarising Fathy's film, ends with the following comment: 'And how, you ask, is this different from Amy Ziering Kofman's movie? Don't ask. Watch both.' Available at http://hydra.humanities.uci.edu/derrida/elsewhere.html (last accessed 18 September 2017). For useful critical engagements with *D'Ailleurs, Derrida*, see David Wills (2004) and Peggy Kamuf (2010); for a comparative analysis of *Derrida* and *D'Ailleurs, Derrida* as works of film-philosophy rather than biography or autobiography, see Robert Sinnerbrink (2016).

18. Ziering Kofman relates this anecdote in 'Making *Derrida*' (2005: 35, n. 2).
19. Polley repeats her fear of appearing narcissistic again in interview with Michael Fox (2013). She tells José Teodoro, 'Most of the time I wished I wasn't doing it at all' (2013: 55).
20. See, for instance, reviews by Nick McCarthy (2013), Richard Porton (2013), José Teodoro (2013), Leah Anderst (2013) and Kate Kellaway (2013).
21. Other feminist experimental personal documentaries include Martha Coolridge's *Not a Pretty Picture* (1974) and Su Friedrich's *The Ties That Bind* (1985). See Robin Blaetz (2007) for collected essays on women's experimental cinema more broadly, and Erens (1988: 562) for a brief overview of 1970s and 1980s feminist experimental documentary filmmaking. I am indebted to Sophie Mayer (2013) for first drawing my attention to the lineage between *Daughter Rite* and *Stories We Tell*: 'Never overt, Polley's documentary embraces both the political and cinematic heritage of feminism, particularly the seminal film *Daughter Rite* which screened internationally in 1978, the year Polley was conceived. Polley, of course, couldn't have seen it at the time but Michelle Citron's unique and influential combination of optically printed home movies, vérité footage revealed to be staged and poetic voiceover is deeply woven into the DNA of *Stories We Tell*.' It is curious that Polley does not cite this feminist heritage when discussing the film, claiming Lars von Trier's *The Five Obstructions* and Orson Welles' *F for Fake* as the most powerful influences among the many personal documentaries she watched in preparation for making *Stories We Tell* (see Polley in Dowd 2013).
22. See Michelle Citron (1999) for details of the source and nature of the different elements of the film's composition.
23. Like Citron, Polley discusses the make-up of the film freely in interview, expressing her surprise that the reconstructed footage in fact fooled audiences; in interview, she tells Kate Kellaway, 'I had been wondering, in my own life, what was real and what wasn't. I wanted people to have the same questions in their minds' (Polley in Kellaway 2013). See also extended discussion of this in interview with Germaine Lussier (2013) and Michael Porton (2013).
24. See Dillon (2015a) for an extended discussion of the relationship between literature and film, and of second-person address, in Isabelle Coixet's narrative feature in which Polley plays the lead, *My Life Without Me* (2003). Fascinatingly, given my attention to it in the closing sections of this chapter, this precise expression also appears in Derrida's 'Circumfession': 'my life without me' (*CM* 282).

25. Peggy Kamuf also gets this sense from 'Circumfession', observing that 'the opening sequence of *Circumfession* thus reads like a film script, with image track and sound track on which a three-word phrase would be spoken first in a ghostly, unidentified voiceover and then repeated by one of the actors in the scene who plays a nurse and who manipulates a complicated apparatus that draws his lifeblood from the child, now adult, remembering the scene' (2010: 113–14).
26. See Christine Boheemen-Saaf (2013) for an excellent discussion of matricidal writing in Joyce and in Derrida's 'The Night Watch' (more properly translated, according to Boheemen-Saaf, as 'The Waking Woman'). See especially Boheemen-Saaf's critique of the way in which the literary style of the end of 'The Night Watch' (which is evocative of 'Circumfession') is embroiled there in killing the mother (2013: 194–5). See also Parker (2012), a book which, as the author explains, 'turned out in some sense to be "about" Jacques Derrida even though his work never occupies center stage for very long' (xiii).

CHAPTER FIVE

How Do I Look?

At the outset of this book, I noted that other than his comments on films in which he appears – on *Ghost Dance*, *Derrida* and *D'Ailleurs, Derrida* – Derrida never published a sustained analysis of a cinematic text. He did, however, write an extended commentary on a photonovel: Marie-Françoise Plissart's *Droit de regards* was first published in French in 1985 accompanied by a 'reading' by Derrida of the same title. In *Screen/Play: Derrida and Film Theory* (1989), Peter Brunette and David Wills propose that in 'Right of Inspection', Derrida 'comes closest to writing "about" the cinema' (Brunette and Wills 1989: 134); it is also the only instance in which he engages directly with a queer feminist visual work. For these reasons, although *Right of Inspection* (the title under which it was first published in English in 1998) is not a film, it demands consideration here.[1] It does so also for a further reason. The French title has multiple semantic valences and possible translations; as Brunette and Wills note, it can translate as 'both "the right to look" and "the law(s) of looking (of the looks)"'; in addition, 'the expression *avoir droit de regard sur* means "to oversee"' (Brunette and Wills 1989: 135–6, n. 31). As its title signals, then, *Right of Inspection* is a work deeply concerned with issues of representation and visibility, with interrogating who has the right to look, who is subject to the look, and what the laws of the look are or, more radically, could be. More specifically, it is concerned with how these issues and laws pertain to women, in particular, queer women. In combining such thematic concerns with a commentary from Derrida, *Right of Inspection* is a fundamental inclusion, if not a paradigmatic text, in any enquiry into the intersections of deconstruction, feminism and film. It seems not just appropriate, then, but essential that it be the subject of this concluding chapter.

Brunette and Wills celebrate 'Right of Inspection' because, they say, in his reading Derrida 'sets out to avoid the inevitable positioning operated by the image' (1989: 135). In doing so, they argue that Derrida demonstrates 'how strategies for reading film might challenge [. . .] the institutions that determine and restrict such reading(s)' (Brunette and Wills 1989: 135). But in relation to *Right of Inspection*, this resistance to the positioning of the work is problematic from a feminist perspective. As I explored in detail in Chapter 1, film (and, we might now add, photography) have historically situated women only as those who can be looked at, not those who can look. One way to respond to this is in the agential feminist spectatorship I theorised in that chapter and have performed throughout this book. But another response to the problematic politics of the gaze is to create feminist works which produce alternative spectatorial positions. This is indeed what *Right of Inspection* does, creating, as I will explore in the first section of this chapter, a lesbian subject position for the viewer. As Teresa de Lauretis notes,

> One, and not the least, reason why spectatorship is pivotal to what I have called a feminist cinema is that its concern with address (whom the film addresses, to whom it speaks, what and for whom it seeks to represent, whom it represents) translates into a conscious effort to address the spectator as female, regardless of the gender of the viewers; and that is what allows the film to draw into its discursive texture something of that 'Real' which is the untheorized experience of women. (de Lauretis 1987: 119)

In resisting the inevitable positioning of these images, Derrida is in fact resisting the queer female spectatorial position created by the text. In doing so, he fails to see *Right of Inspection*'s radical rethinking of who looks, who is looked at and who has the right to look – and the consequences of this for the lived experiences of embodied women – topics which his essay is ostensibly concerned to explore. In contrast, in my close reading of the photonovel I embrace the text's positioning and analyse how it achieves its effect.

While the first section of this chapter demonstrates Derrida's inability to properly read *Right of Inspection* in relation to its engagement with the feminist politics of the gaze, in the second section I explore what Derrida's essay *does* offer the feminist film critic: a theoretical account of *metonymic reading* which delineates and justifies the critical methodology employed throughout this book. In closing the chapter, and the book, I return to Plissart's photonovel in order to expose Derrida's blindness to the literary text which lies at its heart, one which offers a surprising metonymic clue to the power of feminist critical and creative practice.

I He Can't See Queerly

In '*Roman-photo* Revisited' (1986), Plissart and her collaborator Benoît Peeters describe the photonovel as 'an exhausted and much neglected genre' (298). The key issue with the genre is the question of the relationship between, and respective primacy of, text and image. In their earlier work such as *Correspondance* (1980) and *Fugues* (1983), Peeters and Plissart explain that their aim 'was not simply to juxtapose text and image, but to try to achieve a true fusion of the two within a narrative framework' (1986: 298). The problem they encountered, and it is a common one across the genre, is that the text dominated the image, not just typographically in the difficulties of where to place the text so as not to visually dominate or even occlude the image, but also narratively in the sense that the visual images become subordinate to the literary narrative.[2] In an attempt to avoid both of these problems, in *Right of Inspection* Peeters and Plissart decided to do away with text completely, so that 'nothing could be narrated unless it could be photographed' (1986: 299). *Right of Inspection* was therefore born out of the desire to do away with words and their dominance over images, but in a paradoxical circularity befitting – as we will see – the text's own narrative structure, the work has prompted discussion in words about how to write about a text solely consisting of images. This is one of Derrida's main concerns in 'Right of Inspection', a conversation between an unidentifiable number of speakers; it is, as one of them describes it, a 'polylogue' (*RI* 30). (What can be said for sure is that there are at least three speakers and that at least one is gendered as female and one as male.)[3] *Right of Inspection* therefore runs the risk of merely returning its readers to the debates about the very tension between image and text from which it was intended to escape. Such a reductive outcome is countered, however, by the causative way in which monomodality of technique can in fact lead to multimodality of audience response: as Jan Baetens suggests, 'would it not be possible to suppose that the *refusal* of multimodality at [the] technical level is the condition of the *achievement* of multimodality at other levels?' (2009: 80).

In 'How Many is Multi? On the Example of Photo Narrative, High and Low' (2009), Baetens offers up Derrida's reading of *Right of Inspection* as a paradigmatic example of the way in which the very lack of words in the photonovel in fact produces an excess of discourse. Derrida's text performs this effect in both its form – in the multiplicity of voices that converse in 'Right of Inspection' – and in its content – the idea that the images generate almost infinite verbal stories is just one strand in the many threads of the conversation prompted by the photonovel. One of the speakers is concerned that the discussion is becoming 'a homage to the word and to rhetoric, a right of inspection accorded the word, which remains therefore as that which was in the beginning' (*RI* 20). This concern does indeed dominate the discussion but it also encompasses attention to ideas of the pose, gender, genre, the relationship between the photograph and cinema, and a whole series of wordplay and ideas-play in relation to the game of chequers. The strand of the conversation I take up in this section is the text's engagement with the multiple semantic valences of the title of Plissart's work – 'right of inspection' – since this discussion bears explicit relevance to feminist film theory's discussions about the politics of the gaze, although notably Derrida's text does not directly engage with feminist theory. My contention is that while Derrida's essay does attempt to address the questions the photonovel raises about looking – how one does so and who has the right to do so – his reading is limited by a failure on his part to recognise and take up the lesbian subject position created by the photonovel. This subject position is not adopted by any of the multiple voices in Derrida's text, which, similar to Derrida's other ostensibly polyvocal texts, in fact fails to represent a multiplicity of distinct subject positions, not least those of any women.[4]

As early as page three, one of the speakers in 'Right of Inspection' fights back against another speaker's logocentric reading of Plissart's work – the assertion that it is 'conjugated by a photographic grammar' (*RI* 3) – and identifies instead the work's concern with the visual and with looking:[5]

> I would say that, rather than conjugated by a photogrammar, it is declined by the rhetoric and/or the erotics of a certain photographic apparatus, by the power of the lens, the scope of its angles, the montages it can give rise to, the objectifying and capturing of images, the surveillance [*droit de regard*], the order intimated in silence, all the potential gestures, movements, situations, and positions that assign you a particular subject position: looking or looked at in turn, but by no means always alone. (*RI* 3)

What is not identified is the specifically gendered concern of this looking and being looked at within the work; *Right of Inspection* is directly concerned with how women look at women, and is invested in constructing a female spectatorial position outside of the work. This is not acknowledged in Derrida's text, neither in his discussion of the images, nor in his discussion of how to respond to them.

As in other Derrida works which take place on the terrain of gender, Derrida's multiple and multiply gendered voices are an attempt to respond to the politics of the gaze and to break free from the perspective of the male-embodied author. But a crucial exchange early on in the text moves the discussion away from a direct concern with gender. 'Here is what is on trial,' declares one of the speakers: 'since one always addresses more than one other, male or female, will I *in the same breath* speak for a male and female spectator?' (*RI* 4). The answer s/he receives is 'Yes, for these are only images. Everything you say refers to what remains to be seen: photographs proffered to the gaze, nothing more. Photographs of photographs and so on, virtually to infinity' (*RI* 4–5). Rather than acknowledging and exploring, as I will do here, that the self-referentiality of the work *foregrounds* its concern with looking, Derrida's speaker argues the opposite, that 'this abyssal inclusion of photographs within photographs takes something away from looking, it calls for discourse, demands a reading' (*RI* 5). The assertion regarding the images is that 'instead of a spectacle they institute a reader, of either gender, and instead of voyeurism, exegesis' (*RI* 5). Rather than an embodied, gendered, spectator, the argument is that the images produce an androgynous reader. This could not be further from the truth, but with this move Derrida veers away from the most crucial question Plissart's work addresses, that of the gender and nature of the spectatorial position created by the work. As a result, Derrida's speakers are free to move into a literary, not a visual, response to the work – to tell stories, not analyse images. For Derrida, to respond to these images visually – some of them explicit depictions of lesbian sex – is merely to become a 'voyeur'. As such, he retreats from thinking through the text's challenge to ideas of spectatorship into the safety and familiar comfort of 'exegesis'. What this exegesis then does is identify that the politics of looking is a key concern of Plissart's work, but in failing to theorise and take up the spectatorial position constructed by the text, the polylogue is not able to pose an argument about the *content* of *Right of Inspection*'s engagement with this topic.[6]

One of Derrida's speakers is correct when s/he observes that *Right of Inspection* 'analyzes the following: who possesses this right [of inspection], who possesses the other, holding it as the object of its gaze or within its sights [*objectif*]? Who holds the rights as "developer," who "fixes," who "mounts"?'(*RI* 7). The identification of this theme is repeated throughout the polylogue: 'I repeat, this work is only about looking and the right to it' (*RI* 15) but Derrida's engagement makes little further progress in exploring what the work has to say about looking, and the right to it, especially with regard to women. To make that progress here, it is necessary first to provide a sense of the work's narrative movement, something very difficult to do since its story is, as Plissart and Peeters realised, 'impossible to paraphrase [. . .] it really had to be seen' (1995: 299). In a work of written critical commentary, though, it is necessary to at least attempt a paraphrase, in order to orient the reader for the ensuing close analysis.

With apologies for the laboriousness of the following description, then, *Right of Inspection* opens with images of two women making love and shots depicting their surroundings. Postcoitally, one of the women dresses in white shirt and trousers and leaves the other naked on the bed. The woman descends the staircase of a lavish house and exits the building, running across paths surrounding a large lake. We then see an image of a third woman, dressed in black, who is taking photographs of the woman in white. The woman in white chases her, only to be photographed falling down stone steps. The next image shows the woman in white and the woman in black now in bed, the photograph of the former's fall hanging framed above them. The woman in black is now naked and the woman formerly in white is now dressed all in black. The camera pans back to reveal that all the photographs of the opening are also fixed, unframed, on the wall. The woman now in black, one of the subjects of the photographs, rips them from the wall and leaves the woman formerly in black naked in bed. She then gets up, puts on a white dress, and chases after her lover. What she encounters, however, is not the woman she is chasing but another framed photograph which depicts her lover standing to the side of a doorway watching another couple, this time a man and a woman. The next sequence of images takes us into that photograph and plays out a fight between the man and the woman. Eventually the woman now in black appears in the frame, walks across the stage of the fight, opens large glass doors and rips and scatters into the air the photographs she has with her. She turns to leave, the man closes the doors, and the male-female couple have now exchanged their original positions, the man now at the window with his back to us, the woman in profile in the chair. The last we see of them is again as a framed photograph, but now in these exchanged positions. With that we return to the woman now in white who has been looking at the photograph. She turns to leave, descends less glamorous stairs and exits the building to encounter on the ground the scattered fragments of photographs. It is at this point that we get the first images of a bald-headed figure in black, seen only at first from behind, gender indeterminate. Images of this figure are intercut with images of the woman now in white looking at the fragments of photographs, leaving the building's environs and wandering the city at night.

Right of Inspection contains one hundred pages of photographs; at its centre, on page fifty, are two images, from different angles, of the bald-headed figure handwriting with a fountain pen in a lined notebook. On page fifty-one, we get the first images of this figure from the front, and full length, from which it is clear that she too is female. These images at the centre of the work are crucial to analysis of it and I will return to them in the final section of this chapter. But to finish the impossible paraphrase of the second half of *Right of Inspection*: the bald-headed figure, who we will now call the Director, dominates the next sequence of images as she is seen setting up the second bedroom scene, playing chequers, walking upstairs, and setting up the mise-en-scène for the male-female couple's fight. As she returns to her writing desk, we cut back to images of the woman in white, still wandering the city but making her way back to the original building. There is now a parallel scene of the entering into a photograph of someone watching two people through an archway; in this iteration, the watcher is the woman left in bed in the first bedroom scene. She is watching two young girls, disconcertingly made up like women, playing chequers. We enter into this image and stay with the girls as they play, pose and fight. Echoing the end of the first adult bedroom scenes, one of the girls flees, only to be chased by the other. In a further direct echo of the first flight, the leading girl, camera in hand, turns to photograph the girl chasing her as she falls down a flight of stairs. After images of the photographer, and a brief pause to examine the Polaroid image, the chase continues, to end on a mattress on which the girls fight over the photograph, only for one again to up and run off; this is a direct echo of the second bedroom scene. After this re-enactment of the opening scenes with the pairs of lesbian lovers, the girls are then posed to echo the scene of the male-female fight. We exit from this uncanny echoing when one of the girls smashes the very framed photograph of the girls being watched playing chequers that took us into that world. In the next image, the smashed frame lies at the feet of the woman in white who is now being left by the observer of the children; this is the first time these two women, one from each of the initial couplings, are seen together. The woman in white discovers the ripped-up photographs in a drawer and through a fragment of herself in one of them she is transited back into her black clothes and her role as photographer. This transit takes us back full circle to the beginning of the story as she follows the woman who was watching the girls – now in white, not black – as she enters the building in which she makes love to the woman, the photographs of which have opened the work.

In *Right of Inspection*, the characters move between subject positions – in Roland Barthes' terminology, sometimes they are *Spectator* (the one looking), sometimes *Operator* (the one taking the photographs), sometimes *Spectrum* (the subject of the photograph); regularly, they are in more than one of these positions at the same time. This movement between and doubling-up of positions in relation to looking is part of the photonovel's strategy of questioning and challenging any simplistic understanding of the women as only the object of the gaze. This technique also renders the work, in de Lauretis' terms, both one that represents lesbians and one that 'represents the problem of representation' (1991: 224). The mise-en-abyme effects of the work heighten the multiplicity of subject positions, and the very obvious switching of clothes from black to white signals, through costume, the shifting subject positions of the characters. For Derrida, these reversals and inversions are crucial, but it is almost a truism to say that the women in *Right of Inspection* move through a number of subject positions, and inhabit one or more at the same time. This is so obviously the case. What is less obvious, but more crucial, is that this play with positionality is part of a further effect of the work which Derrida does not see – it does not (just) constitute this as a work that represents lesbians and represents the problems of representation. *Right of Inspection* goes even further than this; it denaturalises heterosexuality and places lesbianism not as an outside issue to be, or not to be, represented, but as *the default position* for observing all representation.

136   *Deconstruction, Feminism, Film*

In order to justify this argument, it is necessary to pay attention to a small detail, to read one image metonymically.[7] The impossible paraphrase is helpful as context, but analysis of one photograph provides the argument. Consider the image from *Right of Inspection*, reproduced in Figure 5.1. Every figure in this photograph, by the very nature of it being a photograph, is subject to our gaze. But the woman in the foreground (who was the photographer of the original sequence) is also the *Spectator* who is viewing the woman in black who is both *Spectrum* (in relation to us and the woman in white) and *Spectator*, in relation to the male-female couple. Here we have the shifting subject positions that deconstruct the idea of women as only object of the gaze. But far more interesting in this image is what happens to the heterosexual couple. They become *Spectrum* three times over, being the object of both women's gazes and our own. The framing of this image by these gazes objectifies heterosexual relationality, and the literal frame around the photograph distances it from the layers of 'reality' of the work that the lesbian women inhabit. That this scene is not 'real' is emphasised further when we see the Director setting up the mise-en-scène for the shoot. This is the scene of mainstream cinema whose narratives are driven by heterosexual romance. But in *Right of Inspection*, heterosexuality becomes the object of the lesbian

Figure 5.1   Denaturalising heterosexuality.
Source: *Right of Inspection* © Les Impressions Nouvelles/Marie-Françoise Plissart, 2017.

subject's gaze, and through the mise-en-abyme effect of this image we too are placed in that subject position. Rather than viewing homosexuality from a heterosexual perspective, as some readers may have been inclined to do at the beginning of the work, this image instead causes us to identify with the repeated *ad infinitum* lesbian subject position. In doing so, it denaturalises heterosexuality and makes it the object, not the subject, of our point of view.

This effect is further reinforced by the generic associations of the heterosexual images. The exchange between the man and the woman does not just recall and denaturalise mainstream cinema but also the popular *roman-photo* in France (or *fotonovella* in Latin America) driven by plots of heterosexual romance.[8] As Peeters and Plissart note, their survey of the *roman-photo* revealed that 'by means of a synecdochic seizure, one type – pulp romantic fiction – had succeeded in passing itself off as the be-all and end-all of photographic narration, virtually encompassing the genre' (1995: 198). So disillusioned were they by this survey of the genre that they 'decided to forget, or at least temporarily disregard, the legacy of the *roman-photo* and to start afresh with a *tabula rasa* of sorts, sweeping away all the false assumptions that had taken root over the years' (Peeters and Plissart 1995: 299). In *Right of Inspection*, Plissart places a parody of this genre into her text – framed, however, as unreal – in order to expose both the previous paucity of the genre in which she is working *and* to challenge its commitment to stories that reinforce heteronormativity as the default position for readers and characters alike.

As noted in the summary above, the structure of Figure 5.1 is repeated at another moment in the work when we enter into the photographic world of the girls (see Figure 5.2). This is not a direct replication of the first version since in the second image we do not see the woman in white looking at the photograph. But we have just seen her enter the room in which it hangs. In omitting the actual shot of her looking at the photograph this second rendition actually reinforces our lesbian subject position since we are literally placed in front of the photograph in the position occupied by the woman in white: our subject position unites with hers. The scenes of the young girls we then view are perhaps the most disturbing of the entire work, and Derrida does not find a way to respond to them adequately. When read in the light of the previous analysis, however, their effect becomes clear. The scenes with the young girls echo not just the two lesbian encounters but also the heterosexual one preceding them. In their actions, their heavy make-up, their posing, smoking and drinking, the girls are mimicking adult behaviour, sexual and otherwise. This is disturbing, but it is meant to be. *Right of Inspection* displaces the heteronormativity of looking – that is, both *what* is looked at as well as *how* it is looked at – and constructs in its place a world in which

Figure 5.2 Entering the world of the two young girls.
Source: *Right of Inspection* © Les Impressions Nouvelles/Marie-Françoise Plissart, 2017.

homosexual looking – that is, both *what* is looked at as well as *how* it is looked at – is the norm. Crucial to this radical deconstruction of heteronormativity is a challenge to its presumption that children have no sexuality at all, and that when they do have sexuality it will by default be heterosexual.[9] The scenes of the girls' mimicry of adult behaviour and (hetero and homo)sexual relations challenge both of these assumptions – they do not just sexualise the child, they homosexualise her.

This reading of *Right of Inspection* reveals the limitation of Derrida's ability to respond to a lesbian visual text; he is unable to take up the subject position created by the text, finding himself caught only in voyeurism when thinking through a visual response to the photonovel. Instead, Derrida retreats to the safety of words and to telling stories, but Derrida's words revolve around the images without actually responding to them. He cannot *see queerly* (with the emphasis on both of those words). What Derrida's polylogue does offer, however, is a useful analysis of the methodology I have used to analyse *Right of Inspection*, and employed in my readings throughout this book: close attention to the singular detail and exploration of the access it provides to (often original) general interpretation. In 'Right of Inspection', Derrida calls this 'metonymic reading'.

II Metonymic Reading

When confronted with a whole that actively withdraws from the logic of narrative to which we are so accustomed, Derrida focuses on the detail. He does so not in order to avoid the whole but in order to access it, in order to move from the singular to the general. One of the voices in 'Right of Inspection' calls this 'metonymic reading' and crucial to it is a rhythmic movement between stasis and speed:[10]

> If I understand correctly, one has to bring enormous attention to bear on each detail, enlarge it out of all proportion, slowly penetrate the abyss of these metonymies – and yet manage to skim through, diagonally. Accelerate, speed up the tempo, as if there were no more time. (*RI* 22)

Metonymic reading must be slow, it must focus on the detail, it must go deep in its analysis of the minute and even seemingly inconsequential. But these slow, deep critical abysses, taken together, are the material fabric of a reading that also moves, however obliquely, with sustained speed across the text.[11] Metonymic reading produces the gestalt of a speedy interpretation which is palpably different to, but predicated upon, the slowness of its constituent parts.

Metonymic reading is particularly suited to *Right of Inspection* since it is the type of reading that photography as a non-narrative art in fact demands. To respond to it adequately requires:

> a reading of the significant 'detail' in a blowup, in a process of increasing enlargement, of *découpage* or montage, a reinscription of metonymies, displacement, substitution, restaging, analysis of the figurative function of words in the silent *Darstellbarkeit*, etc. (*RI* 23)

In *Right of Inspection*, the whole is contained within the part, to the extent that 'there is only detail' (*RI* 23). This style is not merely aesthetic, though, it is also political. For if no whole is represented, if the whole is only accessible through the magnification of parts, then, as one of Derrida's voice's recognises, 'there is no right to a complete inspection, it is the opposite of a panopticon' (*RI* 23). Metonymic composition makes us *look* differently, in all the senses of that verb and that pronoun: it makes *us as subjects appear* differently to those who observe us; and it makes *us as observers look at* that which we are observing differently. Metonymic reading exposes how the photographs in *Right of Inspection* – and the other works considered throughout this book – pose a political question. They 'pose and repose the same question, that of the right of inspection: They displace the foundations of an established jurisdiction, they call for another, right before our eyes' (*RI* 24). One of the voices in 'Right of Inspection' attributes this power of displacement to '*Ps* and *Ph*', photography and psychoanalysis, but to do so is to at best misinterpret, at worst unnecessarily delimit, its possibilities. For the interrogation of the right of inspection, the destabilisation of our established understanding of how we look – both how we appear and how we behold – is not the exclusive purview of '*Ps* and *Ph*'. In fact, it is most appropriately the purview of feminist and queer critical and creative practice with its long history of exposing the very complicity of much '*P*sychoanalysis' and '*Ph*otography' in the *ph*allocentric jurisdiction of the gaze. For, as Teresa de Lauretis argues, 'undoubtedly, that is the project of lesbian performance, theatre and film [:] redefining the conditions of vision, as well as the modes of representing' (1988: 170–1).

One of the voices in 'Right of Inspection' recognises that the detail is independent of a general theory and that it must retain this independence in order to mobilise its fragmentary power: 'the silent liturgy of the fragment *should* remain discreet and not give rise to any dream of a *general theory*, which is another name for the panoptical' (*RI* 24). 'At the same time, s/he begins to wonder 'whether, instead of opposing [. . .] this general politics, this politics of the general, the art of magnifying on the contrary . . . ' (RI 24), but the ellipsis signals that the speaker's speculation is interrupted, the thought never directly completed. It is taken up again, but only obliquely, shortly afterwards. The interrupted speculation on how exactly the singular might relate to the general haunts the thoughts that follow, thoughts that are themselves about haunting, about the way in which even as the whole is withdrawn from the detail, this withdrawal remains haunted by that now absent whole. The whole haunts the fragment; the fragment spectrally reproduces the whole. 'Isn't it the case,' asks Derrida's speaker, that 'one reproduces – even as the silhouette of a phantom – something of the whole, the spirit of the whole, the specter that remains present in the magnification of the detail?' (*RI* 24). Details might not *show* the whole, but via a spectral logic they still '*mean* something with respect to the whole' (*RI* 24).

Later in his work, Derrida returns to the idea of metonymy in another reflection on a series of photographs, this time by Jean-François Bonhomme. Derrida's commentary was first published in 1996 in a bilingual French-Modern Greek edition of Bonhomme's images, the English translation only being published fourteen years later, in 2010, under the title *Athens, Still Remains*. At the very opening of this text, Derrida again reflects on *how to write* about a series of photographs, and again he hits upon the idea of finding his way through attention to metonymic substitution – each photograph in the series is both itself and stands for all of the others: 'without compromising in the least its absolute independence, each of them is what it is, no doubt, all on its own, but each one calls at once *some* other one and *all* the others' (*ASR* 3). Derrida repeats this argument regarding the metonymic reading of serial photography elsewhere in his writing on photography. Consider, for example, his comments on one of the photographs in Frédéric Brenner's collection *Diaspora: Homelands in Exile: voices* (2004): 'This photograph thus also photographs *one single time for all*, as their metonymy and exemplary example, what each one of the photographs in the series already encrypts [. . .]' (*D* 21). In his comments on Brenner's photographs, Derrida does not resist the temptation 'to read, in each one of these photographs, a displacement and a condensation, an allegory, a metonymy or a metaphor' (*D* 51). For Derrida, metonymic substitution is a defining characteristic of photographic seriality which in turn, he argues, is structurally essential to photography itself: 'That's photography: seriality does not come to affect it by accident. What is accidental is, for it, essential and ineluctable' (*ASR* 3). If photography is essentially serial, and seriality is essentially metonymic, then metonymic reading is necessarily essential. So much so, in fact, that Derrida asserts that 'every photograph is a fetish' (*ASR* 41) and attention to its detail becomes a fetishistic form of reading.[12]

Here again, the masculine pathology of fetishism recurs as that which names the act of paying close attention to the detail. In 'Female Fetishism' (1986), Naomi Schor attempts a feminist recuperation of fetishistic attention to the detail, only in the end to admit, 'at the very least a certain unease resulting from the continued use of the term fetishism, with its constellation of misogynistic connotations' (Schor 1986: 371). She identifies the continued use of the term 'fetishism' as 'an instance of "paleonymy," the use of an old word for a new concept' and asserts that 'a new word adequate to the notion of female fetishism' needs to be forged (Schor 1986: 371). Schor does not offer such a neologism in the essay, nor in her book *Reading in Detail: Aesthetics and the Feminine* (1987). What she does do in the latter, however, is provide a fascinating history of the genderedness of the detail in Western aesthetics, the way in which 'the patriarchal paradigm – with its divisions of masculine/feminine, general/particular, mass/detail – has held the detail in thrall' (Schor 1987: blurb). Schor's assertion is that the prominence of attention to the detail – evident of course in Derrida's work, as well as in that of Roland Barthes, Michel Foucault and Jürgen Habermas (all the examples Schor gives are of male thinkers) – is a relatively contemporary phenomenon which risks eliding the fact that 'the detail has until very recently been viewed in the West with suspicion if not downright hostility' (Schor 1987: 3). Historically, linked as it has been with the ornamental and the everyday, the detail has been irreducibly associated with the feminine: 'the detail does not occupy a conceptual space beyond the laws of sexual difference: the detail is gendered and doubly gendered as feminine' (Schor 1987: 4). There are two possible responses to this, reflecting the two phases of deconstruction explored at the beginning of this book: the first is to argue that the reversal of this history, the new legitimacy of the detail in Derrida's work and others, heralds also a new valorisation of the feminine with which it is associated; the second is to recognise that with such a reversal, necessary as it is, we remain, in Schor's words, 'prisoners of the paradigms' (Schor 1987: 4). In this second phase, it is necessary to *degender* the detail. In doing so, no new neologism for a 'female fetishism' is needed, for the act of attention to the detail becomes freed from the psychoanalytic framework which renders it a fetishistic act and is sufficiently described in rhetorical terms as metonymic reading.

Metonymic reading remains, however, political. It has been a characteristic of queer reading, for example – both historical and contemporary queer reading of film – which renders visible the invisible queer through attention not to the predominantly overarching heterosexual narratives but by working up new interpretative wholes via metonymic attention to the detail. As Roger Hallas defines it, although retaining the now contested association with fetishism, queer spectatorship includes 'a rejection or neglect of narrative linearity and trajectory; a fetishistic preoccupation with the moment, the detail, the fragment' (2003: 93). To stake a claim for the political power of metonymic reading is to dispel a false dichotomy between close textual attention and political critique. Such a dichotomy is posed, for instance, by de Lauretis at the opening of 'Film and the Visible' when she outlines her intentions in the essay: 'My purpose is not to do a textual reading,' she says, 'however tempting that may be with a film so rich and so eminently "cinematic," but rather to take the film as the ground from which to pose the question of lesbian representation and spectatorship' (1991: 224–5). In contrast, in this book I have argued and performed that close textual reading *is* political, in that it is the very means via which one can interrogate the question of women's representation and spectatorship, both in the texts immediately under consideration here and, metonymically, in general.

Rather than yoking metonymic reading to fetishism by identifying the detail as a fetish, it is more productive to understand both the detail and the act of close reading in the context of Roland Barthes' theory of the *punctum*, to which no doubt Derrida's thought on this topic is indebted. In 'The Deaths of Roland Barthes', Derrida acknowledges that 'this interest in the detail was also his' (*DRB* 268), that 'the word *punctum* [. . .] translates, in *Camera Lucida*, one meaning of the word "detail": a point of singularity' (*DRB* 269), and that 'as the place of irreplaceable singularity and of the unique referential, the *punctum* irradiates and, what is most surprising, lends itself to metonymy' (*DRB* 288). For Derrida, the *punctum*'s relation to metonymy is not accidental but essential; metonymy constitutes the *punctum*'s force, 'its *dynamis*, in other words, its power, potentiality, virtuality, and even its dissimulation, its latency' (*DRB* 288). In *Camera Lucida*, Barthes calls the *punctum* 'this element which rises from the scene, shoots out of it like an arrow, and pierces me' (2000: 26). Barthes chooses the word *punctum* because of its Latin origins, which 'designate this wound, this prick, this mark made by a pointed instrument' (2000: 26), but in addition he chooses it because 'it also refers to the notion of punctuation' (2000: 26). For Barthes, photographs 'are in effect punctuated' by the accidental but arresting '"detail"' (2000: 43). While no analysis is necessary to perceive the *punctum* – 'it suffices that the image be large enough, that I do not have to study it [. . .], that, given right there on the page, I should receive it right here in my eyes' (Barthes 2000: 42–3) – it is still a key provocation to analysis. In fact, crucially for the context of our discussion, the *punctum* has a potentiality, 'a power of expansion', that Barthes indeed defines as 'metonymic' (2000: 45).

The *punctum* is the metonymic detail that one 'stubbornly sees', which provokes one's '"thinking eye"' and 'makes me add something to the photograph' (Barthes 2000: 45). But according to Barthes in *Camera Lucida*, this phenomenon is unique to still photography; it is not possible in the movies:

> Do I add to the images in movies? I don't think so; I don't have time: in front of the screen, I am not free to shut my eyes; otherwise, opening them again, I would not discover the same image; I am constrained to a continuous voracity; a host of other qualities, but not *pensiveness*; whence the interest, for me, of the photogram. (2000: 55)

As Derrida notes in *Right of Inspection*, the origin of the Latin verb 'to think' means 'to be in suspense' (*RI* 25). Like metonymic reading, thought itself requires a slowing of pace, a slowing of pace in fact to a pause, a moment of suspense in which thinking can take place. Barthes states here that this is not possible in relation to film because of the speed of its movement from one image to the next. But Barthes was writing in 1980, before the advent of the video recorder, of DVDs and of the digital technologies that now allow us to break down moving images into their constitutive stills. In twenty-first-century film criticism, it is possible to slow down and to think. One of the most effective ways of doing so is to pay close attention to the affective detail of the still image that makes up the moving one, in order to develop the *punctum*'s metonymic powers of expansion.[13]

More than this, though, there is now compelling evidence that Barthes was disingenuous in his division of the *punctum* from cinema in *Camera Lucida*. There is a body of work that demonstrates the origin of his idea of the *punctum* in his close analysis of stills from the films of Sergei Eisenstein in 'The Third Meaning' and his tentative development there of the idea of an obtuse meaning in images.[14] In that essay, Barthes acknowledges his 'taste for stills'

(1977: 66) and states that 'a theory of the still becomes necessary' (1977: 67). With the idea of metonymic reading, developed out of an engagement with *Right of Inspection*, Derrida provides such a theory. It is therefore perhaps not surprising to discover tucked away in a footnote of 'The Third Meaning' that Barthes intuited that the 'photo-novel' might provide the prompt to such a theory: 'there are other "arts"', he writes, 'which combine still (or at least drawing) and story – namely the photo-novel and the comic-strip. I am convinced that these "arts", born in the lower depths of high culture, possess theoretical qualifications and present a new signifier (related to the obtuse meaning)' (1977: 66). In addition to 'The Third Meaning', the publication of Barthes' *Mourning Diaries* in 2009 provides further proof, laid out in exemplary fashion by Neil Badmington (2012), that Barthes was first pricked by the *punctum* in the cinema, on trips to watch William Wyler's *The Little Foxes*, Christian Gion's *One Two Two* and Hitchcock's *Under Capricorn*. The origins of Barthes' idea of the *punctum* therefore lie in cinema, confirming the authenticity and validity of a film critical practice that pays metonymic attention to the detail.

III Veering from Borges

I began this book by departing from Proust; I want to end it by veering from Borges. To enclose the book in textual engagements with two canonical male literary figures is not to entomb it but to demark its dual feminist practice of critical engagement with masculine texts in order to develop a critique of them, combined with close engagement with feminist works in order to move away from the masculine lineage and generate new thought and ideas. It also signals, I suppose, in my first book on film, my own origins as a literary critic and my medium promiscuity. Derrida shares in such a transgression of the boundaries between disciplines, often introducing a literary interlocutor to aid his philosophical speculations. He does this in 'Right of Inspection', engaging with Edgar Allan Poe – in particular the story 'The Murders in the Rue Morgue' – alongside his reading of Plissart's photonovel. But Poe is an odd choice, since Derrida usually engages an interlocutor offered by the text on which he is writing and *Right of Inspection* does indeed signal its literary intertext in the passage which the Director is writing out by hand in the images at its centre. In this way, the photonovel smuggles in a literary intertext as an image, a method Baetens identifies as part of the genre's commitment to monomodality:

> if text has to be present, it must be transformed in such a way that all traces of multimodality are whipped [sic] out: verbal information is thus no longer

added to the image, it is photographed itself as part of the pictured universe, in order to become itself a visual element (sometimes at the price of its very readability). (2009: 79)

But the text *is* readable here, and it is not from Poe, but from Jorge Luis Borges: the passage is an extract from the anecdote 'Covered Mirrors' in Borges' short-story collection *The Maker* (1960).

Borges' text appears at the centre of *Right of Inspection* on a page containing two photographs of the hand of the Director writing in Spanish in a notebook (see Figures 5.3 and 5.4). Derrida refers to these images and the writing in them on numerous occasions in 'Right of Inspection' but never once identifies the literary source (see, for example, *RI* 9–10, 16 and 24–5). To identify it here, the Borges passage the Director transcribes is translated into English thus:

> As a child, I knew that horror of the spectral duplication or multiplication of reality, but mine would come as I stood before large mirrors. As soon as it began to grow dark outside, the constant, infallible functioning of mirrors, the way they followed my every movement, their cosmic pantomime, would seem eerie to me. One of my insistent pleas to God and my guardian angel was that I not dream of mirrors; I recall clearly that I would keep one eye on them uneasily. I feared sometimes that they would begin to veer off from reality; other times, that I would see my face in them disfigured by strange misfortunes. I have learned that this horror is monstrously abroad in the world again. The story is quite simple, and terribly unpleasant.
> In 1927, I met a young woman (Borges, 'The Maker' 146)

The passage finishes mid-sentence after the word 'woman'; if completed according to Borges' original work, the complete sentence would be 'In 1927, I met a grave young woman, first by telephone (because Julia began as a voice without a name or face) and then on a corner at nightfall' (146). Paying metonymic attention to this literary intertext reveals that within it lies a clue not just to the world created by *Right of Inspection* but to the generative activity of feminist critical and creative work more broadly.

In Borges' anecdote the speaker recalls how he used to go walking with Julia, but that their relationship was not romantic: 'Between us there was neither love itself nor the fiction of love; I sensed in her an intensity that was utterly unlike the intensity of eroticism, and I feared it' (147). The speaker then moves quite suddenly from this personal account and admission of fear to a general truism about what one must do in relation to *all* women in order to develop intimacy with us: 'In order to forge an intimacy with women, one often tells them about true or apocryphal things that happened in one's youth' (147). Signalling this shift from particular to general, the English

146   *Deconstruction, Feminism, Film*

Figure 5.3   The Director transcribes Borges' 'Covered Mirrors'.
Source: *Right of Inspection* © Les Impressions Nouvelles/Marie-Françoise Plissart, 2017.

Figure 5.4   The Director transcribes more of Borges' 'Covered Mirrors'.
Source: *Right of Inspection* © Les Impressions Nouvelles/Marie-François Plissart, 2017.

translation changes here from the personal pronouns that have been used up until this point, 'us' and 'I', to the generality of 'women', 'one' and 'them'. In the original Spanish, the line is: '*Es común referir a las mujeres, para intimar con ellas, rasgos verdaderos o apócrifos del pasado pueril*' (Borges 1960). A literal English translation renders this: 'It is common, in order to forge an intimacy with women, to relate things, both real and apocryphal, from childhood.' The verb '*referir*', rendered as 'one tells' in the published translation, is in the infinitive form in the Spanish. Both the gender neutral 'one' in English and the axiomatic form of the original Spanish ('It is common to relate . . . ') disguise the male subject position of the speaker, turning his specific treatment of one woman into a universally accepted generic practice. In doing so, the speaker's grammar forces the reader – male or female – to align him or herself with the speaker's male subject position by acquiescing to a gender neutrality which is, of course, by default, always coded as male, as Derrida himself has well observed.[15] Women remain 'them', not 'us'. The culmination of the story escalates this male elision of a female subject position into a total inability of the woman to see herself. We learn that the speaker told the woman about his horror of mirrors, and that

> she has gone insane, and [. . .] in her room all the mirrors are covered, because she sees my reflection in them – usurping her own – and she trembles and cannot speak, and says that I am magically following her, watching her, stalking her. (147)

'Covered Mirrors' turns out to be a story about the 'dreadful bondage' that the ever-present image of man imposes on woman: it is a metonym for patriarchal society and culture in which women cannot see ourselves, never mind each other, but only the man or men looking at us; we exist only as the object of his/their gaze.

Borges' story provides a crucial intertext for *Right of Inspection* and the other feminist visual works on which this book has focused because they could all be read as mirror images of Borges' story: they render men incidental; they construct female spectatorial positions; they denaturalise heterosexuality and normalise female homosexuality, that intensity, perhaps, that the narrator of 'Covered Mirrors' so fears in Julia, and which he is unable to equate with his heteronormative conception of 'eroticism'. Women are seen, and see themselves and each other, repeatedly in *Right of Inspection* in a myriad of mirrors, windows and other reflective surfaces. This is a woman's world never haunted, watched or stalked by man. But the end of 'Covered Mirrors', the part that most clearly enables us to see how *Right of Inspection* inverts the story, is not included in the text the Director transcribes. Rather, what she writes out is the passage detailing the narrator's fear of mirrors, in particular that 'they would begin to veer off from reality' or reveal to him his face 'disfigured by strange misfortunes' (146). When one has read the whole story, one understands that when he says 'I have learned that this horror is monstrously abroad in the world again' (Borges 2000: 146) he is referring to its manifestation in the woman to whom he believes he has transferred it. But there is something both cheekily playful and seriously powerful in Plissart's choice of place to cut off the Director's transcription. Just from this fragment, we do not know that the horror is transferred. Rather, the implication is that it has returned *to himself*. And what has prompted it to do so? According to the transcribed fragment, the whole cause of the 'simple' and 'terribly unpleasant' story of the return of this horror is this: 'In 1927, I met a young woman'. This is not of course the full story of 'Covered Mirrors', but the ending of the extract portrays it as such. Meeting a woman who challenges him to relate to her on terms other than those of heterosexual eroticism might very well make the male narrator's horror come true, reflecting back to him a world that veers from reality as he perceives it. For as this book has shown, feminist visual works do indeed powerfully and liberatingly 'veer off from reality' (Borges 2000: 146), creating worlds in which women are no longer bound by the 'dreadful bondage of [man's] face' (Borges 2000: 147). May we yet see such worlds become our reality.

Notes

1. The English translation of Derrida's text is presented in a volume which bears his name and attributes the title *Right of Inspection* to his work. This supplantation of Plissart's photographs, their relegation to the position of supplement to Derrida's text, inverts the proper order of creation and in a dark irony is a publishing decision influenced by precisely the dominance of the word and the masculine that Plissart's photonovel is intended to deconstruct.
2. Jan Baetens (2009) details the reasons behind high-art photonovels' rejection of verbal elements: they claim all the spectator's attention; they disturb the pictures' composition; they displace the images as the driver of the narrative. Even in those photonovels which rid themselves of captions, or speech, however, words still persist, for instance in the photographed text I will analyse at the end of this chapter. *Right of Inspection* did have a script, albeit 'a less elaborate one' (Peeters and Plissart 1995: 299) than those which had guided their previous works. When Peeters and Plissart introduce the photonovel *Aujourd'hui* they state that 'this photographic suite attempts to create a truly visual piece of fiction by allowing the narrative to develop naturally from the images' (1995: 301), but they then provide a paragraph ostensibly setting up 'the basic situation' which in fact provides a written narrative frame which prescribes and proscribes one's individual interpretation of the images.

3. See David Wills (1988: 23–4) for an extended discussion of the question of the number and genders of the speakers, as indicated by Derrida's pronouns.
4. See Chapter 3 for an extended critical engagement with the claimed polyvocality of Derrida's 'Envois'.
5. Derrida's essay is not paginated in the English edition of *Right of Inspection*, so for ease of reference readers may wish to annotate their copies in order to add sequential page numbering from the first page through to the last: pp. 1–37.
6. David Wills also cites and comments upon this moment in Derrida's text: '*Right of Inspection* questions the logic of a written text in apposition to a photographic text; it questions that logic in terms of the law, or institutional restraint. It seeks therefore to perform "looking" as, and to transform "looking" into, a type of reading. Plissart's photographs on the other hand represent mostly female homosexual encounters. They raise the question of overt legal and social restraints on reading and on so-called deviant sexual practices' (1989: 12). Wills does not criticise Derrida directly for this move, but the import of 'on the other hand' is that Derrida's polylogue is doing something quite different to Plissart's photonovel with respect to questions of looking, gender and sexuality.
7. Such an approach to the photonovel has precedent in Derrida's reading, as I will explore below, and elsewhere. For instance, in 'Going to Heaven: A Missing Link in the History of Photonarrative' (2001), Baetens concentrates in some detail on analysing the opening image of a photonarrative before he moves on to the 'proper story' (97). Using an orchestral rather than a rhetorical analogy, he explains that this opening scene 'can be read as a kind of program (maybe in the tradition of the symphonic "ouverture," where the main themes and structures of the work are already presented in a nutshell)' (Baetens 2001: 97).
8. See primarily the work of Cornelia Butler Flora (1980) for analysis of the gender politics of the popular *roman-photo*. In 'The photo-novel, a minor medium?' Baetens (2012) also comments on the conservative gender politics of the medium (54), as does Russel B. Nye (1977), who declares that 'there is no women's liberation here' (746).
9. The figure of the (queer) child has received extensive and illuminating attention in recent queer theory. See, for instance, Steven Bruhm and Natasha Hurley (2004) and Kathryn Bond Stockton (2009).
10. See Dillon (2015b) for an extended discussion of the importance of rhythm when thinking through the relationship between deconstruction and film.
11. In 'Supreme Court' (1988), one of two essays he has written on *Right of Inspection*, David Wills identifies the tension between speed and slowness within deconstruction as a critical practice. Rather than support the traditional reading – that speed is inimical to the slow, careful pace of deconstruction – Wills seeks to recoup speed into the oblique reading practice he performs and proposes (see esp. pp. 24–7).
12. Derrida repeats this association of the photograph and the fetish in *Copy, Archive, Signature*: 'All photography is from the outset a fetish, the immediate possibility of a fetishization, in itself, if I can put it this way, as a photographic thing

(the thing itself is a fetish, that is what must be thought) and sometimes in what it shows . . . ' (*CAS* 33).
13. For Barthes the *punctum* is not the intentional focus of the photographer, the *Operator*, but this does not mean that its inclusion in the frame is accidental: 'the nuns "happened to be there," passing in the background, when Wessing photographed the Nicaraguan soldiers' (2000: 42) but, for the *Operator*, 'a whole causality explains the presence of the "detail": the Church implanted in these Latin-American countries, the nuns allowed to circulate as nurses, etc.' (2000: 42). The perception of the *punctum*'s incidentality lies with the *Spectator*, not the *Operator*: 'but from the *Spectator*'s viewpoint, the detail is offered by chance and for nothing; the scene is in no way "composed" according to a creative logic' (Barthes 2000: 42). The intentionality of set-design in film (the act of the *Operator*) therefore does not compromise the *Spectator*'s perception of certain elements of the mise-en-scène as *punctum*.
14. See Badmington (2012: 315, n. 8) for a comprehensive list of such work.
15. In 'Choreographies', Derrida summarises the critiques of Levinas and Heidegger in relation to the question of Woman, which he works through in detail in 'At This Very Moment in This Work Here I Am' (1984) and '*Geschlecht*: Sexual Difference, Ontological Difference' (1983) respectively. In the first text, he exposes the way in which Levinas' argument that sexual difference is secondary to 'humanity in general' (*C* 73) risks restoring 'the classical interpretation' which 'gives a masculine sexual marking to what is presented either as neutral originariness or, at least, as prior and superior to all sexual markings' (*C* 73). In the second text, he indicates that Heidegger's neutralisation – or, as Derrida suggests in 'Women in the Beehive', 'neuterization' (*WB* 194) – of *Dasein* also risks participating in exactly the same classical interpretation in that 'to the extent which universality implies neutralization, you can be sure that it's only a hidden way of confirming the man in his power' (*C* 194).

Bibliography

Anderst, Leah (2013), 'Memory's Chorus: *Stories We Tell* and Sarah Polley's Theory of Autobiography', *Senses of Cinema* 69 (December), http://sensesofcinema.com/2013/feature-articles/memorys-chorus-stories-we-tell-and-sarah-polleys-theory-of-autobiography/ (last accessed 18 September 2017).

Artmour, Ellen T. (1997), 'Questions of Proximity: "Woman's Place" in Derrida and Irigaray', *Hypatia* 12.1: 63–78.

Attridge, Derek (1992), 'Introduction', in Jacques Derrida, *Acts of Literature*, ed. Derek Attridge (London and New York: Routledge).

Bachmann, Michael (2008), 'Derrida on Film: Staging Spectral Sincerity', in Ernst van Alphen, Mieke Bal and Carel Smith (eds), *The Rhetoric of Sincerity* (Stanford: Stanford University Press), pp. 214–29.

Badmington, Neil (2012), '*Punctum Saliens*: Barthes, Mourning, Film, Photography', *Paragraph* 35.3: 303–19.

Baetens, Jan (2001), 'Going to Heaven: A Missing Link in the History of Photonarrative', *Journal of Narrative Theory* 31.1: 87–105.

Baetens, Jan (2009), 'How Many is Multi? On the example of Photo Narrative, High and Low', *Image & Narrative* 10.3: 73–82.

Baetens, Jan (2012), 'The photo-novel, a minor medium?', *NECSUS: European Journal of Media Studies* 1.1: 54–66.

Baker, Peter (1996), 'Deconstruction and the Question of Violence: *Fictions Letimimes* versus *Pulp Fiction*', *symploke* 4.1/2: 21–40.

Barad, Karen (2007), *Meeting the Universe Halfway: Quantum Physics and the Entanglement of Matter and Meaning* (Durham, NC: Duke University Press).

Barnouw, Erik (1974), *Documentary: A History of the Non-Fiction Film* (Oxford: Oxford University Press).

Barthes, Roland (1977), 'The Third Meaning: Research Notes on Some Eisenstein Stills', in *Image Music Text*, trans. Stephen Heath (New York: Hill and Wang), pp. 44–68.

Barthes, Roland [1980] (2000), *Camera Lucida: Reflections on Photography*, trans. Richard Howard (London: Vintage).

Baudry, Jean-Louis (1974–5), 'Ideological Effects of the Basic Cinematographic Apparatus', *Film Quarterly* 28.2: 39–47.

Bennington, Geoffrey (1993), 'Derridabase', in Geoffrey Bennington and Jacques Derrida, *Jacques Derrida* (Chicago and London: University of Chicago Press).

Bennington, Geoffrey (2008), 'A Life in Philosophy', in *Other Analyses: Reading Philosophy*, Createspace, pp. 403–23.

Bergstrom, Janet and Mary Ann Doane (1989), 'The Female Spectator: Contexts and Directions', *Camera Obscura*, Special Issue on 'The Spectatrix', 20/21: 5–27.

Blackmore, Susan (1999), *The Meme Machine* (Oxford: Oxford University Press).
Blaetz, Robin (2007), *Women's Experimental Cinema: Critical Frameworks* (Durham, NC and London: Duke University Press).
Boheemen-Saaf, Christine van (2013), 'Matricidal Writing: Philosophy's Endgame', in Andrew J. Mitchell and Sam Slote (eds), *Derrida and Joyce: Texts and Contexts* (Albany: State University of New York Press), pp. 183–200.
Bordwell, David and Noël Carroll (eds) (1996), *Post-Theory: Reconstructing Film Studies* (Madison: University of Wisconsin Press).
Borges, Jorge Luis (1960), *El hacedor*, http://www.literatura.us/borges/hacedor.html (last accessed 18 September 2017).
Borges, Jorge Luis (2000), *The Maker* [1960] in *The Aleph and Other Stories*, trans. Andrew Hurley (London: Penguin), pp. 137–78.
Bortolotti, Gary R. and Linda Hutcheon (2007), 'On the Origin of Adaptations: Rethinking Fidelity Discourse and "Success" – Biologically', *New Literary History* 38.3: 443–58.
Bowie, Andrew (2015), 'The "Philosophy of Performance" and the Performance of Philosophy', *Performance Philosophy* 1: 51–8, http://www.performancephilosophy.org/journal/article/view/31/83 (last accessed 18 September 2017).
Brinkema, Eugenie (2014), *The Forms of Affects* (Durham, NC: Duke University Press).
Bronski, Michael (1984), *Culture Clash: The Making of Gay Sensibility* (Boston: South End Press).
Brown, Mark (2017), 'British Cinema's Gender Imbalance Worse in 2017 than 1913, says BFI Study', *The Guardian*, 20 September, available at: https://www.theguardian.com/film/2017/sep/20/british-cinema-gender-imbalance-worse-2017-bfi-filmography?CMP=share_btn_tw (last accessed 21 September 2017).
Bruhm, Steven and Natasha Hurley (eds) (2004), *Curiouser: On the Queerness of Children* (London and Minneapolis: University of Minnesota Press).
Brunette, Peter (1998), 'Poststructuralism and Deconstruction', in John Hill and Pamela Church Gibson (eds), *The Oxford Guide to Film Studies* (Oxford: Oxford University Press), pp. 91–5.
Brunette, Peter and David Wills (1989), *Screen/Play: Derrida and Film Theory* (Princeton and Oxford: Princeton University Press).
Brunette, Peter and David Wills (eds) (1994), *Deconstruction and the Visual Arts: Art, Media, Architecture* (Cambridge: Cambridge University Press).
Bruss, Elizabeth (1980), 'Eye for I: Making and Unmaking Autobiography in Film', in James Olney (ed.), *Autobiography: Essays Theoretical and Critical* (Princeton: Princeton University Press), pp. 296–320.
Burchill, Louise (2009), 'Jacques Derrida', in Felicity Colman (ed.), *Film, Theory and Philosophy: The Key Thinkers* (Durham: Acumen), pp. 164–78.
Burt, Jonathan (2006), 'Morbidity and Vitalism: Derrida, Bergson, Deleuze and Animal Film Imagery', *Configurations* 14: 157–79.
Burton, Julianne (1990), 'Democratizing Documentary: Modes of Address in Latin American Cinema, 1958–1972', in Julianne Burton (ed.), *The Social Documentary in Latin America* (Pittsburgh: University of Pittsburgh Press), pp. 77–86.
Cahill, James Leo and Timothy Holland (eds) (2015a), *Discourse* 37.1–2, Special Issue: Derrida and Cinema.
Cahill, James Leo and Timothy Holland (2015b), 'Double Exposures: Derrida and Cinema, an Introductory Séance', *Discourse* 37.1–2 (Winter/Spring): 3–21.
Callaghan, Joanna (2010), *A Mind's Eye* Feature, *Screenworks* 3 (June), http://screenworks.org.uk/archive/volume-3/a-minds-eye (last accessed 18 September 2017).

Callaghan, Joanna (2012), 'Mashing Up Derrida and Film', *Frames* 1, http://framescinemajournal.com/article/mashing-up-derrida-and-film/ (last accessed 18 September 2017).
Callaghan, Joanna (2014), 'Reflections', in Joanna Callaghan and Martin McQuillan, *Love in the Post: From Plato to Derrida – The Screenplay and Commentary* (London and New York: Rowman & Littlefield), pp. 57–95.
Callaghan, Joanna (2016), *Love in the Post: From Plato to Derrida* Feature, *Screenworks* 6, http://screenworks.org.uk/archive/volume-6/love-in-the-post (last accessed 18 September 2017).
Callaghan, Joanna and Martin McQuillan (2014), *Love in the Post: From Plato to Derrida – The Screenplay and Commentary* (London and New York: Rowman & Littlefield).
Caputo, John D. (1997), *Deconstruction in a Nutshell: A Conversation with Jacques Derrida* (New York: Fordham University Press).
Case, Sue-Ellen (1988–9), 'Toward a Butch-Femme Aesthetic', *Discourse* 11.1, Special Issue: Body / Masquerade (Fall–Winter): 55–73.
Casetti, Francesco (2015), *The Lumière Galaxy: Seven Key words for the Cinema to Come* (Columbia: Columbia University Press).
Castle, Terry (1993), *The Apparitional Lesbian: Female Homosexuality and Modern Culture* (New York: Columbia University Press).
Causseu, Jean-Max (2006), Director: La Filmotéque Quartier Latin (January 2006, Paris), Interview with Ken McMullen, 'Special Features', *Ghost Dance*, Mediabox DVD.
Cavarero, Adriana (1995), *In Spite of Plato: A Feminist Rewriting of Ancient Philosophy* (Cambridge: Polity Press).
Child, Ben and Nigel M. Smith (2015), 'Hollywood Prejudice Against Female Directors to Have US Equal Opportunity Enquiry', *The Guardian*, 7 October, http://www.theguardian.com/film/2015/oct/07/us-hollywood-discrimination-prejudice-female-directors-equal-opportunities (last accessed 18 September 2017).
Chisholm, Ann (2000), 'Missing Persons and Bodies of Evidence', *Camera Obscura* 43 15.1: 123-61.
Chisholm, Dianne (1993), Review of *Screen/Play*, *Screen* 34.2: 190–5.
Cholodenko, Lisa (2004), 'Talking About Women: A Conversation between Frances McDormand, Lisa Cholodenko and Emily Mortimer', *Projections 13 – Women Film-Makers on Film-Making*: 2–26.
Chow, Rey (2006), 'Poststructuralism: Theory as Critical Self-Consciousness', in Ellen Rooney (ed.), *The Cambridge Companion to Feminist Literary Theory* (Cambridge: Cambridge University Press), pp. 195–210.
Chow, Ray (2009), '"I Insist on the Christian Dimension": On Forgiveness . . . and the Outside of the Human', *differences* 20.2/3: 224–49.
Citron, Michelle (1999), 'Fleeing from Documentary: Autobiographical Film/Video and the "Ethics of Responsibility"', in Diane Waldman and Janet Walker (eds), *Feminism and Documentary* (Minneapolis: Minnesota University Press), pp. 271–86.
Clayton, Alex and Andrew Klevan (eds) (2011), *The Language and Style of Film Criticism* (London and New York: Routledge).
Colebrook, Claire (1997), 'Feminist Philosophy and the Philosophy of Feminism: Irigaray and the History of Western Metaphysics', *Hypatia* 12.1: 79–98.
Conley, Tom (1991), *Film Hieroglyphics: Ruptures in Classical Cinema* (Minneapolis: University of Minnesota Press).
Cull Ó Maoilearca, Laura and A. Lagaay (eds) (2014), *Encounters in Performance Philosophy* (Basingstoke: Palgrave Macmillan).

D'Cruz, Carolyn and Glenn D'Cruz (2013), '"Even the Ghost was more than one person: Hauntology and Authenticity in Todd Hayne's *I'm Not There*', *Film-Philosophy* 17.1: 315–30.
Dasgupta, Guatam (1975), 'Juliet Berto & Dominique Labourier', Interview, *Film* 24 (March): 21–3.
Dawkins, Richard (2006), *The Selfish Gene*, 3rd edn (Oxford: Oxford University Press).
de Lauretis, Teresa (1987), *Technologies of Gender* (Bloomington: Indiana University Press).
de Lauretis, Teresa (1988), 'Sexual Indifference and Lesbian Representation', *Theatre Journal* 40.2: 155–77.
de Lauretis, Teresa (1991), 'Film and the Visible' in Bad Object-Choices (eds), *How Do I Look? Queer Film and Video* (Seattle: Bay Press), pp. 223–64.
Deleuze, Gilles [1986] (2005), *Cinema 1: The Movement-Image*, trans. Hugh Tomlinson and Barbara Habberjam (London: Continuum).
Deutscher, Penelope (1997), *Yielding Gender: Feminism, Deconstruction and the History of Philosophy* (London: Routledge).
Deutscher, Penelope (2005), 'Derrida's Impossible Genealogies', *Theory and Event* 8.1: 1–13.
Deutscher, Penelope (2007), '"Women, and so on": Derrida's Rogues and the Auto-Immunity of Feminism', *Symposium: Canadian Journal of Continental Philosophy* 11.1: 101–19.
Deutscher, Penelope (2013), 'The Membrane and the Diaphragm: Derrida and Esposito on Immunity, Community, and Birth', *Angelaki* 18.3: 49–68.
Diawara, Manthia (1990), 'Black British Cinema: Spectatorship and Identity Formation in *Territories*', *Public Culture* 3.1: 33–48.
Dienst, Richard (1995), *Still Life in Real Time: Theory After Television* (Durham, NC: Duke University Press).
Dick, Kirby (2005), 'Resting on the Edge of an Impossible Confidence', in Kirby Dick and Amy Ziering Kofman (eds), *Screenplay and Essays on the Film* Derrida (Manchester: Manchester University Press), pp. 36–49.
Dillon, Sarah (2006), 'Life After Derrida: Anacoluthia and the Agrammaticality of Following', *Research in Phenomenology* 36: 97–114.
Dillon, Sarah (2007), *The Palimpsest* (London: Bloomsbury Academic).
Dillon, Sarah (2011), 'Time for the Gift of Dance', in Ben Davies and Jana Funk (eds), *Sex, Gender and Time in Literature and Culture* (Basingstoke: Palgrave Macmillan), pp. 109–31.
Dillon, Sarah (2015a), 'Cinematic Incorporation: Literature in *My Life Without Me*', *Film Philosophy* 19: 55–66.
Dillon, Sarah (2015b), '"Talking about the same questions but at another rhythm": Deconstruction and Film', in Dragan Kujundžić (ed.), *The First Sail: J. Hillis Miller A Film-Book* (Open Humanities Press/University of Michigan Online Publications), pp. 86–101.
Dillon, Sarah (2015c), 'Literary Equivocation: Reproductive Futurism and *The Ice People*', in Sarah Dillon and Caroline Edwards (eds), *Maggie Gee: Critical Essays* (Canterbury: Gylphi), pp. 101–32.
Dillon, Sarah (2017), 'Derrida and the Question of "Woman"', in Christian Hite (ed.), *Derrida and Queer Theory* (Brooklyn: Punctum Books), pp. 108–30.
Dillon, Sarah and John Schad (eds) (2017), *Derrida Today* 10:2, Special Issue: Imagining Derrida.
Donaldson-McHugh, Shannon and Don Moore (2006), 'Film Adaptation, Co-Authorship, and Hauntology: Gus Van Sant's *Psycho* (1998)', *The Journal of Popular Culture* 39.2: 225–33.
Dowd, A. A. (2013), 'Sarah Polley (Interview)', *A. V. Club*, 17 May, http://www.avclub.com/article/sarah-polley-on-laying-her-family-history-bare-in--97550 (last accessed 18 September 2017).

Dronsfield, Jonathan Lahey (2014), 'Filming Deconstruction/Deconstructing Film', in Joanna Callaghan and Martin McQuillan, *Love in the Post: From Plato to Derrida – The Screenplay and Commentary* (London and New York: Rowman & Littlefield), pp. 213–37.

Easthope, Anthony (1996), 'Derrida and British Film Theory', in John Brannigan, Ruth Robbins and Julian Wolfreys (eds), *Applying: To Derrida* (London: Macmillan), pp. 184–94.

Elam, Diane (1994), *Feminism and Deconstruction: Ms. En Abyme* (London: Routledge).

Élouard, Michele Zoey (2006), 'Missing: On the Politics of Re/Presentation', in Annette Burfoot and Susan Lord (eds), *Killing Women: The Visual Culture of Gender and Violence* (Waterloo, ON: Wilfred Laurier University Press), pp. 47–65.

Ensslin, Astrid, Pawel Frelik and Lisa Swanstrom (eds) (2017), *Paradoxa*, Special Issue: Small Screen Fiction.

Erens, Patricia (1988), 'Women's Documentary Filmmaking: The Personal is Political' [1981], in Alan Rosenthal (ed.), *New Challenges for Documentary* (Berkeley: University of California Press), pp. 554–65.

Fathy, Safaa (2008), 'Images', *diacritics* 38.1–2, https://muse.jhu.edu/article/316969/pdf (last accessed 18 September 2017).

Feder, Ellen K. and Emily Zankin (1997), 'Flirting with the Truth: Derrida's Discourse with "Woman" and Wenches', in Ellen K. Feder, Mary C. Rawlinson and Emily Zankin (eds), *Derrida and Feminism: Recasting the Question of Woman* (New York and London: Routledge), pp. 21–51.

Feder, Ellen K., Mary C. Rawlinson and Emily Zankin (eds) (1997), *Derrida and Feminism: Recasting the Question of Woman* (New York and London: Routledge).

Fisher, Mark (2013), 'The Metaphysics of Crackle: Afrofuturism and Hauntology', *dancecult* 5.2: 42–55.

Flaxman, Gregory, Robert Sinnerbrink and Lisa Trahair (2016), *Understanding Cinematic Thinking: Film-Philosophy in Bresson, von Trier and Haneke* (Edinburgh: Edinburgh University Press).

Flora, Cornelia Butler (1990), '*Fotonovelas*: Message Creation and Reception', *Journal of Popular Culture* 14.3: 524–34.

Fordy, Tom (2015), 'London Film Festival: Why 2015 is the Year for Strong Women', *The Telegraph*, 5 October, http://www.telegraph.co.uk/women/womens-life/11907336/London-Film-Festival-Why-2015-is-the-year-for-strong-women.html (last accessed 18 September 2017).

Fox, Michael (2013), '*Stories We Tell* with Sarah Polley', *Fandor*, 9 May, https://www.fandor.com/keyframe/stories-we-tell-with-sarah-polley (last accessed 18 September 2017).

Frampton, Daniel (2006), *Filmosophy* (New York: Wallflower Press).

Gaines, Jane (1984), 'Women and Representation', *Jump Cut* 29 (February): 25–7.

Gibbs, John and Douglas Pye (eds) (2005), *Style and Meaning: Studies in the Detailed Analysis of Film* (Manchester and New York: Manchester University Press).

Gledhill, Christine and Linda Williams (eds) (2000), *Reinventing Film Studies* (London: Arnold).

Gonzalez-Arnal, Stella, Gill Jagger and Kathleen Lennon (eds) (2012), *Embodied Selves* (Basingstoke: Palgrave).

Grosz, Elizabeth (1997), 'Ontology and Equivocation: Derrida's Politics of Sexual Difference', in Nancy Holland (ed.), *Feminist Interpretations of Jacques Derrida* (University Park: The Pennsylvania State University Press), pp. 73–101.

Guardiola-Rivera, Oscar (2006), Interview, 'Special Features', *Ghost Dance*, dir. Ken McMullen, Mediabox DVD.

Haddad, Samir (2013), *Derrida and the Inheritance of Democracy* (Bloomington: Indiana University Press).
Hallas, Roger (2003), 'Aids and Gay Cinephilia', *Camera Obscura* 52: 84–127.
Harvey, Elizabeth (1992), *Ventriloquized Voices: Feminist Theory and English Renaissance Texts* (London: Routledge).
Heath, Stephen (1976), 'On Screen, In Frame: Film and Ideology', *Quarterly Review of Film Studies* 1.3: 251–65.
Herzogenrath, Bernd (ed.) (2007), *Film as Philosophy* (Minneapolis: University of Minnesota Press).
Hill, Leslie (2010), *Radical Indecision: Barthes, Blanchot, Derrida, and the Future of Criticism* (Notre Dame: University of Notre Dame Press).
Hillis Miller, J. (1987), *The Ethics of Reading* (New York: Columbia University Press).
Hillis Miller, J. (2014), 'But I love literature . . . me too (*moi aussi*)', in Joanna Callaghan and Martin McQuillan, *Love in the Post: From Plato to Derrida – The Screenplay and Commentary* (London and New York: Rowman & Littlefield), pp. 171–84.
Holland, Nancy (ed.) (1997), *Feminist Interpretations of Jacques Derrida* (University Park: The Pennsylvania State University Press).
Holland, Timothy (2015), '*Ses Fantômes*: The Traces of Derrida's Cinema', *Discourse* 37.1–2 (Winter/Spring): 40–62.
hooks, bell (1993), 'The Oppositional Gaze: Black Female Spectators', in Manthia Diawara (ed.), *Black American Cinema* (New York and London: Routledge), pp. 288–302.
Huffer, Lynne (2013), *Are the Lips a Grave? A Queer Feminist on the Ethics of Sex* (New York: Columbia University Press).
Jenkins, Steven (1984), Review of *Ghost Dance*, *Monthly Film Bulletin* 51.600 (1 Jan): 45.
Johnston, Claire (1973), 'Women's Cinema as Counter-Cinema', in Claire Johnston (ed.), *Notes on Women's Cinema* (London: Society for Education in Film and Television).
Juhasz, Alexandra (1994), '"They said we were trying to show reality – all I want to show is my video": the politics of the realist feminist documentary', *Screen* 35.2 (Summer): 171–90.
Kamuf, Peggy (2005), 'The Sacrifice of Sarah', in *Book of Addresses* (Stanford: Stanford University Press), pp. 102–13.
Kamuf, Peggy (2010), 'Stunned: Derrida on Film', in *To Follow: The Wake of Jacques Derrida* (Edinburgh: Edinburgh University Press), pp. 108–19.
Kamuf, Peggy and Samuel Weber (2015), 'Double Features: An Interview with Samuel Weber', *Discourse* 37.1–2 (Winter/Spring): 148–64.
Keegan, Rebecca (2016), 'Gender bias in Hollywood? U.S. digs deeper to investigate the industry's hiring practices', *Los Angeles Times*, 11 May http://www.latimes.com/entertainment/movies/la-et-mn-0512-aclu-women-directors-update-20160509-snap-story.html (last accessed 18 September 2017).
Kellaway, Kate (2013), 'Sarah Polley', *The Guardian*, Sunday 23 June, http://www.theguardian.com/film/2013/jun/23/sarah-polley-stories-we-tell-interview (last accessed 18 September 2017).
Kofman, Gil (2005), '*Derrida*: Film to Text Adaptation', in Kirby Dick and Amy Ziering Kofman, *Screenplay and Essays on the Film* Derrida (Manchester: Manchester University Press), pp. 51–109.
Kumar, Niven, and Lucyna Swiatek (2012), 'Representations of New Terror: "Auto-anomie" in the films of Michael Haneke', *Journal of Postcolonial Writing* 48.3: 311–21.
Ladenson, Elisabeth (2000), *Proust's Lesbianism* (Ithaca: Cornell University Press).

Lapsely, Robert and Michael Westlake (2006), *Film Theory: An Introduction*, 2nd edn (Manchester: Manchester University Press).
Lesage, Julia (1981), '*Céline and Julie Go Boating*: Subversive Fantasy', *Jump Cut* 24–5 (March), http://www.ejumpcut.org/archive/onlinessays/JC24-25folder/CelineJulie.html (last accessed 18 September 2017).
Lesage, Julia (1986), 'Political aesthetics of the Feminist Documentary Film' [1978], in Charlotte Brunsdon (ed.), *Films for Women* (London: BFI Publishing), pp. 14–23.
Liddell, Henry George and Robert Scott (1996), *A Greek Lexicon* (Oxford: Clarendon Press).
Lieberman, Rhonda (2002), 'Jacques Le Narcissiste', *Artforum*, October: 35–7.
Lippit, Akira Mizuta (1990), Review of *Screen/Play*, *MLN* 105.5: 1130–3.
Lippit, Akira Mizuta (2016), *Cinema Without Reflection: Jacques Derrida's Echopoiesis and Narcissism Adrift* (Minneapolis: University of Minnesota Press).
Lodge, Guy (2012), 'Review of *Stories We Tell*', *Variety* 428.4 (3–9 September): 40.
Luckhurst, Roger (1996), '(Touching On) Tele-Technology', in John Brannigan, Ruth Robbins and Julian Wolfreys (eds), *Applying: To Derrida* (London: Macmillan), pp. 171–83.
Lussier, Germain (2013), 'Film Interview: Sarah Polley Explains Secrets of Her Brilliant Documentary: *Stories We Tell*', Slashfilm.com, 17 May, http://www.slashfilm.com/film-interview-sarah-polley-explains-secrets-of-her-brilliant-documentary-stories-we-tell/ (last accessed 18 September 2017).
Macy, Marianne, Kirby Dick and Amy Ziering Kofman (2005), 'Interview with Filmmakers', in Kirby Dick and Amy Ziering Kofman, *Screenplay and Essays on the Film* Derrida (Manchester: Manchester University Press), pp. 128–37.
Malabou, Catherine (2014), 'Cinema is not a brain reading', in Joanna Callaghan and Martin McQuillan, *Love in the Post: From Plato to Derrida – The Screenplay and Commentary* (London and New York: Rowman & Littlefield), pp. 157–69.
Malone, Alice (2017), *Backwards and in Heels: The Past, Present and Future of Women Working in Film* (Miami: Mango).
Manon, Hugh S. (2006), 'Seeing Through Seeing Through: The "Trompe L'Oeil" Effect and Bodily Difference in the Cinema of Tod Browning', *Framework* 47.1 (Spring): 60–82.
Marder, Elissa and Andrew Parker (2013), 'The Maternal Turn: Elissa Marder and Andrew Parker', *The Los Angeles Review of Books*, 28 February, https://lareviewofbooks.org/article/the-maternal-turn-elissa-marder-and-andrew-parker/ (last accessed 18 September 2017).
Marks, Laura U. (2000), *The Skin of the Film: Intercultural Cinema, Embodiment, and the Senses* (Durham, NC: Duke University Press).
Marks, Laura U. (2002), *Sensuous Theory and Multisensory Media* (Minneapolis: University of Minnesota Press).
Marsh, Steven (2013), 'Turns and Returns, *Envois/Renvois*: The Postal Effect in Recent Spanish Filmmaking', *Discourse* 35.1: 24–45.
Maslin, Janet (1984), Review of *Ghost Dance*, *The New York Times*, 31 October, http://www.nytimes.com/movie/review?res=9D06E1D9143AF932A05753C1A962948260 (last accessed 18 September 2017).
Mayer, Sophie (2013), 'Film of the week: *Stories We Tell*', *Sight and Sound* 23.7 (July): 87–8, http://www.bfi.org.uk/news-opinion/sight-sound-magazine/reviews-recommendations/film-week-stories-we-tell (last accessed 18 September 2017).
Mayer, Sophie (2015), *Political Animals: The New Feminist Cinema* (London: I. B. Tauris).
Mayne, Judith (1991), 'Lesbian Looks: Dorothy Arzner and Female Authorship', in Bad Object-Choices (eds), *How Do I Look? Queer Film and Video* (Seattle: Bay Press), pp. 103–43.

McCarthy, Nick (2013), '*Stories We Tell*', *Slate Magazine*, 18 March, http://www.slantmagazine.com/film/review/stories-we-tell (last accessed 18 September 2017).
McFarlane, Brian (1996), *Novel to Film: An Introduction to the Theory of Adaptation* (Oxford: Clarendon).
McGarry, Eileen (1975), 'Documentary, Realism, and Women's Cinema', *Women & Film* 2.7: 50–9, http://www.ejumpcut.org/archive/WomenAndFilm/WF7/50.html (last accessed 18 September 2017).
McMahon, Laura (2012a), 'From Homofraternity to Hospitality: Deconstructing the Political with Derrida and the Dardennes', *French Studies* LXVI.4: 510–24.
McMahon, Laura (2012b), 'Unwinding the Anthropological Machine: Animality, Film and Arnaud des Pallières', *Paragraph* 35.3: 373–88.
McMullen, Ken (1995), 'Back From the Future', *Vertigo* 1:5 (Autumn–Winter).
McMullen, Ken (2009), 'An Organisation of Dreams', *Vertigo* 28.
McMullen, Ken (2012), 'Immortality and Cinema', 27 March, http://backdoorbroadcasting.net/2012/03/ken-mcmullen-immortality-and-cinema/ (last accessed 18 September 2017).
McQuillan, Martin (2014), 'The Legs of Freud: A Note on Autobiography in Derrida's *The Post Card*', in Joanna Callaghan and Martin McQuillan, *Love in the Post: From Plato to Derrida – The Screenplay and Commentary* (London and New York: Rowman & Littlefield), pp. 97–111.
Mellinger, Leonie (2006), In Conversation with Ken McMullen (Jan 2006), 'Special Features', *Ghost Dance*, dir. Ken McMullen, Mediabox DVD.
Morris, Christopher D. (2000), 'Reading the Birds and *The Birds*', *Literature Film Quarterly* 28.4: 250–8.
Morris, Christopher D. (2002), *The Hanging Figure: On Suspense and the Films of Alfred Hitchcock* (Praeger).
Mulhall, Stephen (2008), *On Film*, 2nd edn (London: Routledge).
Mullarkey, John (2009), *Philosophy and the Moving Image: Refractions of Reality* (Basingstoke: Palgrave Macmillan).
Mulvey, Laura (1975), 'Visual Pleasure and Narrative Cinema', *Screen* 16.3: 6–18.
Mulvey, Laura (2006), *Death 24x a Second: Stillness and the Moving Image* (London: Reaktion Books).
Mulvey, Laura and Anna Backman Rogers (eds) (2015), *Feminisms: Diversity, Difference and Multiplicity in Contemporary Film Cultures* (Amsterdam: Amsterdam University Press).
Newton, Judith and Nancy Hoffman (1988), *Feminist Studies* 14.1, Special Issue: Feminism and Deconstruction.
Norman, Barnaby (2013), 'Time of Death: Herzog/Derrida', *The Oxford Literary Review* 35.2: 205–20.
Nye, Russel, B. (1977), '*Miroir de la vie*: The French Photoroman and its Audience', *Journal of Popular Culture* 10.4: 744–51.
Oswald, Laura (1986), 'Semiotics and/or deconstruction: In quest of cinema', *Semiotica* 60.3/4: 315–41.
Park, Eun-Jee (2012), 'The Politics of Friendship and Paternity: The Dardenne Brother's *Rosetta*', *Studies in French Cinema* 12.2: 137–49.
Parker, Andrew (2012), *The Theorist's Mother* (Durham, NC: Duke University Press).
Peeters, Benoît and Marie-François Plissart (1995), '*Roman-photo* Revisited', *History of Photography*, Special Issue: Photo Narrative, ed. Mireille Ribière, 19.4: 298–300.
Peeters, Benoît (2012), *Derrida: A Biography*, trans. Andrew Brown (Cambridge: Polity Press).
Penley, Constance (1985), 'Feminism, Film Theory, and the Bachelor Machines', *m/f* 10: 39–59.

Plato (2009), *Phaedo*, trans. David Gallop (Oxford: Oxford University Press).
Plissart, Marie-Françoise (1995), 'Aujourd'hui: Suite photographique', *History of Photography*, Special Issue: Photo Narrative, ed. Mireille Ribière, 19.4: 301–11.
Plissart, Marie-Françoise [1985] (1998), *Right of Inspection* (New York: The Monacelli Press).
Poore, Benjamin (2015), 'Philosophy on Film', *Time Higher Education Supplement*, 10 September, https://www.timeshighereducation.com/features/philosophy-in-cinema (last accessed 18 September 2017).
Porton, Richard (2013), 'Family Viewing: An Interview with Sarah Polley', *Cineaste* (Summer): 36–40.
Proust, Marcel (2002), *The Prisoner*, trans. Carol Clark, in *The Prisoner and The Fugitive, In Search of Lost Time*, Vol. 5 (London: Penguin).
Read, Rupert and Jerry Goodenough (eds) (2005), *Film as Philosophy: Essays in Cinema after Wittgenstein and Cavell* (Basingstoke: Palgrave Macmillan).
Review of *Ghost Dance*, *Time Out*, no date, http://www.timeout.com/london/film/ghost-dance (last accessed 18 September 2017).
Reynolds, Simon (2006), 'Society of the Spectral', *The Wire* 273 (November): 26–33.
Reynolds, Simon (2011), *Retromania: Pop Culture's Addiction to Its Own Past* (London: Faber & Faber).
Richards, K. Malcolm (2008), *Derrida Reframed: A Guide for the Arts Student* (London: I. B. Tauris).
Riel, Trine (2015), 'The Philosopher Cameo', *Kinema* 44 (Fall): 93–106.
Riffaterre, Michael (1978), *Semiotics of Poetry* (Bloomington and London: Indiana University Press).
Robb, David (2015), 'Feds Officially Probing Hollywood's Lack of Female Directors', *Deadline*, 6 October, http://deadline.com/2015/10/female-directors-hollywood-federal-investigation-eeoc-1201568487/ (last accessed 18 September 2017).
Robb, David (2017), 'EEOC: Major Studios Failed to Hire Female Directors; Lawsuits Loom', *Deadline*, 15 February, http://deadline.com/2017/02/hollywood-studios-female-directors-eeoc-investigation-1201912590/ (last accessed 18 September 2017).
Robertson, Pamela (1996), *Guilty Pleasures: Feminist Camp from Mae West to Madonna* (London and New York: I. B. Tauris).
Ropars-Wuilleumier, Marie-Claire (1980), 'The Disembodied Voice: *India Song*', *Yale French Studies* 60: 241–68.
Ropars-Wuilleumier, Marie-Claire (1981), *Le texte divisé: essai sur l'écriture filmique* (Paris: PUF).
Rosen, Philip (1981), 'The Politics of the Sign and Film Theory', *October* 17 (Summer): 2–21.
Royle, Nicholas (2015), 'Blind Cinema', *Discourse* 37.1–2: 117–37.
Ruby, Jay (2005), 'The Image Mirrored: Reflexivity and the Documentary Film', in Alan Rosenthal (ed.), *New Challenges for Documentary*, 2nd edn (Manchester: Manchester University Press), pp. 34–47.
Schopenhauer, Arthur (2004), *Essays and Aphorisms*, trans. R. J. Hollingdale (London: Penguin. Kindle Edition).
Schor, Naomi (1986), 'Female Fetishism: The Case of George Sand', in Susan Suleiman (ed.), *The Female Body in Western Culture* (Cambridge, MA: Harvard University Press), pp. 363–72.
Schor, Naomi (1987), *Reading in Detail: Aesthetics and the Feminine* (New York: Methuen).
Schwartz, Louis-George (2006), 'Cinema and the Meaning of "Life"', *Discourse* 28.2 & 3: 7–27.

Sedgwick, Eve Kosofsky (1991), *Epistemology of the Closet* (Hemel Hempstead: Harvester Wheatsheaf).
Sedgwick, Eve Kosofsky (1993), *Tendencies* (Durham, NC and London: Duke University Press).
Sinnerbrink, Robert (2011), *New Philosophies of Film: Thinking Images* (London: Continuum).
Sinnerbrink, Robert (2016), 'Photobiographies: The 'Derrida' documentaries as film-philosophy', *NECSUS: European Journal of Media Studies*, 11 July, http://www.necsus-ejms.org/photobiographies-derrida-documentaries-film-philosophy/ (last accessed 18 September 2017).
Smith, Murray and Thomas E. Wartenberg (eds) (2006), *Thinking Through Cinema: Film as Philosophy* (Oxford: Blackwell).
Smith, Robert (1995), *Derrida and Autobiography* (Cambridge: Cambridge University Press).
Smuts, Aaron (2009), 'Film as Philosophy: In Defence of a Bold Thesis', *The Journal of Aesthetics and Art Criticism* 67.4: 409–20.
Snider, Eric. D (2002), Review of *Derrida*, 23 October, http://www.ericdsnider.com/movies/derrida/ (last accessed 18 September 2017).
Sontag, Susan (1982a), 'Notes on "Camp"' [1964], in Elizabeth Hardwick (ed.), *A Susan Sontag Reader* (London: Penguin), pp. 105–19.
Sontag, Susan (1982b), 'The *Salmagundi* Interview' [1975/76], in Elizabeth Hardwick (ed.), *A Susan Sontag Reader* (London: Penguin), pp. 329–46.
Spillers, Hortense J. (1984), 'Interstices: A Small Drama of Words', in Carol Vance (ed.), *Pleasure and Danger: Exploring Female Sexuality* (Boston and London: Routledge & Kegan Paul), pp. 73–100.
Spivak, Gayatri Chakravorty (1984), 'Love Me, Love My Ombre, Elle', *diacritics* 14.4: 19–36.
Spivak, Gayatri Chakravorty (1997), 'Displacement and the Discourse of Woman', in Nancy Holland (ed.), *Feminist Interpretations of Jacques Derrida* (University Park: The Pennsylvania State University Press), pp. 43–71.
Stevens, Brad (2008), 'Review: *Inland Empire/Céline et Julie vont en bateau*', *Sight and Sound* 18.8 (August): 39.
Stewart, Tyson (no date), 'Spectral Media in Ken McMullen's *Ghost Dance* (1983) and *Zina* (1985)', Conference Paper, http://www.academia.edu/9711403/Spectral_Media_in_Ken_McMullen_s_Ghost_Dance_1983_and_Zina_1985_ (last accessed 18 September 2017).
Stockton, Kathryn Bond (2009), *The Queer Child, Or Growing Sideways in the Twentieth Century* (Durham, NC and London: Duke University Press).
Teodoro, José (2013), 'Knowing You, Knowing Me', *Film Comment* 49.3 (May/June): 52–5.
The Midnight Mollusc (2013), Review of *Ghost Dance*, 3 November, http://themidnightmollusc.blogspot.co.uk/2013/11/ghost-dance.html (last accessed 18 September 2017).
Thomson, Stephen (2012), 'Derrida and the Child: Ethics, Pathos, Property, Risk', *Oxford Literary Review* 25.1: 337–59.
Ulmer, Gregory (1981), 'The post-age', review of Jacques Derrida, *La Carte Postale: de Socrate à Freud et au-delà*, *diacritics* 11.3 (Autumn): 39–56.
Ulmer, Gregory L. (1985), *Applied Grammatology: Post(e)-Pedagogy from Jacques Derrida to Joseph Beuys* (Baltimore: The Johns Hopkins University Press).
Ulmer, Gregory L. (1994), *Heuretics: The Logic of Invention* (Baltimore: The Johns Hopkins University Press).
Ulmer, Gregory L. (2004), *Teletheory*, 2nd edn. (New York: Atropos Press).
Walker, Janet and Diane Waldman (1999), 'Introduction', in Diane Waldman and Janet Walker (eds), *Feminism and Documentary* (Minneapolis: Minnesota University Press), pp. 1–35.

Wartenberg, Thomas E. (2007), *Thinking on Screen: Film as Philosophy* (New York: Routledge).
Weber, Samuel (2014), 'The rubric of narcissism that no one escapes', in Joanna Callaghan and Martin McQuillan, *Love in the Post: From Plato to Derrida – The Screenplay and Commentary* (London and New York: Rowman & Littlefield), pp. 185–98.
Weber, Samuel (2015), 'Double Features: An Interview with Samuel Weber', with Peggy Kamuf, trans. Peggy Kamuf, *Discourse* 37.1–2: 148–64.
West, Dennis and Joan M. West (2012), 'The Invisible War Within the Military: An Interview with Kirby Dick', *Cineaste* 37.4 (Fall): 10–15.
Wills, David (1984), 'Post/Card/Match/Book/"Envois"/Derrida', *Substance* 43, 13.2: 19–38.
Wills, David (1988), 'Supreme Court', *Diacritics* 18.3: 20–31.
Wills, David (1989), 'Deposition: Introduction to *Right of Inspection* [*Droit de Regards*]', *Art & Text* 32 (Autumn): 10–18.
Wills, David (2004), 'Derrida, Now and Then, Here and There', *Theory & Event* 7.2: no pagination.
Witt, Michael (2003), Review of *Derrida*, *Sight and Sound* 37 (March): 37–8.
Ziarek, Ewa Plonowska (1997), 'From Euthanasia to the Other of Reason: Performativity and the Deconstruction of Sexual Difference', in Ellen K. Feder, Mary C. Rawlinson and Emily Zankin (eds), *Derrida and Feminism: Recasting the Question of Woman* (New York and London: Routledge), pp. 115–40.
Ziering Kofman, Amy (2005), 'Making *Derrida* – An Impression Or . . . ', in Kirby Dick and Amy Ziering Kofman, *Screenplay and Essays on the Film* Derrida (Manchester: Manchester University Press), pp. 22–35.

Filmography

A Mind's Eye, short, directed by Joanna Callaghan. UK: Heraclitus Pictures, 2008.

'Adaptation', video essay, produced by Joanna Callaghan. UK: Heraclitus Pictures, 2010, http://loveinthepost.co.uk/research-in-progress/

Céline et Julie vont en bateau: Phantom Ladies Over Paris, feature, directed by Jacques Rivette. France: Les Films du Losange et al., 1974.

D'Ailleurs, Derrida, documentary, directed by Safaa Fathy. France: Gloria Films, La Sept Arte, Kinotar Oy, 1999.

Daughter Rite, feature, directed by Michelle Citron. USA: Iris Films, 1978, http://www.cinenova.org/

'Deconstructive Film', HDV, produced by Joanna Callaghan. London, UK: Heraclitus Pictures, 2010, http://loveinthepost.co.uk/research-in-progress/

Derrida, documentary, directed by Kirby Dick and Amy Ziering Kofman. USA: Jane Doe Films, 2002.

DO NOT READ THIS, short, directed by Joanna Callaghan. London, UK: Heraclitus Pictures, 2012.

Ghost Dance, feature, directed by Ken McMullen. UK: Channel Four Films et al., 1983.

Grey Gardens, documentary, directed by Ellen Hovde, Albert Maysles, David Maysles and Muffie Meyer. USA: 1975.

'Letters', HDV, directed by Joanna Callaghan, UK: Heraclitus Pictures, 2010, http://loveinthepost.co.uk/research-in-progress/

'Love', short documentary, directed by Joanna Callaghan. UK: Heraclitus Pictures, 2010, http://loveinthepost.co.uk/research-in-progress/

Love in the Post: From Plato to Derrida, feature, directed by Joanna Callaghan. UK: Heraclitus Pictures, 2014.

Meshes of the Afternoon, short, directed by Maya Deren. USA: 1943.

'Postal', animation, directed by Joanna Callaghan. UK: Heraclitus Pictures, 2010, http://loveinthepost.co.uk/research-in-progress/

Stories We Tell, documentary, directed by Sarah Polley. Canada: National Film Board of Canada, 2012.

Index

Note: *italic* page number indicates figure; n indicates note

A Mind's Eye (Callaghan, 2008), 70
Abraham, Nicolas, 40
Adami, Camilla, 24
adaptation, 78–9
Albertine (Rose), 5
Allegories of Reading (De Man), 1
anacolutha, 1, 2–5
Archive Fever (Derrida), 45
Arquette, Patricia, 10
art, 14–16, 17
Artmour, Ellen T., 22
'*As if* I were Dead' (Derrida), 33
Athens, Still Remains (Derrida), 140–1
Attridge, Derek, 101
autobiography, 8, 97–8, 120–1
  and Derrida, 105, 109, 121–4
  and *quer*, 112, 114–15, 116–20
  see also *Daughter Rite*; *Stories We Tell*
avant-garde film, 30, 31, 45

Backman Rogers, Anna, 11
Badmington, Neil, 144
Baetens, Jan, 131, 144–5
Barad, Karen, 22
Barison, David, 90
Barker, Stephen, 72, 109
Barthes, Roland, 141, 142–4
Bennington, Geoffrey, 22, 23, 101, 105, *106*, 124
Bernstein, Maxine, 57
Berto, Juliet, 59, 60
biography, 8, 98–100, 105, 108–9
Black feminist film theory, 30–1
body, the, 14, 15, 17, 50
Boheemen-Saaf, Christine van, 83–4
Bonhomme, Jean-François, 16, 140
Borges, Jorge Luis, 9, 144, 145, *146*, 147–8
Bortolotti, Gary, 79
Boyars, Robert, 57

Boyde, Jessica, *81*
Braidotti, Rosi, 19
Brenner, Frédéric, 141
Brisley, Stuart, 53, *54*, 64n19
British Film Institute (BFI), 11
Bronski, Michael, 57
Browning, Tod, 48, 50
Brunette, Peter, 27, 129
Bruss, Elizabeth, 120–1
Burchill, Louise, 27
Burton, Julianne, 106–7
butch-femme dynamic, 56–7, 59–60

Cahiers du cinéma (magazine), 25, 29
Cahill, James Leo, 26, 27, 62n3
Callaghan, Joanna, 7, 66, 69–71, 86, 101;
  see also *Love in the Post*
Camera Lucida (Barthes), 142, 143
camp, 57, *58*, 59
Carte postale, La **see** *Post Card, The*
Case, Sue-Ellen, 56, 57, 59–60
Castle, Terry, 4, 5
Causseu, Jean-Max, 55
Céline et Julie vont en bateau: Phantom Ladies Over Paris (Rivette, 1974), 7, 40, 57, 59, 60
children, 78–81, 137–8
'Choreographies' (Derrida), 46–7
cinema **see** film
'Cinema and its Ghosts' (Derrida), 50–1
cinema verité, 101, 106, 125n7
'Circumfession' (Derrida), 8, 98, 105, 122–4
Citron, Michelle, 8, 98, 114, 123; **see also** *Daughter Rite*
Clayton, Curtiss, 111
close reading, 6, 8, 25, 33–4, 142–3
Club des Femmes, 10
Colebrook, Clare, 24

collectivism, 29
colour, 90
Correspondence (Plissart/Peeters, 1980), 130–1
countersignature, 7, 66–7, 90–1
'Covered Mirrors' (Borges), 145, *146*, 147–8
Crito (Plato), 16
Croft, Stephen, 33

D'Ailleurs, Derrida (Fathy, 1999), 97–8, 111–12
Dasgupta, Gautam, 60
Daughter Rite (Citron, 1978), 8, 98, 122
　and home movies, 103, 115–16
　and *quer* autobiography, 112, 114
de Lauretis, Teresa, 5, 9, 23, 142
　and *Right of Inspection*, 130, 135, 140
De Man, Paul, 1
death, 14, 15, 41–2; **see also** mourning; spectrality
Death 24x a Second (Mulvey), 32
deconstruction, 5–6, 9, 27–8, 33, 101
　and autobiography, 121–2, 123
　and fidelity, 73–4
　and *Ghost Dance*, 46–7
　and philosophy, 99–100
　and Woman, 17–22
Deleuze, Gilles, 88
Deren, Maya, 45
Derrida, Jacques, 3, 4
　and anacoluthon, 1, 2
　and autobiography, 121–4
　and biography, 98–100
　and children, 79–81
　and deconstruction, 5–6, 9
　and 'Envois', 66, 67–9
　and fidelity, 70–1
　and film, 6–8, 24–30, 37n13, 38n23, 88
　and *Ghost Dance*, 40, 41–2, 46–7, 55
　and hospitality, 76–8
　and literature, 83–5
　and metonymic reading, 139–44
　and Plato, 14, 16–17, 35n7
　and *Right of Inspection*, 129–30, 131–3, 135, 137, 138, 144, 145
　and singularity, 32, 33
　and spectrality, 45, 50–1, 62n3, 63n14
　and Woman, 17–24
　see also *D'Ailleurs, Derrida*; *Derrida* (film); *Love in the Post*
Derrida, Marguerite, 103, 104
Derrida (Dick/Kofman, 2002), 7–8, 97–8, 99–106, 108, 109–12, *113*

Deutscher, Penelope, 75–8
Diaspora: Homelands in Exile: voices (Brenner), 141
Diawara, Manthia, 31
Dick, Kirby, 7–8, 106–8, 126n14; **see also** *Derrida*
digital technology, 32, 44
directors, 10
discrimination, 10
DO NOT READ THIS (Callaghan, 2012), 70
documentaries, 73, 115
　and feminism, 102–3, 105–8, 123, 127n21
　see also *Daughter Rite*; *Derrida*; *Stories We Tell*
Dorich House Museum, 86
Droit de regards **see** *Right of Inspection*
Dronsfield, Jonathan Lahey, 90

Easthope, Anthony, 27
Echographies of Television, 28, 32
Eisenstein, Sergei, 143
'Envois' (Derrida), 7, 66, 67–9, 83–5
　and *Love In the Post*, 71–2, 73–5, 78–9, 82–4, 88, 90–1, 92
Equal Employment Opportunity Commission (EEOC), 10
equality, 10, 11

Fathy, Safaa, 97, 111–12
Feder, Ellen K., 22
female agency, 7, 30–2, 41
feminism, 5–6, 9–12
　and camp, 5, *58*
　and closeting, 56–7
　and Derrida, 17, 19–22, 23–4, 28, 29
　and documentaries, 102–3, 105–8, 123, 127n21
　and festishism, 141–2
　and the gaze, 130, 131–2
　and *Ghost Dance*, 40–1, 44–7
　and realism, 108–9
Feminisms: Diversity, Difference and Multiplicity in Contemporary Film Cultures (Mulvey/Rogers), 11
fetishism, 33–4, 141–2
fidelity, 2, 7, 70–1, 73–5
film, 6, 32
　and autobiography, 120–1
　and Derrida, 24–30, 37n13, 38n23
　and 'Envois', 68–9
　and feminism, 9–12, 22–4

and metonymic reading, 143, 144
and philosophy, 69–70, 72–4
Film Portrait (Hill, 1972), 115
Films Fatales, 10
Foucault, Michel, 141
fraternity, 76–7
friendship, 76–7
Fugues (Plissart/Peeters, 1983), 130–1

Gaines, Jane, 106
gaze, 30–2, 129–30, 131–3, 136–7
gender, 18–19, 132–3, 147; **see also** women
Ghost Dance (McMullen, 1983), 6–7, 28, 40–7, 52–3, *54*, 55, *58*
  and butch-femme, 57, 59–60
  and director, 60–1
  and *Love in the Post*, 89–90
  and myth, 51–2
  and reception, 55–6
  and Rivette, 57, 59, 65n23
  and *trompe l'oeil*, 47–8, *49*, 50–1
ghosts **see** spectrality
Gift of Death, The (Derrida), 14, 16
Gordine, Nora, 86
Grey Gardens (Hovde/Maysles/Meyer, 1975), 103
Grosz, Elizabeth, 6, 19
Gulkin, Harry, 114, 116, 118, 119

Habermas, Jürgen, 141
Hallas, Roger, 142
Harvey, Elizabeth, 23
Heath, Stephen, 34
Heidegger, Martin, 14, 70, 90
heterosexuality, 136–8
Hill, Jerome, 115
Hillis Miller, J., 1, 2, 4, 68
Hobson, Marian, 91, 92
Hölderlin, Friedrich, 90
Holland, Timothy, 26, 27, 62n3
Hollywood, 30, 33
homology, 79
homosexuality, 4, 57; **see also** lesbianism
hooks, bell, 30–2
hospitality, 77–8
Houllebecq, Michel, 102
Hovde, Ellen, 103
Hunting Ground, The (Dick/Ziering Kofman, 2015), 106–8
Hutcheon, Linda, 79

'I', 120–3, 124
In Search of Lost Time (Proust), 2

inequality, 10
infidelity, 2, 3, 7, 73–5
Invisible War, The (Dick/Ziering Kofman, 2012), 106–7

Jacques Derrida (Bennington), 105, 122, 124
Johnston, Claire, 106
Joyce, James, 68, 71
Juhasz, Alexandra, 106, 107

Kamuf, Peggy, 29, 101, 111
Kidnapping of Michel Houellebecq, The (Nicloux, 2014), 102
Kierkegaard, Søren, 14
knife, 40, 43, 44–5, 52, 55
Kreines, Jeff, 115

Labourier, Dominique, 59, 60
Lapsley, Robert, 27
Lesage, Julia, 59, 60, 106, 107–8
lesbianism, 3, 4–5, 7, 8, 9, 34
  and apparitionality, 12n1
  and camp, 57
  and *Céline et Julie vont en bateau*, 60
  and *Right of Inspection*, 130, 132, 133–4, 135, 136–8
'Life After Theory' conference, 1
Lippit, Akira Mizuta, 26–7
Living with Peter (Weinstein, 1973), 115
Lloyd, Lucinda, *80*
'Love Me, Love my Ombre, Elle' (Derrida), 17, 19–20, 21
London Feminist Film Festival, 10
looking, 8, 129–30, 131–3, 135, 137–8, 139
Love in the Post: From Plato to Derrida (Callaghan, 2014), 7, 66–7, 70, 71–6, 82–4
  and children, 80–1
  and mise en scène, 91–2
  and philosophy, 86, *87*, 88–91
  and pregnancy, 78–9
  and women, 81–2, 85–6
Ludwig, Birgit, *87*

McDonald, Christie V., 46–7
McGarry, Eileen, 106
McMahon, Laura, 27
McMullen, Ken, 6–7, 42, 47, 51–2, 60–1, 89–90; **see also** *Ghost Dance*
McQuillan, Martin, 71, 72, 80–1
MAI: Journal of Feminism and Visual Culture (journal), 11

Malabou, Catharine, 83, 88
Malone, Alicia, 10
Manon, Hugh S., 48, 50, 89
Marder, Elissa, 72
Marx, Karl, 48, 50
Mayer, Sophie, 10
Mayne, Judith, 34
Maysles, Albert and David, 103
Mellinger, Leonie, *49*, 50, 55, 56, *58*, 60–1
memes, 79, 94n16
Meshes of the Afternoon (Deren, 1943), 45
metonymy, 34, 46, 136, 139–44
Meyer, Muffie, 103
mirrors, 145, 147–8
mise en scène, 91–2
Mother Right (Citron, 1999), 123
mothers, 115–16, 123–4
mourning, 40, 103–4
Mourning Diaries (Barthes), 144
Mulvey, Laura, 11, 23, 30, 31–2, 33–4, 52
music, 16, 62n8, 111, 125n5; **see also** soundtrack
myth, 51–2, 59–60

Nana, Mom, and Me (Rothschild, 1974), 115
narcissism, 101, 114
narrative, 1, 3–4, 33–4, 43–4
'Night Watch, The' (Derrida), 83–4
Norman, Barnaby, 32–3

Of Hospitality (Derrida), 77–8
Ogier, Pascale, 6, 28, 40, 41–2, 45–7
and camp, *58*
and Mellinger, 55, 56, 60, 61
Ontological Narratives (Callaghan, 2003–14), 69–70
othering, 6

Parain, Brian, 62n11
Parjure, Le (Thomas), 1, 2–3
'"Parjure," Perhaps, Le' (Derrida), 1, 3
Parker, Andrew, 123
Patočka, Jan, 14
Peeters, Benoît, 24–5, 100, 130–1
perjury, 1, 3
Phaedo (Plato), 6, 14–15, 16
phallogocentrism, 17–18, 19, 22
philosophy, 14–15, 16, 20
and film, 69–70, 72–4
and *Love in the Post*, 86, 88–91
photography, 139–41, 143–4
photonovels, 8, 129, 130–1, 137, 144–5, 148n2; **see also** *Right of Inspection*

Plaint of Steve Kreines as Recorded by His Younger Brother Jeff (Kreines, 1974), 115
Plato, 6, 14–15, 70
Plissart, Marie Françoise, 8, 130–1; **see also** *Right of Inspection*
Poe, Edgar Allan, 144
poetry, 15, 43
politics, 107, 126n13, 139, 140, 142
and the gaze, 132
Politics of Friendship, The (Derrida), 76–7
Polley, Michael, 114, 116, 117–19
Polley, Sarah, 8, 98; **see also** *Stories We Tell*
Poore, Benjamin, 67
Post Card, The (Derrida), 7, 17, 19–20, 21; **see also** 'Envois'; *Love in the Post*
pregnancy, 78–9, 82
Prisoner, The (Proust), 2, 3–5
pronouns, 119–20
Proust, Marcel, 1, 2, 3–5
psychoanalysis, 139–40
punctum, 142–3, 144

queer reading, 142
queer autobiography, 97–8, 112, *113*, 114–15, 116–17, 121

race, 30–1
Rand, Richard, 102
realism, 50–1, 57, 59, 105–7, 108–9; **see also** cinema verité
reflexivity, 101, 103, 109, 112
Riel, Trine, 62n11
Riffaterre, Michael, 7, 43–4
Right of Inspection (Plissart), 8–9, 60, 129–30, 131–8, 144
and Borges, 145, *146*, 147–8
and metonymic reading, 139–40
Rivette, Jacques, 7; **see also** *Céline et Julie vont en bateau*
Robertson, Pamela, 57
'*Roman-photo* Revisited' (Plissart/Peeters, 1986), 130
roman-photo **see** photonovels
Romeo and Juliet (Luhrmann, 1996), 79
Rose, Jacqueline, 5
Ross, Daniel, 90
Rothschild, Amalie, 115
Ruby, Jay, 103, 109, 115

Sakamoto, Ryuichi, 111
Schad, John, 1
Schor, Naomi, 141–2

Schwartz, Louis-George, 41–2
score *see* music
Sedgwick, Eve Kosofsky, 4
Semiotics of Poetry (Riffaterre), 43–4
sexism, 10
sexual violence, 45, 51–2
'Signature, Event, Context' (Derrida), 121
singularity, 29–30, 32–3, 44
slavery, 30–1
Smith, Robert Rowland, 72, 100
Socrates, 14–15, 16
Sontag, Susan, 57
soundtrack, 48, 110–11
spectators, 29–32, 48, 50–1
    and *Right of Inspection*, 130, 132–3, 136
    and women, 52–3
Specters of Marx (Derrida), 50, 66
spectrality, 6–7, 27, 28–9, 33, 59
    and Derrida, 62n3, 63n14
    and *Ghost Dance*, 40, 41–2, 45, 50–1
Spivak, Gayatri Chakravorty, 6, 17–18, 19–22, 35n7
Spurs (Derrida), 18
Stories We Tell (Polley, 2012), 8, 98, 114–15, 116–20
symbolism, 51

technology, 28, 32, 42–3, 45–6
theatre, 122
'Third Meaning, The' (Barthes), 143–4
Thomas, Henri, 1, 2–3
Thrownness (Callaghan, 2004), 70

Torok, Mària, 40
Trilling, Jacques, 71
trompe l'oeil, 47–8, *49*, 50–1, 89

ungrammaticality, 43–4, 48, 50
US Military, 106, 107

violence, 26, 45, 51–2
Vivre sa vie (Godard, 1962), 62n11
voice, 23–4

Weber, Samuel, 29–30
Weinstein, Miriam, 115
Westlake, Michael, 27
Wills, David, 24, 67, 68, 129
Witt, Michael, 105
Woman, 16–24, 42
women, 11, 16–24
    and fetishisation, 33–4
    and friendship, 75–7
    and infidelity, 74–5
    and intimacy, 6, 7, 9, 51, 52, 55–6, 59
    and looking, 129–30, 132, 136, 147
    and *Love in the Post*, 81–2, 85–6
    and spectators, 30–2, 52–3
    see also butch-femme dynamic; feminism; lesbianism; mothers
Woodstock Film Festival, 10

Zankin, Emily, 22
Ziering Kofman, Amy, 7–8, 100–1, 106–8, 110, 126n14; **see also** *Derrida*